The Survival of a

Counterculture

The Survival

TALK ABOUT IMPERSONATING AN IDENTITY, about locking into a role, about irony: I went to cover the war and the war covered me; an old story, unless of course you've never heard it. I went there behind the crude but serious belief that you had to be able to look at anything, serious because I acted on it and went, crude because I didn't know, it took the war to teach it, that you were as responsible for everything you saw as you were for everything you did. The problem was that you didn't always know what you were seeing until later, maybe years later, that a lot of it never made it in at all, it just stayed stored there in your eyes. Time and information, rock and roll, life itself, the information isn't frozen, you are.

Michael Herr
Dispatches

# of a
Counterculture

IDEOLOGICAL WORK AND
EVERYDAY LIFE AMONG RURAL
COMMUNARDS BY Bennett M. Berger

University of California Press / Berkeley • Los Angeles • London

University of California Press
Berkeley and Los Angeles, California
University of California Press, Ltd.
London, England
© 1981 by The Regents of the University of California
Printed in the United States of America
1 2 3 4 5 6 7 8 9

Library of Congress Cataloging in Publication Data

Berger, Bennett M.
  The Survival of a Counterculture. Ideological work
and everyday life among rural communards
  Bibliography: p.
  Includes index.
    1. Communal living—California—Case studies.
2. Social sciences—Field work.   3. Ideology.
4. Knowledge, Sociology of.   I. Title.
HQ971.5.C2B47   307.7   72-93531
ISBN 0-520-02388-9
OCLC 6625387

CONTENTS

THIS BOOK IS FOR Bruce and Diane, who were there when it was happening; and for Chandra, without whom the book might never have been written.

A NOTE TO
SOCIOLOGISTS AND
OTHER READERS

I have put the author, myself, front and center in this book instead of bunkering him behind devices such as the passive voice, the Royalist We, and the presentation of findings with no visible, sentient finder. Some readers may find that odd, even tasteless in a book which, violating W. H. Auden's commandment, deliberately tries to commit a social science.

Nevertheless, I hope that the prominence of the first person singular will be taken neither as narcissim nor confession nor as grounds for imputing to me a "subjectivism" I do not hold. I delayed writing this book for several years because I couldn't find an interpretive frame to put around the social life I observed. Without that frame, I wasn't sure that I understood the meaning of what I was seeing. Without that understanding, I had no posture toward the data, and that reduced my motivation to write. And when that understanding finally began to emerge, I didn't like the "cynical" posture it invited me to take.

My solution to this problem was to try to take the reader along with me as I dealt with it, working toward a theoretical understanding of the data and toward a conscious grasp of the interpretive frame which shaped the meaning I gave to the data. Although communards may agree with some of the interpretations made here, they will disagree with others; the meanings asserted here are mine, not theirs. Thus the prominence of the first person singular.

In giving these reasons (which I take to be "good reasons") for adopting a style which is likely to offend some social-scientist readers, I am also exemplifying what in this book I call "ideological work": I am attempting to provide persuasive explanations and justifications to reduce the tension caused by an apparent discrepancy between my claim to be doing "objective" sociological research while using "subjective" devices like the first person singular and the autobiographical mode.

Like other ideological work, these explanations and justifications are self-serving; I am, after all, a "member" of the diffuse sub-group of sociologists with common professional interests in legitimating as "sociology" the kind of work this book represents.

At the same time, my awareness of the self-serving character of my own interpretive and analytic convictions cannot help but carry with it some of the skepticism we have all learned to adopt almost automatically toward self-congratulatory postures. I regard my effort to be skeptical about my own interpretive frame as an effort of detachment—not from the commune people and the data they provided, but from the mode by which I imputed meaning to what I observed. Given the bondage of researchers to never-fully-explicit paradigmatic habits, objectivity must be a *co-operative* effort between authors and reader-critics to be self-consciously and critically reflexive about the never-fully-conscious modes by which we seek to find meaning in social life.

PREFACE AND
ACKNOWLEDGMENTS

I have reached for two goals in this book that are not usually reached for simultaneously. First of all, I aim to do a partial ethnography of a commune—more specifically, a description of some of its beliefs and the practices that reveal them. Second, I aim to do a sociology of knowledge: I will not regard the meaning of the beliefs as self-evident. I will attempt to find that meaning in the relationships between the beliefs and the pressures exercised by the practical circumstances in which communards must live out their day-to-day existence.

Not only are these two aims seldom reached for simultaneously, but the audiences for each effort do not usually overlap much. Like historians, ethnographers usually look for detail, and ethnographies are likely to be praised to the extent that they are rich in directly observed empirical material, for example, descriptions of or quotations from the people who are studied that evoke the sense of their authentically lived lives. In the literature of the sociology of knowledge, one is lucky to find any live people at all. The data are frequently texts, and sociologists of knowledge usually look for logically rigorous relationships between abstract (usually highly abstract) categories devised from those texts and the social structures or existential conditions in which those texts appeared. Ethnographers are usually interested in accuracy, verisimilitude, and vivid detail; sociologists of knowledge are usually interested in historical sweep, analytic depth, and the relevances of ideology and epistemology to stratified political interests. The latter is a very different business indeed from sociological ethnography.

I want to try to thread my way between them, even to combine the two, but I do not delude myself that I'm likely to satisfy either audience fully. Ethnography fans will probably find too little descriptive detail. For some of them there won't be enough "warm and human" stuff; others will complain that persons are insufficiently evoked and insufficiently quoted in these pages. Sociologists of knowledge will probably wonder why I bother with as much humble detail as I do. Some of them may think the ideas I deal with hardly worth troubling oneself with analytically; others may think the practical circumstances to which I try to relate the ideas hardly deserving of membership in such grand categories as "social structure" or "existential conditions." Ethnographers will find me too abstract and too ambitious; sociologists of knowledge will find me too unambitious and not abstract enough.

That may be as it must be. Inner dialogues with imagined critics must end in order for a book to get written. The curse of ironic self-consciousness is an inability to articulate an assertion fully without stopping in the middle to comment on an anticipated response to one's not-yet-completed argument. Such defensive reflexivity can generate wonderfully spontaneous and staccato nonlinear talk. But a book like this provides an occasion for full assertion, and it is time to put aside responding to not-yet-made criticism of what I have not yet said, and begin to say it.

First I must acknowledge those who helped me get the work done. For a book that has been so long in the making by a person who is a notoriously poor keeper of records, it will be virtually impossible for me to remember all of them and thank them properly. What I say about the commune I call "The Ranch"* (where I gathered most—but not all—of the

---

*The communards at "The Ranch" are properly concerned about the protection of their anonymity. They do not wish to be publicly known and located. I have attempted to be no more specific than saying that The Ranch exists somewhere in "rural California," and "The Ranch" is as bland and unrevealing a name as I could invent.

data for this book) has been informed by the research conducted by my collaborators in communes both similar to and very different from The Ranch. First of all, my thanks go to Bruce Hackett, my friend and co-principal investigator, and to Diane Hackett Rizzo, core persons in the group that sustained me. Bruce and I argued for years over the meaning of our data—he the pragmatic idealist, I the reluctantly skeptical materialist. Were it not for our disagreements, this book would be as much his as mine, for the argument of this book is a dialectical outcome of our disagreements.

I want to thank also our former graduate students and assistants: Joseph Damrell, Dick Farrell, Mervyn Millar, Marilyn Noble, Arthur Seeger, Sue Thieman, and Gilbert Zicklin. Thanks also to Vinod Agarwal, Margaret Albertson, Molly Freeman, and Ben Rosenbluth; to Sherri Cavan and Amelia Fitts (to whom was done a disservice for which I apologize); to commune researchers Jud Jerome, Paul Kagan, Rosabeth Kanter, and Benjamin Zablocki; to Howie Becker and Barney Glaser; to Dorothy Miller, Ann-Marie Garrigues, and the staff of Scientific Analysis Corporation, which administered the grant; to the National Institute of Mental Health, whose generous grant (#RO1 MH 16579) made it all possible; to Ruth Fleshman, David Smith and the staff of San Francisco's Haight-Ashbury Clinic; and to Max Scherr and the Berkeley *Barb*. My thanks, of course, also go to the people of The Ranch, who showed me more hospitality and cordiality than I probably deserved. I am grateful for that and I hope they will not think ill of my book, though I do not expect them to agree with or approve of everything in it.

I have greatly benefited from critical readings of an early draft of the manuscript by Lewis Coser, Murray S. Davis, Joseph Gusfield, Bruce Hackett, Kristin Luker, Suzanne Wedow, and Norbert Wiley. Stanley Aronowitz, Randall Collins, Aaron Cicourel, and Bennetta Jules-Rosette commented usefully on an early draft of my theoretical approach, as did Judith Sherer and Jerzy Michaelowicz, students in a short seminar I gave in 1976.

Grant Barnes, my friend at the University of California Press, was patient far beyond the call of duty with an unconscionably tardy author. But Grant is above all a gentleman, and he kept prodding me, with just the right combination of encouragement and severity, to let go of my retentiveness and finish the book. Thanks are due Grant also for having given the first draft of the manuscript to Elisabeth Vodola, who provided a relentless and enormously helpful line-by-line critique of the language and logic of the entire first draft.

I cannot imagine any book that would not be much improved by so close a reading—so long as the author could recover from the blow to the ego of seeing his (or her) clumsiness, illogic, and other fatuities revealed by an impersonal reader. My friend and colleague Chandra Mukerji read each chapter, some of them fresh from the typewriter, and I regard myself as very lucky indeed to have had a reader who could maintain my sense of her enthusiasm, while at the same time she scrutinized almost every idea critically and checked it against her own communal experience.

I always thought it a cliché for an author to absolve from responsibility all those who helped make a book. Now I understand the caveat. Not only are these people not accountable for what I say in the following pages, but it also seems unlikely that any of them will subscribe thoroughly to all the things I say here. They are off the hook. Nevertheless, it remains true that I would not have been able to say some of them without the help these friends provided in the not-quite-endless, day-to-day discipline of putting down these words.

La Jolla, California
October 1979

CHAPTER 1

INTRODUCTION

THE RESEARCH: RELUCTANT BEGINNINGS

In 1970, I, together with my University of California colleague Bruce Hackett, was awarded a grant by the Social Problems Division of the National Institute of Mental Health to study child-rearing in counterculture communes. Applying for the grant was an unusual thing for me to do, since I had never before applied to any funding agency for a substantial grant to do research or anything else. I was, in fact, more than a little vain about that virginal status. I liked to think of myself as comparable to Alexander Pope, the eighteenth-century poet who was the first Englishman of his profession to get his work done and earn a living through it without grants, either in the form of patronage from wealthy or noble families or sinecures from the government; and like him, I was suitably and self-servingly disdainful of both kinds of support. By 1970, I had established a good enough reputation as a sociologist among those whose opinion I cared about, on the strength of a not-very-lengthy bibliography of theoretical, critical, and research publications. And having achieved that, together with a secure faculty position in a good university, I had no great motive to start off on the new path of Big Research. I would rather have continued doing the kinds of small things I had done well in the past without grants.

I was prevailed upon otherwise. As a senior faculty member in a graduate department of sociology, I was told, I was obliged to help support our graduate students by bringing in research money for assistantships. As a teacher of graduate students in a department that emphasized the importance of field research, I was obliged to provide our students with opportunities for practical research experience in the field. I was reluctant to get involved in a big research project for what I took to be good reasons. In my own graduate student days, I had never been a very good assistant to anyone else; I took direction poorly; I preferred to do the work my way rather than my boss's way; I had been dropped from one research project for "not working well with others." Moreover, I had never been able to use assistants successfully myself. I didn't know how to delegate work efficiently. As a researcher and writer, I developed a style that was largely improvisational— playing with perspective, revising design, and reinventing logics as I went along, frequently discovering what I wanted to say (and my warrant for saying it) only in the process of trying to say it—habits that made it almost mandatory for me to work alone.

As a teacher, I had no gift for helping graduate students who did not already seem to know what they were interested in. I preferred self-directed students, those strongly moti- vated to pursue their own intellectual visions, to whose work I could contribute such gifts as I did have: critical and analyti- cal skills for seeing and repairing troubles like logical gaps, half-truths, latent contradictions, unexplored connections, confusing organization, and stylistic excesses. Faced with the prospect of directing a large and complex research project, I had little reason to believe that I would be a particularly com- petent research administrator, one capable of supervising staffs of secretaries, research assistants, typists, and consul- tants, or keeping track of field locations, organizing meetings, verifying salary claims, checking expense vouchers, and the thousand other unnatural shocks that a principal inves- tigator's flesh is heir to.

I was reluctant to get involved in big organized research for other reasons too. My image of big organized researchers fixed them in my mind as people whose weight in Theory or Method or Substantive Expertise was so heavy that wherever they put their feet money seemed to run downhill toward them like water, and along with the money, the troops of would-be students and assistants. But the American sociologists whose work I admired most seemed to me less concerned with Theory or Method than with style and sensibility. They sometimes worked with assistants or collaborators, and they often had money and student-admirers. But they were not "Experts," and they were largely people without influential Theories or Methods sufficient to found a "school of thought" and attract Disciples. Bendix, Bittner, Goffman, Gouldner, Hughes, Riesman—all very different from each other—would leave no disciples; a heritage, yes, but no intellectual heirs; no school of thought to invoke the names of the sacred Founders. Whereas Methods and Theories can be practiced competently by anyone who learns the rules for using them, and whereas expertise can be achieved through the diligent mastery of literatures, the excellence of the work of each of these men lay not in its formal adherence to the codifiable properties of good social science (although it often had that merit), but in its unique style and sensibility, its *moral* rigor, even wisdom, which, apparently uncodifiable, could not be passed on for disciples to practice, whatever the intensity of their dedication to the Master.[1]

There were more personal reasons for my reluctance to get involved in organized commune research. As a graduate student, I had been strongly influenced by my mentor, Reinhard Bendix, who had rejected my first Ph.D. dissertation proposal (on stereotypes of sociology by "humanistic" intellectuals) with the advice that it was a waste of time and effort to undertake research on questions to which I thought I already knew most of the answers. I didn't know much about child-rearing (except what I'd learned from experience as a father and from books about socialization) and I hadn't had much experience with communes, but I thought I already knew most of what

1. The two categories are not neat, and I do not wish to exaggerate. Robert Merton, for example, whose work I admire as much as that of any of the men I have cited, has been an organized researcher with troops of disciples. But I always thought that Merton's most valuable qualities were not his "theories" or his command of substantive fields (like the sociology of science), but his learnedness, his clarity, and the almost rococo elegance of his mind, which made him interesting on whatever topic he touched.

the hippies were about.[2] There is a story about a man who, having read a book on penguins, was asked what he thought about it. His apocryphal reply was that the book taught him more about penguins than he cared to know. I thought I already knew more about hippies than I cared to know. I had lived among the "Beatniks," their ideological predecessors, for much of the previous twenty years; I had also written about them previously; they were, moreover, a major presence in the San Francisco Bay Area, where I lived, and I knew enough of them to be sufficiently aware of what was traditional and what was new in their style of life.[3]

In part, too, I was put off by my feeling that they were "my people," and I felt that I knew so much about them that I could imagine no manuscript I might produce being sufficiently thorough and subtle to satisfy my sense of their complexity. I felt the prospect of becoming some damn academic "expert" on them as a betrayal of the kinship I felt (or remembered I once felt—memory and identity are elusive in matters like this) for them. Betrayal? Yes. I wanted to be neither their Boswell nor their critic nor their "catcher in the rye,"[4] and I could anticipate no way of being simultaneously loyal to my own analytic convictions as a sociologist and to my respect for the seriousness of the communal vision. Puffery, advocacy, "warm" ethnography would have been easy enough; there was already plenty of that. There was also plenty of outraged criticism and viewings-with-alarm.

2. "Hippies": in 1980 the word falls from the tongue queer and quaint and dated. I can remember the first time I heard the word, in 1964 or '65, used by Jesse Pitts, who had an early interest in them. It embarrassed me then too because I ignorantly "heard" it as a vulgar and unhip corruption of the older "hipster," of whom I had known many in the 1940s and of whom Norman Mailer (among others) had written in the 1950s. In the space of little more than a decade, "hippie" had gone from embarrassing me at hearing it to embarrassing me (for different reasons) at using it—a comment, perhaps, on the fragility of "current" usage.

3. See "Hippie Morality" in Bennett M. Berger, *Looking for America* (Englewood Cliffs, N.J.: Prentice-Hall, 1971).

4. For those who do not remember, the title of Salinger's famous novel referred to his protagonist's fantasy of watching a group of children playing in a field of rye near the edge of a cliff. When one of the children would fall over the edge, Salinger's hero would "catch" the child.

But the kind of quasi-detached, interpretive ethnography I liked to think I practiced was no insurance against the probable betrayal. The ethnographer neither sees nor interprets in the same ways that participants do, even when phenomenological Theory and Method constrain the ethnographer to try; and adherence to the validity of my own perceptions, I imagined, could be maintained only at the probable cost of discounting theirs. Like some Lord Jim with a too vivid anticipation of disaster, I imagined my expertise sought after by eager journalists with a deadline to meet, whose editors demanded the latest scoop on counterculture "far-outness" to satisfy their audience's craving for vicarious deviance. And like Conrad's sailor, I was ready to abandon ship before it had been tested by the full force of the storm.

The storm I imagined blew from the pressures of focusing my attention on the relationship between the ideological claims made by whatever human groups I happened to be studying and the day-to-day behavior in those groups. It seemed to me almost inevitable both that the ideals articulated by hippie communards would be transparently self-congratulatory, *and* that there would be glaring discrepancies between their ideological claims and their everyday behavior. Such discrepancies and self-congratulations are, I think, typical of all human groups, in communes as anywhere else. But pointing these out (which was my analytic habit) would be received, I imagined, as a malicious effort to impugn their ideas by focusing on their self-serving character, and to "expose" or "unmask" the pretentiousness of their ideology by holding it up to the mirror of their everyday life.[5] Moreover, my own sociological perspective led me to be pessimistic about the efforts of radical cultural innovators to create social structures adequate to carry and sustain their moral visions (and hence reduce the discrepancies), and I was reluctant to let my own pessimism add a self-fulfilling dimension to the already considerable obstacles they had to overcome. Like

5. What makes this especially intense in the case of the hippies is the assumption that, because they see their ideals as more elevated and self-consciously articulated than those of other groups, they are therefore more vulnerable when discrepancies, fatuities, or self-congratulations are pointed out.

other sociologists of knowledge, in short, I feared exposing
ideas I had sympathy for to the knife of ideological analysis.

But these were exquisite doubts I carried (a result, perhaps,
of an excessively perfervid imagination), whereas the arguments in favor of applying for the grant were practical and
blunt. So we drew up a research proposal, and after the usual
delays the funds were granted. I never did use a research
assistant, although half a dozen or more graduate students
worked on the project over its three-year life. I remembered
Morris Janowitz telling me, years earlier, how he had received
a substantial grant for graduate students, not to work as assistants on a professor's project, but to do their own independent work. That model appealed to me, and we used it in a
modified form. The graduate students we recruited to the
project were informed of our general mandate, were familiar
with the counterculture, and interested in doing commune
research. We agreed on a minimal definition of a commune (at
least five adults plus two children living together and self-
identified in quasi-kinship terms), and the graduate assistants were instructed only to get out there in the field, locate a
commune or two or three, and find out what goes on with
respect to the children. We senior researchers did the same,
except for Sherri Cavan, who studied rural hippies living in
nuclear families and whose work we supported for the comparative family perspective it could provide.

The difficulties of access to research sites (the biggest single
problem of such research among groups who generally have
no desire to be studied) were reduced because most of our
assistants were visibly indistinguishable from the people they
set out to study. An enviable role for them: hip camp followers living off the "Establishment" for doing what they'd like
to be doing in any case. But they were also graduate students
in one or another stage of compound ambivalence: ambivalent disaffection from the movement, some of whose aims
they shared, and ambivalent disaffection from their image of
Establishment sociology, working for journeymen sociologists, long-haired and/or bearded with their own ambivalences.
I figured that if 30 percent of our efforts turned out successfully, we'd have a good study.

We did not attempt to sample communes rigorously because we had no way of knowing the population from which a sample could be drawn. "Snowball sampling" (find one and through it find another and so on) is the not-quite-technical term used to rationalize the selection of cases when the universe those cases presumably represent is unknown and perhaps unknowable. We did, however, make special efforts to find the types of communes that we reasoned would represent some of the bases of variation in the phenomenon: urban and rural, creedal and noncreedal, open and closed, missionary and reclusive, large and small.

The staff met periodically to hear our consultants (on communes, on field work, on participant observation) and to discuss our findings. When our findings were consistent, we explored interpretations and checked with each other to find out whether any of us was in possession of data that cast doubt on the generalizations to be drawn from an interpretation. When our findings varied, we discussed the probable reasons for that variation and went back to the field with questions more sharply focused. We wrote reports, circulated them, and discussed them. Although our mandate was to study communal child-rearing, we discovered early in the research that we could not begin to understand the lives of communal children without paying close attention to the social structure of family life and to the culture that envelops the lives of children in these families. Our research, then, was concerned not only with the specific character of child-child and child-adult interaction, but also with the basic economic arrangements of commune life, the structure of nuclear units within it, and the problems of leadership, authority, decision making, recruitment, and ideology—in which settings the lives of children are made meaningful.

The project produced three Ph.D. dissertations,[6] an additional book-length manuscript (Sherri Cavan's *Hippies of the Redwood Forest*), about a dozen articles in books and journals,

6. The dissertations are by Joseph Damrell (University of California, Davis, 1972), Arthur Seeger (University of California, Davis, 1975), and Gilbert Zicklin (University of California, Davis, 1977).

the appropriate reports to NIMH, and the present manuscript. We also contributed support to the work of Paul
Kagan, eventually published as *New World Utopias*.[7] The project also produced many adventures, several friendships and
romances, one marriage, and (after the research was finished)
a purchase of rural property by the two principal investigators. It also provided the support for graduate students
and their opportunities for research experience. Whether the
taxpayers got their money's worth is a question perhaps best
left for others to judge.

WHAT THIS BOOK IS ABOUT

Although I have drawn freely on the more or less independent work of some of my collaborators, this book is less the
product of "our" research than the result of my own reflections on that part of the ethnography I did myself, which is
one (but not the only) reason for the prominence of the first-
person pronoun. Many ethnographies attempt to render the
ethnographer invisible, sometimes on the grounds that the
data are "out there" to be recorded by a passive observer
trained in providing objective accounts of events whose meanings "emerge naturally" from those events. Such "nonobtru-
sive" procedures frequently adopt literary devices like the
passive voice, the Olympian or Royalist "we," and an impersonal "there is . . ." and "there are . . . ," which typically
downplay or disguise the role of investigators in *eliciting* the
information provided to them.

I have adopted another strategy. (I could have said "this
book adopts another strategy.") This book is to some extent
the record of a research *experience*; it is not only about communards, but about my relationship to them, which was in
fact a recurrently salient issue in the research. I was also in
fact strongly affected by that research experience, and to
write as if I had not been so affected would be a falsification.
I also in principle urge a "reflexive" practice regarding such
experience. The ubiquitous "I," then, is not only an "I" record-

7. Baltimore: Penguin Books, 1975.

ing the research experience, but also an "I" reflecting upon the affect of the experience. The book, in short, is a "personal" book, but not, I hope, less objective because of that. Any objective account that denies the existence of the accountant is merely "objective."

Most of the data are drawn from the field work I did at the rural commune I call "The Ranch," and by reporting some of those data I hope to make a contribution to the ethnographic literature on this curious subject.[8] I call it curious because public interest in communes has been far out of proportion to the apparent magnitude of their importance. Like the hippie phenomenon in general, the commune movement never attracted more than a small percentage of its potential constituency, even at the height of its appeal between 1968 and 1971. But it did attract the mass media, which saw in it the apotheosis of counterculture "liberation," prominent (but never even close to dominant) among middle-class youth in the 1960s. Communes (read: hippies, sex, drugs, fevered transcendence, Dionysius incarnate) were such sufficiently resonant news that journalists seeking expert sanction to inform or slant a story would pursue social scientists (if not communards themselves) with questions: how many communes are there? why have these people dropped out? how do they survive? what are they *doing*? And however early the stage of a social scientist's research or however tentative the initial findings, a superficial impression, an *ad hoc* interview, or an idle remark dropped over a long distance telephone conversation would appear a short time later in print or image

---

8. To the extent that it focuses on "The Ranch," this book is a case study; it does not even attempt to be ethnographically exhaustive of "our" work. Indeed, the descriptive ethnography is not even the major aim of the book. For this reason the text is not as rich with quotations from communards as is usual in sociological ethnographies. Quotations constitute most of the raw data of qualitative ethnographies (although they are not nearly as "raw" as many researchers seem to imply) and are essential when the major task at hand is to establish the accuracy of the presented facts. In this case most of the facts are not at issue, for they will surprise few readers who are knowledgeable about communes. This book offers an interpretation of the ideas conveyed by those data, and I have used my own language to carry the burden of the argument.

as an authoritative account by a certified expert to be quoted and then requoted in that self-fulfilling process by which news becomes history.

Now that the movement has abated somewhat and lost much of its chic, the news media leave it largely alone, except, perhaps, when unusual religious communes are charged with "brainwashing" their young members, and "kidnappings" occur under the auspices of agents retained by parents to "reeducate" their wayward children; or when litigation tests residential zoning laws apparently violated by "nonkin" families occupying single-family dwellings; or when Charles Dederich, the charismatic leader of Synanon, decides to divorce his wife and remarry, thereby inducing almost all other members of Synanon to "change partners."[9]

But that communes are not nearly as newsworthy in 1979 as they were ten or even five years ago should not be regarded as evidence of their disappearance. In this respect, communes are not unlike political scandals—their disappearance from the headlines does not mean that governmental corruption has ceased. The waning chic of the movement has unquestionably discouraged frivolous attempts to make a commune by finding a rentable house and a group of willing people adrift in the world. But parts of rural California are still generously populated with serious post-hippies, living both communally and in nuclear families, and this fact was inadvertently brought to public light by a recent story in the Los Angeles *Times* announcing that Governor Brown had taken an option to buy some rural property in what the story's headline called "hippie country."

A curious subject, then, to which I hope to add some ethnographic knowledge. But that is not my greatest hope. Ethnographic description even at its best is time-bound and ephemeral; like newsprint, it yellows with age. It can be valu-

9. I wrote this as the bizarre events at Jonestown in Guyana and the arrest of Charles Dederich on suspicion of attempted murder dominated the headlines in December 1978.

able as a contemporary account (and eventually as an historical record) of what life was like among a certain group at a certain time in a certain place. But between its immediate, contemporary relevance and its eventual historical value there is likely to be a long period when it seems merely quaint and "dated," unless ethnographic data are *used* to reveal fundamental social processes that transcend the time and place in which the data were gathered.

Because communes have been interesting for a variety of mostly topical reasons (e.g., fascination with the deviance or rebellion of gilded youth; communal forms as a response to "alienation"; the prominence of gurus and charismatic leaders), relatively few of the many books on communes over the past decade have attempted to deal with the fundamental issues of sociological theory raised by the study of communes.[10] My greatest hope is to impose on the commune data I gathered at The Ranch a theoretical frame whose relevance transcends the time and place in which the data were gathered. If that relevance is there, it must be discovered and imposed on the data by the ethnographer.[11] Like art, sociological theory is an imposed order, and like contemporary art it need not be beautiful to be good.

The theoretical order I hope to impose is drawn from the sociology of knowledge, which deals with the relationship of

10. The important exceptions: Rosabeth Kanter's book, *Commitment and Community* (Cambridge: Harvard University Press, 1972), makes important contributions to the theory of commitment and boundary maintenance in communes. Ben Zablocki's *The Joyful Community* (Baltimore: Penguin Books, 1971) also reveals consistent theoretical preoccupation with the idea of community. *Communes, Sociology and Society*, by Philip Abrams and Andrew McCulloch (London: Cambridge University Press, 1976), is thoroughly Durkheimian; and Laurence Veysey's *The Communal Experience* (New York: Harper and Row, 1973) seriously treats the relevance of contemporary communes to the anarchist tradition. Hugh Gardner's *The Children of Prosperity* (New York: St. Martin's Press, 1978) is an attempt to test Kanter's theory of commitment.

11. Even theories that emphasize the privileged cognitive status of phenomenological understandings are *imposed* orders to the extent that the theorist-investigator decides that a phenomenological reality is more equal than others in a world of multiple cultural realities.

ideas to the social contexts in which they are embedded.[12] The sociology of knowledge is not beautiful because its dominant skepticism tends to impugn the felt authenticity of beliefs and hence implicitly discount (and thus, perhaps, weaken) the subjective "reality" of a person's identification with what he or she believes—or as I like to say (to emphasize the sociologically contingent character of beliefs), what people "believe they believe they believe . . ." and so on toward the infinite regress.

In the past, the sociology of knowledge, if it was at all empirical (as it usually was not), was concerned with the relation of "macro" ideologies (e.g., political, religious, or esthetic doctrines like liberalism, Calvinism, or romanticism) to "macro" social structures (feudal, capitalist, socialist, industrial).[13] In this book I want to concern myself empirically with

12. The literature on the sociology of knowledge is large, and I will not cite the bulk of it here because this is not a formal treatise on the sociology of knowledge. For good and fairly recent bibliographies, see Gunter Remmling, *Towards the Sociology of Knowledge* (New York: Humanities Press, 1973); and Kurt Wolff, *Trying Sociology* (New York: John Wiley and Sons, 1974). These bibliographies do not strongly reflect the recent renewal of interest in the sociology of knowledge by Neo-Marxists, which seems to have developed from the failures of the socialist movement in Western industrial countries and the defeat of the New Left. The question raised for Neo-Marxists by these setbacks was: why? And the answers were formulated as a sociology of knowledge that stressed the dominating role of established institutions (e.g., education and mass media) in reproducing a capitalist culture and capitalist mentality that systematically distorted or distracted the understanding of capitalism by its citizens, thus impeding their capacities for seeing and acting on the good sense of the socialist critique of capitalist civilization. The interpretation is, of course, self-serving, but (as I will argue below) should not be dismissed simply for this reason. See Antonio Gramsci, *Selections from the Prison Notebooks*, edited and translated by Quentin Hoare and Geoffrey Nowell Smith (New York: International Publishers, 1971); and Louis Althusser, "Ideology and Ideological State Apparatuses," in his *Lenin and Philosophy* (New York: Monthly Review Press, 1972). See also Herbert Marcuse, *One-Dimensional Man* (Boston: Beacon Press, 1964); if you can bear to read him, see also Jurgen Habermas, *Knowledge and Human Interests* (Boston: Beacon Press, 1971).

13. Although most of the literature is programmatic and/or theoretical and hortatory, again there are exceptions. My favorite (and relatively little-

the relationship of the small moral ideas of communards to the small social structures of communes—with what I call the *microsociology of knowledge.*[14] In this effort I am deliberately attempting to marry two intellectual traditions: the American tradition of participant-observer ethnography to the European tradition of ideological analysis. I hope also to exemplify one way of linking "microsociology" to "macrosociology" by showing that analytic techniques normally associated with conceptually distant or comprehensive subjects may be used to understand relatively intimate ideas when seen close-up.

In speaking of "small ideas" and "small social structures," I realize that there is no clear line between big and small, and that ideas that seem small (or large) at first glance may turn out to be larger (or smaller) than one initially thought. But I make the distinction because relatively specific ideas are more

---

known) exception is Reinhard Bendix, *Work and Authority in Industry* (New York: John Wiley and Sons, 1956); though it is widely used in university courses on work, politics, and industrialization, the book is to a large extent a study of managerial *ideas* and their relation to the political and industrial contexts in which they appeared and gathered strength. For an interesting and unusual case study in the sociology of knowledge see Clifford Geertz, "Ritual and Social Change: A Javanese Example," in his *The Interpretation of Cultures* (New York: Basic Books, 1973). Robert Merton probably does the best consistent empirical work in the sociology of knowledge. See some of the essays collected in his *The Sociology of Science* (Chicago: University of Chicago Press, 1973). In addition to Bendix, Geertz, and Merton, my own thinking on this subject has been most influenced by *The German Ideology* of Marx and Engels; Georg Lukács' *History and Class Consciousness*; and, of course, Karl Mannheim's *Ideology and Utopia*, and his *Essays on the Sociology of Knowledge*. More recently the work of Raymond Aron, Alvin Gouldner, and Thomas Kuhn has also shaped my thinking. Like nearly every other sociologist, I have also been influenced by the efforts of Peter Berger and Thomas Luckmann to integrate theoretically the Marxist tradition of the sociology of knowledge with the Durkheimian tradition, phenomenology, and American Symbolic Interactionism. See *The Social Construction of Reality* (New York: Doubleday and Co., 1966).

14. To my knowledge, Peter Berger was the first sociologist to use the term "Microsociology of Knowledge." See "Marriage and the Construction of Reality" in his *Facing Up to Modernity* (New York: Basic Books, 1977). The term is awkward, and "sociology of microknowledge" might well be more accurate, except that it is even more awkward.

empirically manageable than highly abstract ones and can therefore be used to illustrate more clearly than the latter the relationship of ideas to interests and circumstances.

An injunction to "get in touch with your feelings" is a small idea—which may or may not be espoused in association with a more comprehensive and abstract set of ideas, for example, "romanticism." "Kids should settle their own quarrels" is a small idea; "sexual preference is a private affair" is also a relatively small idea; and so is the belief that one should try to overcome jealousy. A belief that one ought to earn one's rewards through labor is a somewhat larger but still relatively small idea that may or may not be part of a still larger idea like "the Protestant ethic." By small social structures I mean those recurrent patterns of behavior that define relatively small groups like families, workgroups, schools, and friendship networks (in whose settings the ideas are manifested), rather than the larger structures of social classes, institutions, or nations.

If the sociology of knowledge is to be useful for the understanding of ideas in context, it must somehow transcend both the tendency to discount or impugn ideas by attending exclusively to their material circumstances or by reducing them to the interests they serve, and the tendency to reify ideas by ignoring their embeddedness in society and history.[15] More useful than either the skepticism of the materialist perspective or the ethereality of the idealist perspective on this matter is a perspective that emphasizes the interaction or dialectic between ideas and circumstances. This perspective combines Marxist and Weberian ideas in the analysis of everyday life.[16] It acknowledges the relevance of material interests and circumstances to the formulation, maintenance, and development of ideas; but it also acknowledges the tendency of believers to

15. "Reification": a term usually employed pejoratively to suggest that an idea is mystified when it is removed from the social and historical context from which it derives its meaning. An idea, that is, becomes a "thing" when it is used in sentences as a subject that carries the action of a verb, and it therefore obscures the role of historically embedded actors who "really carry the action."

16. To say that "this perspective combines . . ." is a reification, but I do not use the term pejoratively here.

believe (and to behave) *as if* their convictions were autonomous, not simply an "expression of" (or reducible to) interests and practical circumstances.[17] This perspective, therefore, seeks to understand the meaning of beliefs in the attempts of human beings to cope with the relationship between the ideas they bring to a social context and the practical
pressures of day-to-day living in it, as though through their
copings they gradually or suddenly become aware of that
meaning. When beliefs do not seem to be very effective in
serving the interests of believers (from their own point of
view) or when routine behavior is in apparent contradiction
with professed belief, tensions are added to that relationship
that constrain people to resolve or reduce them by some

17. The Neo-Marxist debate about "ideology" disinterred once again the
old issue in Marxist circles about the relationship of "infrastructure"
(technology and the relations of economic production) to "superstructure"
(the dominant ideas produced and reproduced within the other established
institutions). Were the superstructures of capitalist society simply "reflections of" (or "expressions of") the necessities generated by the economic
infrastructure? Or were these superstructures "relatively autonomous," i.e.,
capable of exerting their own causal force on the infrastructure? The debate
has gone on since Engels's famous letters after Marx's death, explicating his
and Marx's views on the interaction of cultural superstructures and economic
infrastructures. See, for example, the account in Tom Bottomore and Patrick
Goode, eds., *Austro-Marxism* (Oxford: Clarendon Press, 1978). The debate
was intensified by the permanent influence of Max Weber's *The Protestant
Ethic and the Spirit of Capitalism* (New York: Scribner's, 1930) and by his insistence on the relative autonomy of "status" from "class." For the most persuasive recent argument against the orthodox Marxist view, see Marshall
Sahlins, *Culture and Practical Reason* (Chicago: University of Chicago Press,
1976). Sahlins argues that the dominance (long or short run) of "materialist"
factors is not an historical universal but a variable, dependent upon the symbolic (i.e., the "cultural") prescription of legitimate priorities. Although
Sahlins's ethnographic evidence is persuasive, I see little prospect of the
theoretical argument being finally resolved. It seems to me, rather, that it is a
reification to speak of infrastructure and superstructure (and their various influences) as if they were separably "real"—rather than human conceptual
inventions that, like other powerful cultural inventions, can certainly *feel* real.
But although Sahlins is correct in seeing that "economic" events *are* cultural
events (to the extent that they invoke and imply symbols and priorities of
value), he does not seem to acknowledge that cultural events are equally
economic events (to the extent that they reproduce or influence changes in
economic production and exchange). Engels attributed his (and Marx's) ne-

alteration in their ideas or their circumstances or both,[18] despite the general reluctance of people to give up either their ideas or their interests, and despite the obstacles to altering their actual circumstances.

Reified or abstract ideas are by themselves a generally poor guide to the resolution or reduction of those tensions because such ideas usually turn out so sufficiently contingent as to require interpretation to be applied in specific situations. Even so apparently unambiguous a moral dictum like "thou shalt not kill" requires interpretation to be applied in war or self-defense or defense of others—although the authoritative source of that particular commandment does not state it contingently. Moral injunctions are seldom stated contingently, and although I may "believe in" honoring my mother and father, my belief may be a poor guide should I discover them pushing heroin in the junior high school cafeteria. Moreover, local social contexts can usually be relied on to generate (by interactions with their larger environments) unanticipated conditions or situations that further exacerbate the practical ambiguity of ideas, render them difficult to "live up to," and hence make the ways in which they will be interpreted difficult to predict or anticipate. Who would have guessed that George Wallace's invocation of the principle of local control to defend the segregation of Alabama schools would be duplicated only a few years later by black leaders in northern ghettos in behalf of attempts to promote black interests? "Identi-

---

glect of the dialectical feedback influence of superstructure on infrastructure to the fact that they were involved in the rough-and-tumble of political combat. It may well be that Sahlins's insistence that cultural symbols and values govern the salience of "material" factors in history, and his *neglect* of the questions regarding the genesis of those symbols and values themselves, may be attributed to his own participation in the rough-and-tumble of Marxist polemics. Which determines or influences what to what extent may well be a perennial theoretical question that will remain unanswered definitively. In the meantime, historical and empirical studies of groups coping with ideal and material constraints on their behavior can conceivably build up a body of evidence on the ways in which the interactions between ideal and material constraints operate. Max Weber seems to have understood all this.

18. These can be seen as cognitive dissonances. See Leon Festinger, *A Theory of Cognitive Dissonance* (New York: Harper and Row, 1957).

cal" principles produce different meanings under changed conditions.

In Weber's terms, representatives of the moral ideas that define what he called a "status group," or a style of life,[19] resist to some extent the characterization of those ideas as determined by, dependent on, or as rationalizations for gross material interests. But neither can the ideas of a group be institutionally embodied and sustained in utter disregard to practical exigencies like class, family, occupational, or other group interests, or the need for minimal group stability. *The empirical study of interaction in real communities enables a researcher to see in microcosm the ways in which the practical pressures of daily life do or do not affect the beliefs that groups bring with them to that life* — either by sustaining them and strengthening them or by modifying or undermining them through experience that "tests" their workability; that tests, in effect, the meaning of what people believe they believe they believe. . . .

In our commune research, originally concerned with the study of child-rearing, my habitual preoccupation with the relationship of ideas to interests was alerted by our difficulties in interpreting the data that indicated an unambiguous diminution of age-graded differences in the commune population — compared with what I was used to in mainstream urban society. There was clear evidence that showed the communal ideal of equality was being extended to include children. Was this evidence a direct expression of the equalitarian beliefs hippie parents brought with them to the rural communes from the urban counterculture and the New Left? (This was the view of some of my radically partisan graduate-student-collaborators — Marxist idealism, I called it.) Or was including children a circumstantially convenient and self-serving adaptation by counterculture adults, embarked from scratch on a difficult community-building enterprise, who had little time or inclination or resources for assuming the heavy burdens of middle-class parenting, and for whom, therefore, the exten-

19. Or what Herbert Gans in a narrower context calls a "taste public" and a "taste culture." See Herbert Gans, *Popular Culture and High Culture* (New York: Basic Books, 1974).

sion of the principle of equality to children conveniently provided an ennobling ideology to lighten that burden?[20]

It was both; it was neither. What seemed increasingly clear
and demonstrable was that the communards brought with
them to their rural settings a strong set of moral ideals, not
only about children and childhood, but about a variety of
other matters as well (which constitute most of the data of
this book). Indeed, moving to these rural settings was in part
a deliberate result of their desire for a more hospitable ambience in which to attempt to realize these ideals. The circumstances that they encounter facilitate or obstruct, reinforce
or weaken their ability or their will to institutionalize their
ideas by embodying them in routine practices. Through such
processes ideas may be modified or maintained, strengthened
or discarded. In either case, a lot of *ideological work* seems necessary to keep a group's convictions in some viable relationship to its interests and circumstances, and the commune
situation provides an opportunity to test the microsociology
of knowledge by observing these processes of ideological
work occurring.

I intend to take some basic beliefs of the counterculture, as
they were (and are) expressed in the commune movement,
and to show empirically how these ideas fared when attempts
were made to create a community that lived by them. It is not
feasible to do so for *all* the major ideas of the counterculture
reported by its students.[21] I intend to concentrate on three
sets of ideas that struck me most forcefully during the period
of our research:

1. The decline of age-grading; the equality of children and
   adults; the natural child; devaluation of "grown-ups";
   early maturity for the young; the "inclusion-disattention"
   pattern; children as "small persons" with the rights of or-

20. There are parents who, when interviewed about their occupational
hopes for their children, disguise their powerlessness to affect a child's occupational future by saying such things as "I want him to be whatever he wants
to be," thus transforming powerlessness into permissiveness—a form of
ideological work.

21. For a good summary, see Fred Davis, *On Youth Subcultures: The Hippie
Variant* (New York: General Learning Press, 1971).

dinary members to sex, drugs, and autonomy in resolving their disputes; the education of children.

2. Pastoralism; simple living in harmony with nature in the country; continuities with the "suburban" ideal; negative predispositions toward "technology"; pride in survival "on the land"; pride in development of manual skills; frugality, ecological consciousness; apocalypse: impending doom for the cities.

3. Intimacy; coupling and uncoupling and recoupling; sex; group marriage; negative attitudes toward the fixing of differentiated roles; "out-frontness"; emotional candor; nonpossessiveness; bisexuality; feminism; serial monogamy; the "burning out" of sexual jealousy.

Using the microsociology of knowledge for the analysis of these ideas means that I will not take them at their face value. I mean to treat the ideas *as data*, without reference to my own feelings about them; when I have such feelings I will try to make them clear to make optimum the reflexivity of the analysis. Although I do care about whether these ideas are true or beautiful or good, I will direct my attention to the *relationship* between these ideas and the circumstances in which they must live—if they are to have any "life" at all.

But I am not primarily interested either in "laying bare" that these ideas are "merely" self-serving or that they are compromised by the exigencies of circumstance. I take it as a matter of course that beliefs are likely to have a self-serving component for the individuals or groups who espouse them. Therefore I regard it as juvenile for scholars (though not for ideological combatants)[22] to take as their task "exposing" the

---

22. A couple of examples of ideological work from recent political and economic combat: conservatives responded favorably a few years back to James Q. Wilson's argument for treating the *symptoms* of crime with swift and severe punishment because "rehabilitation" had failed, and seeking the causes of crime seemed unpromising because even if we found them we might be unwilling to pay the price of eliminating those causes. See James Q. Wilson, *Thinking About Crime* (New York: Basic Books, 1975). But another conservative spokesman for industry, when recently asked how big business regarded the proposals to reduce inflation through wage and price controls,

"real" interests served by ideas or "unmasking" or debunking ideas by revealing the contradictions between what ideas
apparently profess and the day-to-day behavior of those who
profess them. Ideas are human creations, and they are
created *for purposes, in contexts, and are definable in time and
place*, by living people who invested themselves in *these*
(rather than *those*) ideas for discoverable reasons.

The reasons for this investment are frequently not the same
as the results brought about by the action dedicated to them
(that is the nature of unanticipated consequences). But to
react to discrepancies between ideological profession and behavior with a smug "aha!" (as if one had caught a pretender
with his pretenses down) is juvenile in the sense that it seems
to assume that a perfect or nearly perfect correspondence between doctrine and practice is normal or to be expected. That
seems on the face of it to be a patently false assumption, since
it is clear that day-to-day behavior is obviously and routinely
affected by a variety of circumstances other than professed
belief (habit, unconscious feelings, emergencies, power or
pressure by others, fear, prior socialization, institutionalized
evasion, calculation of illicit self-interest, etc.), to say nothing
of assumptions buried or taken for granted, not all of which
may be logically or intuitively "consistent" with each other.

Some circumstances encourage or sustain a line of behavior
consistent with professed belief; these circumstances tend to
affirm and strengthen ideology in ways that leave relatively

---

replied contemptuously that federally imposed controls would *merely* treat
the symptoms of inflation rather than its causes. Another example: new
technology has recently made it possible for small independent companies to
compete with ITT in the highly profitable long-distance telephone business.
ITT, well known for its conservative ideological stance against federal regulation, appeals to the government to regulate its competition on the grounds
that such competition would impede ITT's capacity to provide what is generally agreed to be the best telephone system in the world. In the first instance
the ideological work consists in shifting one's judgment of the merits of
"treating symptoms rather than causes." In the second instance the ideological work consists in shifting the grounds of assertion from principle (anti-
government interference in business) to performance ("the best telephone
system in the world"), the maintenance of which apparently requires a federally sanctioned monopoly.

little *new* ideological work to do. Other circumstances may obstruct such lines of behavior or make them impossible. In this case an ideology is threatened, and to the extent that a group defines itself in terms of its ideology, the group itself will be threatened and much remedial ideological work will be left to do. When problems or "crises" like these occur (and it is well to remember that they are *routine* in complex societies and especially salient in *intentional* communities), a variety of solutions are conceivable (although "solutions" is probably not the right word since these problems are seldom clearly solved—"negotiations" may be a better word). A group, for example, may alter or "sell out" its beliefs for the sake of survival under powerfully oppressive conditions that prevent realizing these beliefs; in this case ideological work will probably attempt to rationalize the alteration or the "selling out," or redefine their behavior as something other than selling out. Or a group may struggle against oppressive circumstances to make its beliefs more probably realizable; in this case ideological work is likely to attempt to mobilize the energies of believers in behalf of the struggle. Or somewhere between these two, a group may accommodate its beliefs to the circumstances it cannot alter, while manipulating those it can to achieve the best bargain it can get—somewhat in the manner of the Alcoholics Anonymous prayer, which beseeches the Almighty for the guidance to change what can be changed, to accept what can't be changed, and for the wisdom to recognize the difference. All of these solutions require ideological work.

In Bernard Shaw's play *Major Barbara*, Mr. Undershaft (the liquor and munitions tycoon) takes his daughter, the Salvation Army officer, for a tour through the neat and pleasant garden-apartment community he has built for the workers in his factories. She, frustrated and desperate at the failure of her noble ideas and efforts to help the miserable and the wretched at the army's mission, is utterly crushed at seeing the wholesome lives and happy faces in the garden community, which her father's ill-gotten gains have made possible. She dissolves into tears. Her father provides comfort: "You've learned something," he says to her, "which always appears at first as if you've lost something." He, presumably without illusions (but clearly doing ideological work), suggests that disillusion is the first step toward wisdom. His comment is obviously self-serving (although not necessarily less persuasive because it is) and seems to contain an implicit recommendation to his daughter that she sell out her apparently counterproductive Christian ideas or accommodate them to conditions that she cannot change: people will both drink and make war on each other, and entrepreneurs will profit by providing them the wherewithal to do both, perhaps doing a little good for their workers in the process.

But like "false consciousness," which, however clearly it may be defined conceptually, is likely to be contested (that is, ambiguous) in the concrete case, "selling out," "struggling," and "accommodating" are seldom unambiguously self-evident *while they are occurring.* Ideologies are usually sufficiently ambiguous that these terms are actually interpretations of events they ostensibly describe or summarize, and the interpretations are likely to serve the interests of the groups who make them. Few people (communards included) probably *like* selling out their ideas, unless the price is a very good one indeed (cost-benefit analysis may be applicable even in this extreme case). And like everyone else, communards struggle to some extent toward realizing their ideas. They also, when they have to, accommodate their ideas to recalcitrant circumstances, while at the same time they attempt to maintain some semblance of consistency, coherence, and continuity in what they believe they believe they believe. That is what ideological work is about. How communards go about getting that work done is what the rest of this book is about. But before I get to that, I want to describe The Ranch and my involvement with it.

CHAPTER **2**

THE RANCH

THE SETTING AND THE PEOPLE

The Ranch occupies 140 acres of meadow, orchard, and canyoned forest of redwood, fir, pine, alder, laurel, and madrone, somewhere in rural California. The land was bought in the 1960s by two affluent dropouts, wealthy enough to afford the $50,000 price. Along with some friends and acquaintances, they moved in and attempted to make a commune. That was in 1968, when the streets of San Francisco's Haight-Ashbury had begun to turn mean, and the counterculture was already beginning to go desperate, violent, apocalyptic. Twelve years later The Ranch is still there, surviving, a very long time by the standards of post-hippie communes without formal religious organization.[1]

Over this period, membership has varied between fewer than a dozen to around two dozen adults, plus increasing numbers of children. But it is less accurate to characterize this variation as "turnover" (although there was a good bit of turnover in the first few years) than as a gradual decline in adult membership from its high in the first couple of years to its present low, as the essentially *communal* character of the enterprise emerged. Despite the variation in the size of The Ranch's membership, several of the original members are still there, and former members return occasionally to often for longer or shorter visits, which may turn into another "permanent" stay.

1. Most informed guesses by students of communes estimate the modal duration of "hippie" communes (i.e., those without formal creeds or religions or reliable sources of stable income) as from one to two years.

The Ranch is not the kind of commune that is easily accessible or open to anyone who wants to crash—as, for example, Morningstar Ranch was, a place whose very openness and accessibility brought it widespread publicity (and disaster) in the early phase of the commune movement.[2] The Ranch is more than two miles from the nearest paved road, and the paved road is neither major nor always in good repair, used regularly, as it is, by loaded logging trucks rolling out of the woods. The Ranch is about ten miles from the nearest village and grocery store, about sixteen miles from the nearest town of any size, and about twenty-five miles from the nearest town big enough to sustain a supermarket, a movie theater, or a fast-food outlet.

The Ranch protects its privacy rather well too. Although the signs at the gate to its access road are not encouraging ("No Trespassing"), visitors may be welcomed if they are friends of someone who lives there, or even friends of friends, but they are generally not welcome to stay for very long, at least not without considerable discussion. There are many reasons for this policy, perhaps the foremost of which is the group's understanding that the wrong kind of person can seriously damage their fragile solidarity. But the most obviously convenient (and polite) reason is that facilities are limited.

The main building is a wood-frame ranch house, built early in this century. It is built around an inner courtyard, and contains a kitchen, dining room, living room, and several other rooms that were once presumably bedrooms, but which the commune uses as a library, a children's playroom, a storage room for old or communal clothing, a sewing room, a pantry, and a room sometimes used for guests. The ranch house, in short, is the "communal" house and is used primarily for collective purposes, which means in effect that nobody "lives" (i.e., *sleeps*) there, or nobody is supposed to routinely, except,

2. See Sara Davidson, "Open Land," *Harper's* (June, 1970). See also William Hedgepath and Dennis Stock, *The Alternative* (New York: The MacMillan Co., 1970). See also Hugh Gardner, *The Children of Prosperity* (New York: St. Martin's Press, 1978); and Lewis Yablonsky, *The Hippie Trip* (New York: Pegasus, 1968).

perhaps, the ancient, black, dusty Labrador retriever who survived during my eight-year association with The Ranch despite everybody's expectation that she would die of old age at any moment. People who live at The Ranch sleep in "their own" houses, some of which have been built by their own hands. Indeed, the building of one's own house on the land is informally taken as an indication of one's serious commitment to "permanent" residence or membership.

The private residences are scattered about clearings in the woods and are connected by paths. There are perhaps a dozen or more such houses, usually of one or two rooms, sometimes with a sleeping loft, and almost always of primitive (i.e., noncode) construction; some have unique touches, for example, irregularly shaped window frames made from small tree branches. In the summer, a few large tipis may be seen on the land. People not only sleep in their private houses but also keep most of their personal possessions there: mattress and blanket or sleeping bag, clothes they regularly wear, pictures, religious objects, books they're currently reading, crafts they may be working on, and minor cooking equipment, like something to boil water in and the makings of tea.

The existence of the communal house plus the private residences provides a nice balance between needs for privacy and collective sociability. People will gather for meals in the communal house, irregularly wandering in for a breakfast of bread and jam or honey, tea or coffee (or grain coffee-substitutes) or oatmeal, and more formally when summoned for dinner by the ringing of a bell or the blowing of a conch shell or a ram's horn, the latter two a privilege to which the children look forward eagerly. The communal house is also used for meetings, entertaining, casual or ceremonial occasions, or just hanging out, although spontaneous and small-scale visiting also occurs at the private residences.

The kitchen, which is of course the center of action in the communal house, is large, and for most of my association with The Ranch contained a restaurant-sized gas range, one or two big gas refrigerators, a wood-burning cookstove, a double sink with hot (sometimes) and cold running water, and storage space for dishes and other kitchen equipment. In an unenclosed corner of the kitchen there is a bathtub, a stall shower, a medicine cabinet with mirror, and another deep sink alongside which are hung many toothbrushes. Naked people are often in the kitchen in one or another stage of pre- or post-bathing. A large worktable stands between the gas range and the "bathroom" corner. There is no indoor toilet. An outhouse was located about twenty yards from the kitchen door, and in 1977 a grandly conceived "composter-shitter" was constructed near the kitchen, with a handsome slatted redwood ramp leading to the impressive doorway.

The dining room is sparse: a big, old dining table with benches and old chairs, a serving table in the corner stacked with chipped bowls and dishes of various sizes, a large bulletin board containing schedules for household work and other chores; notes, letters from friends, children's drawings, godseyes and other art and craft work done by members and friends past and present. The living room has a big stone fireplace, a ratty old rug on the floor, a rope swing hung from the exposed beams, an old double mattress and box spring (the Labrador slept there a lot of the time; I did too several times), a few ancient and overstuffed chairs in various stages of disrepair. A door from the living room leads out to a decaying porch (perhaps ten feet above the ground), which overlooks the apple orchard (one can reach out and pick the blossoms in April), a favorite gathering place on Sunday afternoons or warm evenings in summer for after-dinner smokes and talk. Also off the living room, the library contains perhaps two thousand books, heavy on literature; poetry; religion; philosophy; and practical, how-to books.

The Ranch is blessed with good land, good water, and a temperate coastal California climate. Residents grow much of their own food in two gardens, a small one planted shortly after they arrived, in the center of which sat a shaded Buddha on a pedestal; a crudely lettered sign on grayed redwood announced "love of seed nourishes." A much larger garden was planted in 1972, and in 1973 a large and elaborate greenhouse was constructed. In the meadow alongside the dirt and gravel road that runs from the gate through the woods and the meadow to the communal house can be seen not only the greenhouse and the gardens but also (at various times) a goat pen, an American-Indian sweat house constructed from redwood bark, an old washing machine using water piped from a spring, geese, chickens, cats, cords of firewood stacked and aging, laundry drying on a clothesline attached to two enormous trees, and a large Quonset hut containing a forge, workshops, and great quantities of automobile parts and scrap steel from the junked cars (grown from five or six in 1971 to thirty-five or thirty-six in 1978) lying in a field nearby. Another sign on the road nailed to a tree said "the seed is nourished in silence."[3]

California has recurrent, fierce rainstorms out of the north Pacific in the winter; but the temperature only rarely drops below freezing along the coast, although overnight frosts are not uncommon a few miles inland. The dry summers are pleasant, sunny or foggy depending on one's distance from the coast, but hardly ever unpleasantly hot (within eight or ten miles of the coast) by the standards of the rest of the country. Frequent, long rainy spells in the winter sometimes give communards (and others) "cabin fever," stretches when mud makes the road almost impassable and when there's nowhere to go and nothing to do without getting utterly soaked, chilled, or both. It's rural life, although not nearly as comfortable as modern rural life can be, because The Ranch lives without electricity or telephone or vehicles whose reliability can always be counted upon. I performed as chauffeur for The Ranch on several occasions when its cars or trucks were not running or were otherwise unavailable; and one night when a woman with a tubal pregnancy needed emergency hospital care, my car was the only one sufficiently reliable to negotiate the fifty miles of twisting mountain road to get her

3. The first time I saw that sign I remember my defensive response to what I took to be its ostentatious reverence: I thought of the old Jewish joke about the wise and ancient rabbi who told a member of his congregation that "life is like a fountain." Perplexed, the member asked what that meant. The rabbi looked puzzled, thought a while, then replied, "So maybe it's not like a fountain." So maybe the seed is not nourished in silence, I thought. The sign made me nervous.

the medical attention she needed at the county seat. Kerosene lamps provide nighttime light, and wood is the major source of heat in both the communal house and the private cabins. The cabins use small stoves, sometimes homemade from an old milk can or cast-iron tank.

What do they do? How do they live? The Ranch is what I call (without any particular commitment to the label) an anarchist commune (some of them prefer the term "consensus" commune). Not that all or most of its population are formally anarchists; they aren't. I call it anarchist to emphasize their negative predisposition to formal rules, organization, and hierarchy, and to distinguish communes like The Ranch from those communes that are heavy with organization, stable role differentiation, an official creed, a dedicated mission, ritual discipline, and a formal hierarchy of leaderships and followerships. These latter groups are themselves differentiated, ranging from secular groups like Synanon through Jesus communes to Hare Krishna groups and other Eastern religious ashrams, and to secular communal groups like Twin Oaks in Virginia (with its Skinnerian creed and formal organization and its commercial hammock-making enterprise) to Steve Gaskin's The Farm in Tennessee, with its charismatic leader, its missionary character, and its enormous membership, to "The Family of Taos" (now defunct) with its pseudo-aristocratic hierarchy of titles and its sexual jungle.[4] I will not

4. On Synanon, see Lewis Yablonsky, *Synanon: The Tunnel Back* (Baltimore: Penguin Books, 1967); for Hare Krishna communes, see J. Stillson Judah, *Hare Krishna and the Counterculture* (New York: John Wiley, 1974); see also Francine Daner, *The American Children of Krsna* (New York: Holt, Rinehart and Winston, 1974); on Twin Oaks, see Kathleen Kincade, *A Walden Two Experiment* (New York: Morrow and Co., 1973); for The Farm, see Stephen Gaskin ("Stephen and the Farm"), *Hey Beatnik!* (Summertown, Tenn.: The Book Publishing Co., 1974); there is also a chapter on The Farm in John Rothchild and Susan Wolf, *The Children of the Counterculture* (New York: Doubleday and Co., 1975); on The Family of Taos, see Margaret Hollenbach, "Relationships and Regulation in 'The Family' of Taos," in R. M. Kanter, *Communes: Creating and Managing the Collective Life* (New York: Harper and Row, 1973); for a variety of analyses and comment on religious communes, see Charles Glock and Robert Bellah, *The New Religious Consciousness* (Berkeley: University of California Press, 1976), especially the essay by Richard Ofshe on Synanon: "Synanon: The People Business."

be concerned with any of these types of communes, except
for occasional *ad hoc* comparisons.

During my association with it, The Ranch was a post-
hippie "family" commune, several of the members going so
far as to call themselves by a common family name. But this,
like most of their practices, was not obligatory for all; the
point is simply that the *family* was their major enterprise;
maintaining and developing the *communal* idea (itself never
entirely clear and still in the process of emerging) was their
main business, rather than the promotion of a political or religious or psychotherapeutic doctrine. The Ranch had no formal creed, no self-appointed or elected leaders or permanent
official representatives. No one would even admit to the role
temporarily, although of course not all members were equally
influential in communal affairs; and the occasionally excessive influence of a few was at times a source of grumbling or
resentment by the relatively uninfluential others, very much
like an extended family.[5]

Unlike many other communes, The Ranch had no single
income-producing collective enterprise around which it was
organized (like hammocks for Twin Oaks, or Volkswagen repair shops, restaurants, incense manufacture, or candle-
making enterprises for other communes), no charisma, no
missionary zealotry. This is not to say they had no ideas; they
had (and have) more than you can shake a stick at. But few, if
any, of their ideas were compulsory, and virtually all of them
were ideas already familiar around the counterculture by
1968: peace, freedom, love, spontaneity, spiritual questing
(through drugs and otherwise), nature, survival, health,
equality, intimacy, brotherhood-sisterhood (the latter later—
and very important), the do-it-yourself therapies (from Eastern yogic practices to Esalen westernisms, and involving a
great deal of talk about "consciousness," "spaces," and
"working through" hang-ups), and living with as few pos-

5. J. David Hawkins, "The Dynamics of Conformity in Communal
Groups of the Counterculture Movement" (unpublished ms., 1978) contains
some data on The Ranch indicating some of this grumbling. There are, of
course, inequalities of power and influence at The Ranch, and I have not paid
any systematic attention to its internal stratification.

sessions as were useful or necessary, rather than with as many as one could be induced to want.

Alongside these "values" lay the equally familiar negative-critical postures toward urban, middle-class life: against bureaucracy, impersonality, war, competition, consumerism, careerism, technology, alienated work, suburbia, Mammon worship, buttoned-up repression, hierarchy, authority, corporate capitalism, sexual possessiveness, and the isolated nuclear family. When I asked a small group of them once whether they had any one, basic value, Patricia replied: "Yes, wash your own dish."

In succeeding chapters I will have a good deal to say about some of these ideas, about their ambiguity and their ambiguous relevance to the circumstances of communal living. For now, it is sufficient to say that The Ranch's residents and extended visitors (who was or was not a "member" was sometimes a matter of some dispute) over the years have been composed mostly of serious, bright, talented, and verbal people (some, of course, more so than others), several of them usually ready to lay a rap on at short notice. The following is a brief sketch of some of The Ranch's communards over the past ten years, to which readers may refer when I mention some of them later:

1. BOB: 37, short, dark-haired, wiry; a practical philosopher (with graduate school training); all sorts of useful skills: mechanics, gardening waste disposal, blacksmithing; serious, thoughtful, given to the hard decisions; rural Alabama born and raised; very influential; coupled for a time with Linda.[6]

2. LINDA: late twenties; mother of Birch (by Bob); strong, quiet woman; works very hard; sensible, laid-back, unpushy, but cannot be pushed; usually very busy—in the kitchen, or repairing cars (learned from Bob) or upholstering or gardening.

---

6. Where I know the ages of the persons involved, it is stated specifically; in other cases it is estimated (as of 1978). The names of all persons are, of course, changed.

3. PATRICIA: mid-thirties; mother of Tanya and Kashfi, each by different fathers, neither of whom were members of the family; an energetic catalyst; thin; bursts of energy; given to sudden angers and just-as-sudden sweetnesses. A major influence since the beginning, particularly in the organization and maintenance of the school run by (and at) The Ranch; was also influential in the establishment of a now-successful feminist magazine with a national circulation; her name is now on the deed to the property.

4. MAXWELL: mid-forties; sometimes called "Maxwell McNice" (the latter a play on his real name) to indicate his sweetness of temperament; tall, craggy, Lincolnesque; gentle and relatively isolate; came to The Ranch with his wife and children, who left after a short time—some sadness and guilt about this; loves children; children love him; geese too, as well as practically everyone else; does not usually press his views on others, although he has doubts about the wholesomeness of bisexuality; coupled presently with Sheila—although he was uncoupled for most of the years of my association with The Ranch.

5. SHEILA: early to mid-thirties; matronly, very unhippieish; personally unaggressive, although she has been active in worthy causes like ecology and fighting the big lumber companies; teaches at the school; mother of Snowbird (by Paul); she came to The Ranch with Paul, with whom she was then coupled.

6. PAUL: 36; dark, curly-haired, intellectual; strongly attractive to women; given to American-Indian lore, mystic visions; working through sexual and psychological hang-ups; son of an eastern physician; coupled for three or four years with Vickie, although he sleeps with other women, which was a problem for Vickie; he and Sheila share the care of their child; Paul's name is also on the deed to The Ranch.

7. VICKIE: early to mid-thirties; tall, long-limbed, sexy, prematurely weathered; wonderful, straight-out, spontaneous talker; lucidly self-conscious and reflexive; mother of Grove and Rainbow (by different fathers); she left The

Ranch for a while to live with Sid, the father of her second child, on the Monterey Peninsula; returned with him
a few months later; left The Ranch after breakup with
Paul in 1979, although her daughter remains.

8. SID: mid-forties; tall, dark, balding; into Eastern philosophy, massage, and other physically manipulative
therapies; came to The Ranch with Vickie, with whom he
had developed a liaison outside The Ranch. He left The
Ranch shortly after Vickie's coupling with Paul began to
look as if it would last a long time. He returned for visits
while Vickie and their child were living at The Ranch.

9. ABE: 38, poet, bard, reciter of the Upanishads; interpreter
of mystic texts; founding editor of one of San Francisco's
earliest underground, psychedelic newspapers; co-
author of book of poetry-photography documenting the
birth of Swallow, "his" (but see below) son; never wholly
committed to dropout life as a communard; periodically
asked me to arrange poetry readings for him at universities; philosopher of "burning out" sexual jealousy; returned to the city in 1975 to pursue career as writer; now
"hanging out with poets and artists"; "still falling in and
out of love"; returns to The Ranch for visits, the last visit
being for a big birthday party in his honor.

10. BONNIE: early thirties; coupled with Abe during first few
years of the research; beautiful Jewish princess; ex-
flowerchild; Abe and Bonnie (with their son, Swallow)
lived in a tipi; converted to Christianity by nearby Jesus
commune in 1972, after considerable difficulty with Abe;
she took Swallow with her and denied Abe's paternity to
keep him away from Swallow, to whom Abe was closely
attached. Much tension between the two communes for a
short while, involving an aborted "kidnapping" attempt.
Bonnie now lives a Christian life in New Jersey and tells
Abe (whom she regards as the Devil) that, if he wants to
see Swallow, he will have to go through Jews for Jesus.

11. ANNE: early thirties; fierce, intellectual, razor-tongued woman; hard-working, handsome, independent; coupled at

first with Ernest (later cailed Hawk) by whom she is the mother of Starlight; coupled later with Jack by whom she later gave birth to Valle; left The Ranch with Jack and Hawk in 1975 to go to New Mexico; returned with Jack in 1976, pregnant with Valle; now trying to establish commune some sixty miles from The Ranch; returns to The Ranch for visits.

12. HAWK (Ernest): early thirties; tall, blond, poetic, romantic; accomplished guitarist and banjoist; seemed to suffer a good deal during Anne's transfer of her primary affections to Jack; frequently tense; seemed like a relatively immature seeker to me. I was present during an interesting visit to The Ranch by Hawk's Jewish parents from New York. Most of the other communards seemed to enjoy the lively aggressiveness of Hawk's father; he seemed tense and uncomfortable with it, which put Hawk's smoldering passivity in a new light for me. Hawk is now running a successful shop for the sale, repair, and trading of stringed instruments in New Mexico; would like to return to California to do the same thing.

13. JACK: early thirties; handsome, curly-haired, good and energetic worker; bright and self-contained; unintellectual; strong practical bent.

14. COLLEEN: early thirties; strawberry blonde, freckled, sexy; occasional topless dancer in the city to make money; coupled with George and mother of Thunder (by George); coupling with George never was stable; several other lovers; left The Ranch in 1974 with Thunder but without George; now described (without rancor) as "into money and cosmetics"; still has good relations with The Ranch's communards and entertains some when they visit the city.

15. GEORGE: mid-thirties; short, balding, short-tempered; utterly out-front, staccato, speedy personality; supercritical at family meetings; well-liked in spite of frequently bad temper; now farming in northwest; has returned occasionally to The Ranch for visits.

16. JOSEPH (Celt): 27; tall, rangy, cowboy-hippie; came to The Ranch as a teen-aged dropout from family of Marin County artists; had been deeply into psychedelic drugs; younger, less intellectual, less mature than most of the other Ranch communards; hard worker; full of energy and schemes, but regarded as impulsive and unreliable by most of the group, which treated him as a sort of perpetual juvenile; he increasingly resentful; increasingly attracted to town life and its amenities; wants to find a woman and settle down to conventional family life; left The Ranch in 1978 to live at nearby nearly abandoned commune; scrapes a living together with his ancient pickup truck by hauling and selling slash from logging sites.

17. MANFRED: was in his mid-thirties when killed in a fight unrelated to The Ranch; one of the first communards I met; a peculiar combination of violence and gentleness in his bony face, with thin skin pulled taut over its sculptured prominence; expert on tipis; "crazy," high, full of weird energies; left the commune in 1971, a fugitive from the FBI; returned to the region (but not to The Ranch) in 1974 with his legal troubles settled; worked for a while as equipment manager and bouncer for a local rock band; deceased 1976.

18. GABY: early thirties; dour, relatively uncommunicative woman; hard-working, practical, occasionally sharp tongue; coupled with no one I knew of; left The Ranch in 1977 to live in another commune in the far north of California, forty miles from nearest paved road (I visited this place once, which regards itself as a sister commune to The Ranch, since many of their members know each other well from pre-commune days).

19. SHIRLEY: late twenties-early thirties; British accent; thin, delicate, pretty; came to The Ranch with her child but without its father in 1973; works hard; never visibly coupled.

20. SEENA: late twenties-early thirties; like Shirley, came to The Ranch without a man but with child during the same

period in 1973–74; some tension between her and Vickie (who was originally against permitting Seena to become a member of the family) over the affections of Paul.

21. KATHY: late twenties; blonde and pink and smooth-skinned and apple-cheeked; always looked like a wholesome Swiss milkmaid to me; on-and-off member of the family from the beginning; occasional topless dancer in the city; now married to an Englishman and no longer at The Ranch; returns for visits.

There were others over the years, for example, Arthur, a tall, mustached, published poet, Brooklyn-Jewish, who had learned his Eastern philosophy on pilgrimages through the Orient; and Rita, a short, chunky, gap-toothed woman and mother of their child, born, like many others at The Ranch, without benefit of professional medical help. They stayed less than a year, although they did build a cabin. Rincon, a tall and angular Buffalo Billish figure with big mustache and buckskin with fringe, a mandala artist in his forties, was coupled for a while with Esme, a movie-star-beautiful, black, young woman; their child was called Rami. Rincon, Esme, and Rami left The Ranch, early in my association with it, when Esme won a scholarship to study in France, where she eventually married the leader of a Muslim sect. There was Piper, a relatively harmless, nearly psychotic young man who spent most of his time whittling flutes, expounding his eccentric ideas on botany and zoology, and living off his disability pension from the state. He stayed only briefly. Tim was a leather craftsman with a deformed arm whose stump did not seem to impede the quality of his work; he was in and out of residence at The Ranch for a long period. Finally, there was Candice, a thin, nervous, dark-haired young woman given to colds and sniveling and perpetual searches for vitamin C, mother of Nicole. Candice was coupled for a time with Flint, who came to The Ranch with his troubled young son, Freddy, obviously mothered by a black woman with whom Flint had been previously coupled.

Some of these people stayed only a short time, some for two or three years, some for five or six years, and others have been at The Ranch continuously from the beginning; but on the whole they were a group of educated dropouts, fed up with urban hip life (as well as middle-class life) and disillusioned by the politics of the New Left, who went to the country with some of their friends to see if they could create an intentional family, the good society in microcosm, the revolution by example; if not socialism in one country, communalism in one commune, a counterculture in one setting. Their image was friends-as-family: working, playing, singing, dancing, living, loving, hanging out together.[7]

Common sense and "the literature" tell us that such communes are prime candidates for disaster; such places almost always "fail." But unlike the great majority of such groups (anarchist, retreatist, or hippie communes), The Ranch is still there, past celebrating its tenth birthday, tending its gardens, repairing its vehicles, keeping the moss off the apple trees, milking its goats, making cheese and yogurt, participating in local political affairs, and now educating its children formally; building greenhouses and schoolhouses and compostershitters. The Ranch is living its life, "just trying to make it, same as everybody."[8]

I do not know why The Ranch is a "successful" commune, if, indeed, survival for more than ten years is a measure of success. It may be, as Bob thinks, that they now own their land free and clear; that it is good land; that the core members have known each other for a very long time, indeed, some of them before they ever took up residence at The Ranch. They are also bright and resourceful people, respectful of the variety of paths and personal changes that lead people in and out of the commune. Perhaps they have survived because they "believe in" what they're doing, or because they have no

7. Rosabeth Kanter calls such groups "retreat communes." The term, I think, is misleading if it is taken to imply a retreat from some former ideal or a withdrawal from the "real world." Urban communards would often talk about the possibilities of their groups moving collectively to a rural life. I have never heard any rural communards talk about collectively moving "back" to the city.

8. From a "note about the author" (a communard) in Raymond Mungo, *Total Loss Farm* (New York: E. P. Dutton, 1970). They are, of course, trying to make it, but "same as everybody" stretches the point more than a little.

more attractive alternatives; perhaps because they were sensible enough not to establish "rules" that no one was willing to enforce; perhaps because they've gradually modified some of their more extreme counterculture views; and perhaps because they have gradually and largely *ad hoc* been able to cope with (if not permanently "solve") the two most important problems that break up communal efforts: the economics of survival and the cooperative difficulties stemming from sexual-interpersonal jealousies.

In any case, the causes of success and failure are less interesting to communards than to journalists, social scientists, and other outsiders, sympathetic or hostile, who are interested in explaining to their audiences why communes like The Ranch must almost inevitably fail, or why the evidence of their success should hearten us to keep seeking the means to restore our lost sense of community and solidarity, which—as Carl Becker said of God in the eighteenth century—stole quietly away during the night of industrialization, leaving liberated man triumphant, affluent, alone, and in the lurch. I am interested in something else.

ACCESS: THE RANCH AND I

The biggest methodological problem of this research at The Ranch was always that of access, and after initial access, the problem of continued access, because access is never *finally* "won." I was lucky to get in initially on the coattails of a Medical Clinic team that, around the turn of the last decade, would tour the rural communes in its region to provide minor medical care and advice on home remedies. Those were the days not only of "Woodstock Nation" but also of smaller regional and local varieties of the same thing. The locale around The Ranch was often referred to by local communards as a nation in the Woodstock sense, and there seemed to be rock festivals and crafts fairs for almost every conceivable holiday, with flat-bed trucks backed rear-to-rear serving as bandstands, the tall grass full of flower-decked hippies picnicking in the sun, the pond full of naked swimmers, the woods full of lovers, and the trees hung like Christmas, with trinkets for sale.

There were several other communes of substantial size not far from The Ranch. Indeed, on my first trip with the medical team to the region, I had never even heard of The Ranch and certainly had no idea that it would wind up occupying my thoughts (and dreams) for many years. Before we ever arrived at The Ranch, we had spent much of the previous day (and night) at a much more accessible commune (entered directly from a paved county road) called Gertrud's Land, whose seventy-five acres were dotted with tree stumps that had fresh foliage growing out of the decaying wood, giving the stumps the look of enormous bushes. Gertrud, a beautiful, middle-aged woman with deep sympathies for troubled hippies, had "opened" her land to transient young people looking for a new life. There were about twenty people living on the land, "dedicated" (according to Gertrud) to the communal ideal and in the process of building their houses. Gertrud took us on a tour of the land to inspect the houses and the types of construction, which included one geodesic dome and a couple of charming "gingerbread" cottages, among other more nondescript construction. Many of the doors on these houses had the stylistic mark of the land's resident craftsman, who took some pride in building and hanging his plank doors entirely without hardware.

Gertrud's own house, then still unfinished, was being constructed by the cooperative labor of the people there, using mostly old beams and old barn lumber, but with utterly luxurious touches like a very large stained-glass window over her bed and delicately leaded windows of clear glass on either side of the massive front door. The house had just two rooms: a large kitchen with a fireplace, a wood burning stove, and a bright yellow refrigerator (Gertrud's house had both electricity and a telephone), and a large bedroom with a ladder leading up to a spacious loft. During the day the loft was used primarily for sewing, but at night it became a sort of dormitory-crash-pad for the transient hippies.

About fifty yards from Gertrud's house stood (barely) a decaying barn where we had dinner that night. We had brought some barbecued chickens, rice, and a jar of curry—which turned out to be the core of the dinner, although there were

also several salads, a thick potato-onion-celery soup, and a
variety of home-baked breads, cakes, pies, and hot cherries
for dessert. A few people I spoke with remarked that it was a
far better dinner than usual. As the food was put out on a
large smorgasbord, most of the twenty-or-so people present
sat on or stood near some benches, spread around a big
campfire in the barn, talking or meditating. At someone's
signal, the sitting people stood, joined hands with the others,
and began chanting a fugal "Om." I looked around that circle
of freaky faces, with the firelight flickering across them, the
godseyes fluttering, the stars visible through the holes in the
barn roof, I sniffed the mixed odors of the barn animals, the
food, the wood smoke, and the greasy jeans, and listened to
the rise and fall of the "Om-ing," and I felt the ethnographer's familiar rush of panic: how did I get into this? how
am I going to get out of it?

I got my sleeping bag and went back to the loft relatively
early after dinner (about 9 P.M.) because the long day and the
tensions of these first encounters had made me very tired, but
there were two guitarists and a banjoist up there jamming.
The music gradually attracted more people until the floor of
the loft supported wall-to-wall bodies responding enthusias-
tically to the music. Gertrud's elder son (about fourteen years
old) brought in a lid of marihuana, started rolling joints and
passing them around faster than the group could consume
them. The audience became even more animated in response
to the music when the three musicians were joined by two
visiting members of a locally celebrated rock group (a female
guitarist and a Hasidic-looking country violinist) who evoked
cries of "far-out!" and "too much!" as, backed by the other
three, they played a series of apparently well-rehearsed duets.
It was amid all this doping, music, and noisy enthusiasm
that I simply fell asleep in my bag.

In the morning (had it all been a dream?) I woke early,
stepped gingerly over the dozen-or-so bodies still sleeping on
the floor of the loft, and wandered over to the barn area,
where I saw a hot and cold shower that had been rigged up
inside a hollowed-out, half-burned tree whose floor had been
tiled and cemented. A Sears water heater stood alongside the

tree on the bare earth under the sky. I used the shower and
went into the barn where another fire had been started from
the embers of the previous night. There was a kettle of hot
water on the flame, and gathered round it were three people,
including Ron, a blond-bearded man in his thirties and his
seven-year-old daughter (visitors from an Oregon commune), whose faces I recognized from a cover of *Life* magazine, which had run a story on their commune the previous
summer. We chatted amiably about goats and granola and
Viet Nam and about what a blessing it was that marihuana
produced no hangover. Ron then informed me that Gertrud
had promised to prepare a wheat-germ-waffle breakfast with
melted butter and preserves, and if we didn't want to miss it
we'd better get over to the house.

After the delicious breakfast, the medical team got its work
done at Gertrud's Land around noon, and one of the musicians from the previous night's party in the loft volunteered
to come along and show us how to get to The Ranch, our next
stop, and, as it turned out, my research destination. We arrived at The Ranch on a sunny midwinter afternoon in 1970.
There had been a lot of rain for several weeks, and a sign at
the gate said "no vehicles beyond this point." So we walked
the more than two miles of muddy road, washed out in
places, to the main house at The Ranch. It was memorable
because in a clearing about halfway we came upon Maxwell
and Manfred, two communards who had been repairing the
road but who had stopped for lunch and were sitting on the
ground eating oranges and drinking hard cider (made from
apples off their own trees). After the introductions, a gallon
jug was passed around several times, while we chatted about
what we were there for. By the time we got to the house,
accompanied by the two communards, we were all fairly
high on the cider, and the good spirits generated by it lubri-
cated our introductions to the rest of the commune present
that day.

That first afternoon went well. The medical team did its
work; we got a short tour of The Ranch and a brief history of
it; Abe showed us photographs of the birth of his son and
talked with me of the possibilities of having them published

as a book. I was invited to visit again, and I was glad about that because, whereas Gertrud's Land had about it the frantic feel of transience in which people barely knew each other, the people at The Ranch seemed more settled and familiar with each other. Finally, that first afternoon was memorable too for the ride out we were given at the end of the day, back over the two-plus miles of muddy road to the gate where our car was parked: in an old van (driven by Celt, then nineteen) at about 35 MPH (to avoid getting stuck) shredding branches from overhead trees, bouncing across bumps and holes in the road, on one of which bounces I was literally lifted out of my seat and given a good hard knock on the head by the roof of the van. I remember my first encounter with The Ranch.

But even with access initially won, it was never secure because some of the communards at The Ranch did not like "sociology." The communards at The Ranch were typical of the counterculture in a variety of senses, not least of which were their middle-class manners and their generally high level of education. Most had been to college, and many had contacts with social science courses. The attitudes they revealed toward social science were largely (though far from exclusively) suspicious and in a few cases plainly hostile. The grounds of these suspicions were familiar ones to me, for I had encountered them among "humanistically" oriented people for many years and had even written about them while I was still a graduate student.[9] Sociology was identified as being implicated in the ethos of dehumanized science, which they had rejected. Cold and objective, it was part and parcel of the bureaucratic spirit of modern life that they regarded as the spirit of death. Moreover, it was identified with the universities, with which several communards had had a conflictive and/or unsuccessful experience—some had been involved in the struggles at Berkeley or San Francisco State, or other universities, or had strong opinions about those struggles. In its ethnographic efforts, voyeuristic sociology was identified with the journalistic spirit and the hordes of

9. See Bennett M. Berger, "Sociology and the Intellectuals," *Antioch Review* (Fall 1957).

media reporters who had descended on the Haight like (in their view) a proverbial plague of locusts in 1964–65, only to help transform a thriving neighborhood with an interesting population mix of black and white blue-collar workers, shop-keepers and hippie-bohemians into a locus of national fantasy, beginning its long slide into nightmarish decline.

The communards, then, had reason to be suspicious. They didn't much like sociology; and when they asked, as they repeatedly did, why the U.S. government was interested in studying them, I had no ready answer. When a government funding agency hands over a lot of money with apparently no strings attached, one doesn't think to look that particular gift horse in the mouth. "If you want to know about communes, take your money and go create one yourself" was a frequently repeated recommendation.[10] (Some of us researchers entertained the notion that our money was granted because there were people at NIMH whose own children had disappeared into communes, and their parental anxieties about the fate of their children might be allayed by funding a study to find out what life was like in them.) There were in fact no strings attached; we had very little contact with NIMH, and I didn't have to know "why" they funded the study, beyond the self-evident interest that studying communal child-rearing had—although it did become clear later that the Nixon administration turned out to be considering family policy and day care for children.

Nevertheless, the major point is that some of the communards at The Ranch did not like sociology and were skeptical of our interest in them; they had chosen after all to live as they did partly to get away from what we represented: universities, middle-class life, professionalism, urbanity. But they seemed to like me and Bruce Hackett well enough; sociology, no!—we long-haired sociologists, si! Hence the role problem in the research was always salient: the ambiguity created by their devaluation of the researcher's role,

10. McCulloch and Abrams report an identical response from their study of British communes. See Philip Abrams and Andrew McCulloch, *Communes, Sociology, and Society* (Cambridge: Cambridge University Press, 1976).

combined with their apparent affection for me and my co-investigator. There's a worthy ambiguity there. Not that they didn't know the difference between a person and a role; the distinction was obvious enough to them and ironically observed on more than one occasion (over an early coffee: "have you taken any notes yet this morning?" or "how is our sociologist today?"). I would sometimes be introduced to people who did not know me as "our sociologist," but there was also that one morning a year or so into the research, when, in my presence, a letter was read aloud from a social scientist to The Ranch informing them in stilted and pompous language of his intention to visit for research purposes and explaining that, if he did not hear from them by the following week, he would appear shortly thereafter. They thought it was all very funny. I was never certain whether the letter was read aloud in my presence to make me uneasy or to signify that I had finally been accepted as a trusted person.

But although they were conscious enough of the ambiguity of my role, their knowledge was no help in quickly resolving the ambivalence between their apparent willingness to tolerate my hanging around and their distrust of the manifest reasons for my being there. Given the delicateness of the situation, the demeanor of the research had to be delicate, at least at the start. Not that it was so deliberately and continually; I had to be careful, but if it had been necessary for me to be deliberately and consciously careful *all the time*, the research would simply have been too difficult, too exhausting. I never deluded myself (or attempted to delude them) that the research was of the sort that would "help" them in any way I could think of—as, for example, the medical team helped, or research designed to solve social problems may sometimes (but not usually) help. Instead, as it gradually became clear to me that several of the communards at The Ranch were fond of me (not me the sociologist, the researcher, the ethnographer, the professor, but me the skeptical, ironic *philosophe*), I became increasingly interested in them, curious about what they might teach me.

Not that I actually expected to be taught; I surely wasn't ready for that. But one of my "natural" selves suited their context. Like them, I was a seeker too, a professor come to them asking to be taken in as a welcome visitor for shorter or longer periods; unaggressively, even passively, asking permission to hang around, work sometimes, cook, sweep, wash dishes, build, crash wherever a place was available. A professor of some achievement, middle-aged, never having been completely at home in any of the environments that had sheltered me, above all skeptical, uncommitted, but sympathetic. I felt like an elder, not like a father—in part because I was only too aware that paternal attitudes would not be well received. Nor did I actually feel avuncular or paternalistic—like a "catcher in the rye" intent upon saving the *bubalas* from a fate that I might be able to anticipate but that they could not foresee—rather, an older brother, senior friend, sometime neighbor (I rented houses nearby on several occasions, eventually bought a few acres not far away, and built a house), gradually and increasingly trusted figure.

From 1970 to 1974, my visits lasted from a day, to a week or more, to frequent visits during three whole summers and one entire winter quarter when I was in residence nearby and visited often. From 1974 to 1979, I visited perhaps three or four times a year. In the early periods, I'd often come laden with gifts (discreet ones: a gallon of wine, a three-pound can of coffee, a gift for the children—never any marihuana or other psychedelic), bring news of the city, ask how things were, what's new? who's come? who's gone? any new projects? how's the garden? the kids? the moss on the apple trees? the mood? Driving in, I would sometimes infer the mood from the condition of the dirt road: bumpy, rutty road—bumpy, rutty mood. I'd talk about myself, my life, evoke talk about other selves, other lives; get philosophical; move into a "spiritual" mode; we're all interested in the problems and dynamics of communal living; participate, observe, comment (no unobtrusive observer I) on an emergent collective life.

I showed them a lot of me, and I realized later that I had to (although at the time it was not calculated) to establish my human credentials, as distinguished from my professional credentials, which did not impress them. I brought my kids;

my mother, once;[11] the woman I was going with. I brought Rosabeth Kanter once too. I inscribed a copy of my then-recently-published book to them, entertained some of them at my house in Oakland when they visited the Bay Area. I spent one day at The Ranch making gallons of jam from plums picked off my own tree in Oakland and hauled 150 miles to cook. I spent another morning making potato *latkes* for the whole commune, helped build a corral, weeded beets, ran errands, and shelled nuts for a *Seder*. The whole group came to dinner at my rented house near The Ranch. I aided one of them, Manfred, who had jumped bail on a drug charge in Boston, toward a dramatic escape to Canada from the FBI, which had traced him to The Ranch. When I moved in 1973 from the University of California at Davis to the University's campus in La Jolla, I arranged for my moving expenses to be paid to them in exchange for loading my household goods onto their big old schoolbus, and delivering them to me in southern California. No loss or breakage, by the way; I wish I could say the same for commercial movers.

We had a relationship then; I knew those people, and they knew me. But my relationship to them *as a researcher* was never secure. They knew who I was and why I was there. They knew that I was not a communard, *manqué* or otherwise, and that I was not even toying with the idea of becoming one. This was no Establishment professor seeking to be greened.[12] They knew I liked my life as it was and would not trade it for any other I could realistically imagine. Yet they continued to

---

11. This lower-middle class, provincial Jewish lady knew exactly what to do: She headed straight for the babies and immediately assumed a grand-motherly role, which evoked a spontaneous discussion of how communes need older men and women to reproduce the sense of a real family. The nudity in the kitchen did not disturb my mother from The Bronx, but the outhouse was too much for her to take.

12. Probably the three best books of the early 1970s with a counterculture point of view were written by "greened" professors. See Charles Reich, *The Greening of America* (New York: Random House, 1970); Philip Slater, *The Pursuit of Loneliness* (Boston: Beacon Press, 1970); Theodore Roszak, *The Making of a Counterculture* (New York: Anchor Books, 1969).

receive my visits cordially and liked having me around, no matter that some of them continued to dislike the idea of being "studied" under a U.S. government grant.

Perhaps they continued to let me come because it was palpable that I was very happy while I was there. I was truly touched by those people. Although I liked some of them better than others, I thought them very brave on the whole and I continually felt it a privilege to be among them. On leaving after a visit, I often remarked to myself how good I felt, how strong and restored and lucidly in touch with my understandings—even though I usually left with fewer field notes than I had solemnly resolved to make. But not really sorry about that because I had never been the kind of student who could understand a subject by cramming or otherwise recording a lot of material. Only after I *felt* a subject could I begin to think my way through it, using data to *make* meaning instead of memorizing or recording it to reproduce someone else's meaning. I respected them for being serious about what they were doing: building, gardening, mechanics, arts, crafts, cooking, solar power, composter-shitters, educating children— to say nothing now of the delicate interpersonal stuff with which they experimented and, of course, suffered a lot.

But the role ambiguity between researcher and person was still not resolved. One evening a few of us sat around talking after dinner. Bob, one of the founding members of the group (perhaps the central figure in the commune, with respected skills in mechanics, gardening, waste disposal, and other technical matters), talked about the formal ownership of the land (then still in the hands of the two men who bought it) and the legal status of their residence there, which evoked a few questions from me. He then revealed that he had been raised on a marginal farm in the deep South and had received a graduate degree in philosophy from a southern state university. It seemed a rather unusual life-course to me, and my curiosity was so touched that, before I could repress it, I fell into the interviewer's mode, "probing," attempting to elicit more information about how he had gone from rural poverty in the South to graduate education in philosophy to a different kind of rural poverty in California. A bad mistake for which I was immediately sorry; the group visibly stiffened; talk ceased; I had insulted the integrity of the conversation by treating one of its participants as a respondent.[13]

Shortly thereafter I received a letter at my home in Oakland; it summoned me to a family meeting to discuss the nature of my relationship to them:

Dear Bennett—

I have been selected by a [Ranch] council to ask you to come to a council meeting at your earliest convenience in order to evaluate our relationship to your study and to consider whether or not to continue that relationship whatever it is which is the cause of much confusion about the personal heart to heart presence of you. Perhaps some clarification will help us and you.

So could you write us to tell us when you can come so that we can all be present at that prearranged time.

The letter was signed by Abe, another original member of the group, a poet and former editor of a San Francisco underground newspaper, and he concluded the summons (which I read almost as a subpoena) with an exhortation to "let your lovelight shine."

The council meeting turned out to be a small one: seven or eight people (the adult population was more than double that at the time), prominent among them a few (Anne and Hawk, particularly) who had shown the most distrust of the study and the greatest overt hostility to social research in general—although even that was not flagrant hostility. The issue some of those present handed me was a simple one: they didn't want to be studied, but they were fond of me and did not want me to cease coming to visit them. Simple and complex; they liked my being there, but did not want to be part of any government study; come stay with us but don't

13. Richard Sennett makes some sour comments about interviewers behaving in an emotionally reciprocal way toward respondents. In a research setting like The Ranch, "professionally" detached postures would have made the research impossible. See Richard Sennett, *The Fall of Public Man* (New York: Alfred Knopf, 1976).

study us. I told them what they must already have known:
that, given the *kind* of research I was doing, there was no way
that I could continue my visits without at the same time
"studying" them. What they seemed to want from me was a
verbal promise that could not be sustained, and that it could
not be sustained seemed less important than the promise itself. It reminded me a little of what I imagined a Soviet purge
trial might have been like: confession and self-criticism, but
without any real possibility of substantive self-correction because, short of a radical transformation of my own consciousness, there was no way that I could imagine continuing my
visits without making observations and at least mental notes.

A discussion followed, the most memorable part of which
for me was an eloquent defense of social science by Abe, who
had written the letter summoning me to the meeting. Abe's
defense pointed out to my prosecutors that two generations
of social-science ethnography (he cited Benedict, Mead, and
the Lynds by name), by bringing home the message of cultural relativism to the American public, had gone far to create
the atmosphere of tolerance for "deviants," permitting them
to live, relatively unharassed, in the style they had chosen.
And rather than regard social science as their enemy, they
had every reason to be grateful to it for furthering progress
and enlightenment and toleration for unusual styles of life.

His speech seemed to have substantial effect. I had never
heard a more persuasive defense of our business (I still haven't).
I thanked him for his help, but muttered politely that I was
reluctant to be the occasion of any intra-family disputation
and that, rather than let it go on further, I would prefer to
withdraw. I told them plainly that I respected the feelings of
those with antipathies to being "studied," though I disagreed
with their reasons, which I thought mostly groundless. I told
them that I could not simply erase my professional researcher's consciousness and would not even if I could.
Hence I could not promise to continue my visits without
studying them, and since there was no way that I could fulfill
the promise, the emptiness of the verbal affirmation would be
an affront both to them and to me.

There was pressure there, and my response was not uncalculated. I had been in the field on and off for more than a year by the time the summons came; I had already seen much of their child-rearing, and I could always move on to another commune. I could afford to withdraw. But knowing them as I did, I also gambled that their personal knowledge of me would take precedence over their categorical feelings about "sociology." My bet was that in time their knowledge that they could trust me not to do them any gratuitous injury would prove to be more important than their distrust of my sociologist's role. In any case, I had a term of heavy teaching responsibilities in front of me as a visiting professor at a relatively distant campus, which meant that I would not be able to see much of them for a while. But I felt that eventually I would be invited back, and a short time later I was. I still go back there now and then.

CHAPTER 3

COMMUNE CHILDREN: EQUALITARIANISM AND THE DECLINE OF AGE-GRADING

> I am an anthropologist who lost faith in her own method, who stopped believing that observable activity defined anthropos. I studied under Kroeber at California and worked with Levi-Strauss at Sao Paulo, classified several societies, catalogued their rites and attitudes on occasions of birth, copulation, initiation and death; did extensive and well-regarded studies on the rearing of female children in the Mato Grosso and along certain tributaries of the Rio Xingu, and I still did not know why any one of these female children did or did not do anything at all.
>
> Let me go further.
>
> I did not know why I did or did not do anything at all.
>
> Joan Didion
> *A Book of Common Prayer*

      The experience of doing this reseach was fun sometimes. Bruce Hackett spent a lot of time at Gertrud's Land, and I spent a lot of time at The Ranch, but we were not *always* at our commune sites dutifully participating, observing, and making field notes. Residing near these research

NOTE: Some of the material in this chapter is adapted and revised from Bennett M. Berger and Bruce M. Hackett, "The Decline of Age Grading in Rural Hippie Communes," *The Journal of Social Issues* (Winter 1974); and from Bennett M. Berger, Bruce M. Hackett, and R. Mervyn Millar, "Child-Rearing sites in rented houses for three summers and other periods, we also spent time getting to know the environing community and living our lives in what I think is one of the most beautiful and spectacular regions in the world. My colleague brought with him to our rented house his old canvas-over-mahogany canoe, and when we were not working we began taking it out on one of the sheltered coves along the coast— for fishing, for getting to otherwise inaccessible beaches below sheer, rocky cliffs, diving for abalone. As we got to know the ocean in some of the infinite variety of its moods, we would even take the canoe further out on calm days, sometimes almost as far as a mile from shore, rising and falling on the gentle swells, watching seals poke their heads above the water. We would also sometimes careen through the narrow tunnels the ocean had bored through the rocky headlands, using our paddles to keep the boat from crashing the sides, timing the incoming waves to keep the boat from crashing against the roofs of tunnels where, in the higher ones, sea birds nested in the rocks. One time a flock of cormorants took off with a frightening whoosh only a few feet over our heads.

The Ranch was accessible not only by road but also by the canoe—three or four miles up a tidal river to an abandoned logging site from early in the century (the ruins of the apparatus were still there by which the logs were transported to the river, then floated down to the coast, and finally loaded on barges), then on foot through swamp and up a steep, wooded hill to The Ranch itself. One Sunday when we had friends visiting, we decided to paddle up river (with the incoming tide), picnic, visit with our commune friends, and paddle back with the outgoing tide.

The day started out sunny and bright. We put the canoe on the pickup, drove to the mouth of the river, and put the boat in the water. There were five of us in the big canoe, including my then-nine-year-old daughter. The silence of the river was broken only by occasional bird calls, the plop of the paddles hitting the water, and the flap of the wings of great blue her-

Practices in the Communal Family," in Hans Peter Dreitzel, ed., *Family, Marriage, and the Struggle of the Sexes*, Recent Sociology, No. 4 (New York: The MacMillan Co., 1972).

ons that lighted on the tops of the tallest trees, swaying the branches in what seemed like slow-motion. The day went quickly and idyllically, and dependent (as we were) on the tide table, we left early in the evening to paddle downstream. A thick, cold fog had come in from the coast, plunging the warm midday temperature into the 40s. It was already beginning to get dark when about halfway down the river, I peered through the gloom toward the north bank of the river and said, "Isn't that a naked woman over there?"

She was standing there quietly watching us. We paddled over toward the shore and she came down the bank toward us. Before any of us in the canoe could say a word she, like a casual urban tourist asking directions, said "Can you tell me how to get to [name of village]?" Her tone was so routinely matter-of-fact that I almost began to answer routinely until I realized that the question—and the answer I was preparing— were absurd. It was cold and getting dark fast. The village was miles away through thick woods and brush, probably filled with poison oak and blackberry thorns. We could see that her shivering, stark-naked body was scratched in several places and stained with blackberry juice. It seemed clear that she was in trouble but didn't know it. The canoe was already crowded, but it was plain she'd have to come with us. We helped her and her small dog into the boat. I put my jacket around her shivering shoulders, and we went on down the river.

She turned out to be fifteen years old, a girl from Arkansas who, with her migrant parents, had been back and forth to California several times. This time she had left her family to come alone and was staying temporarily (her status as a minor—and, presumably, a "runaway," made it necessarily temporary) with a nearby commune. Nudity was commonplace there on warm days; she had gone out that morning to pick berries, and got lost.

At the mouth of the river, we got the canoe out of the water and onto the pickup, and dropped her near the place she was staying. I helped her out of the truck; she gave me my jacket, kissed me on the cheek politely, then shyly looking down she said, "I got pine tar in my pubic hair; pubic hair, that's what you call it, isn't it?" "Yes," I said, "that's what you call it."

Then, like a sprinter, she took off at a full run, the headlights of the pickup illuminating her pumping haunches until she disappeared into the darkness.

A naked woman; fifteen years old. We researchers were sensitive to age because we were mandated to study child-rearing in a movement dominated by the youth of its own members. I had written a good bit on youth and had developed a strong interest in age-grading. What was a child? When did childhood end? Was adolescence a cultural invention rather than a natural stage of physiological development? Why did age-groups seem to segregate themselves? Was the postponement of adulthood a good idea? Why did we "shelter" and protect children from the experience of adult worlds? I had expressed myself previously on some of these questions, and the commune movement seemed a good place to study them further.

One of the movement's dominant themes was an emphasis on the importance of equality. Would it be extended to age? In *Total Loss Farm*, one of the earliest and still one of the best first-hand accounts by a communard of life at a "New Age" commune, Raymond Mungo comments: "we have children of our own, though they are fully peers by the time they've learned to eat and eliminate without physical help, and soon become more our masters than our students."[1] More our masters than our students: another of the movement's important ideas entailed a devaluation of most modern middle-class models of adulthood as a bad bargain with life in which one gave up more than one got in return. "Grownups are dead" is the way one communard tersely expressed it to me. Mungo put it more extensively: "It is awfully hard to be nine once you'll never see nineteen again. I am never quite free of the forces attempting to make me grow up, sign contracts, get an agent, be a man. I have seen what happens to men. It is curious how helpless, pathetic, and cowardly is what adults call a Real Man. . . . If that is manhood, no thank you."[2]

1. Raymond Mungo, *Total Loss Farm* (New York: E.P. Dutton, 1970), p. 157.
2. Ibid., pp. 136–37.

The other side of the coin that rejects adult models is an idea that affirms the natural virtue and wisdom of children unspoiled by repressive institutions. Thin, wiry, severe Patricia, midwife to The Ranch and other groups, a fierce and gentle woman Massachusetts-reared and Brandeis-educated, with two children of her own by different fathers, was describing the difficulty a friend of hers had (at another commune) in explaining the meaning of "lie" to her young daughter. "Don't worry," I said ironically, "she'll learn." Patricia's retort was characteristically quick: "Not if she stays home," she countered.

Of the many children born at The Ranch in the first six years of its existence, there are no Toms, Dicks, Harrys, Cathies, or Debbies. The children are called by such names as Birch, Snowbird, Rainbow, Swallow, and Starlight, names that convey no specific sexual identity, that express the kinship the family at The Ranch feels toward the American-Indian tradition, and that connect the children to the natural environment, although some names were selected for the children by adults trying to "tune in" to the childrens' natures.

The Ranch was well known in regional communal circles as a place devoted to natural childbirth. The birth of a child in a rural hippie commune—particularly if the birth is "natural" (as many of them are)—is sometimes the occasion of a collective celebration of great significance. For "first-generation" communards, the event can have a virtual constitutional meaning, signifying the collective property as a home to its occupants, and the occupants themselves as members of a single family. That the father will often participate directly in the delivery, receiving the baby into his own hands, and that no officials certified by the state (e.g., a physician) are present, symbolize the kinship-character of the event, that the child belongs to the family, not to the state. During our first visit to The Ranch, Abe showed us the photographs taken of Bonnie while she was in labor with their son. In one of these photographs, the heads of two small children may be seen watching the proceedings as the baby is drawn from its mother's body. The birth was a family celebration, involving massage, chanting, and music. Many members of the group were present, and Abe wrote a long poem to commemorate the event (later published as a book together with the photographs). Appended to the poem is a list of fifteen "Items for Ceremonial Childbirth at Home," and as if to emphasize the ritual character of the event, Abe speaks thus of the placenta:

> . . . deep purple silken pouch
> and we place it in a bowl
> and offer everyone a taste
> of this elixir, builder and nourisher
> of bodies, and I decide
> to bury it in our garden
> to nourish our soil . . .

AGE-GRADING

In spite of the praise of childhood and the dispraise of grownups, age is still one of the universal criteria for role allocation and social stratification, in communes as anywhere else, and there is no good reason to expect it to disappear soon. But over the past twenty years age-grading has been made more problematic as attacks have been mounted with increasing success on some of the traditional and enduring bases of ascriptive inequality, like race and sex. In this process, the status of chronological age as a "natural" criterion of social differentiation and inequality has become more vulnerable to criticism. Age may well be the last major ascriptive structural barrier to the pervasive equalitarianism that writers as early as de Tocqueville saw as an irresistible force in democracies.

Changes in the ascriptive meaning of race and sex have been occurring in recent years in a context of increasing controversy over the "oppression" of groups burdened by ascriptive characterizations of them made primarily by people other than themselves. Blacks argued, for example, that regardless of any other measures of their oppression, the fact that most "knowledge" about who and what they are was formulated by whites constituted a part of the racism oppressing them. Feminists have argued similarly about men regarding sexism. And in the process both groups have created whole libraries of monographs helping to correct the situation that was the source of their complaint.

Protests against age discrimination have not been nearly as insistent. But this may have something to do with the fact that sociological interest in age has been disproportionately concentrated on both ends of the life cycle, on groups perhaps least able to speak for themselves. The prolongation of childhood and other less-than-adult age statuses created one set of problems concerned with schools as age ghettoes and as the nurseries of youth subcultures, and the prolongation of life itself created another set of problems concerned with old age and retirement—indeed, a whole new field of social gerontology.

This should be no surprise. From its very inception, sociology has preoccupied itself more often with the study of relatively vulnerable and dependent groups than with those who have the power to refuse access to them by investigators or to define the terms of the investigation. Children and the aged perhaps lack the resources, the words, or the vigor to object. Nevertheless, apparently caught up in the movement of black, female, and other "liberation" movements, there have recently been at least more middle-adult voices talking about children's rights and children's liberation.[3] In any case, interest in the rights of children comes at a time of increasing suspicion regarding ideas about groups that are formulated by people who aren't members of those groups; at a time when we are predisposed to be sensitive to the self- and group-serving functions of white definitions of black, male definitions of female, and by extension, adult definitions of children.

3. See, for example, two recent anthologies: *Children's Liberation*, edited by David Gottlieb (Englewood Cliffs, N.J.: Prentice-Hall, 1973); and *The Children's Rights Movement*, edited by Beatrice and Ronald Gross (New York: Anchor Books, 1977). "Children's rights" and "children's liberation" tend to connote quite different postures. My impression is that those who use the term "children's rights" are primarily interested in guaranteeing the *protection* of children from abusive treatment by adults, whereas those who use the term "children's liberation" are more interested in *freeing* children from even the benevolent authority of adults. See also, *The Rights of Children*, edited by Albert Wilkerson (Philadelphia: Temple University Press, 1973).

It is a volatile topic. Tampering with any ascriptive system, age or otherwise, is "radical" in both senses of the term: in striking at the very roots of social structure, it threatens the interests based upon them. Ascriptive statuses tend to be taken for granted; hence, challenges to them tend to threaten the very sense of order and propriety of those who take them for granted (and who are thus not readily prepared to *argue* for them). Moreover, age-grading (the differential allocation of proper behavior and demeanor according to age) is universal and subtle and profound.[4] A sixteen year old may be jailed and labeled delinquent for behavior completely legal in an eighteen year old. A forty-year-old man may be humiliated as a "dirty old man" for behavior that is commonplace and expected in a twenty-one year old. Tom Cottle describes a college girl's disgust at her mother's wearing a mini-skirt and the actual nausea of another girl whose roommate's mother became a college student, poring over catalogues and gossiping about courses and professors as if she were a—kid![5] And, as is well known, child molesters evoke a special disgust not solely from the general public; they evoke the scorn and contempt of even the most hardened convicts in prison.

Still, despite the universality and profundity of age-grading, cultural definitions of behavior appropriate to specific age-groups vary enormously over time and place. Philippe Aries has shown how historically recent in Western civilization are our now-dominant conceptions of what childhood and adolescence "are"[6]—as if they are anything other

4. M.W. Riley, M. Johnson, and A. Foner, *Aging and Society: A Sociology of Age Stratification*, Vol. 3 (New York: Russell Sage Foundation, 1972).

5. Thomas Cottle, "Parent and Child: The Hazards of Equality," in David Gottlieb, ed., *Children's Liberation*.

6. Philippe Aries, *Centuries of Childhood* (New York: Vintage, 1962). Aries's influence has helped stimulate a great boom in recent years in historical studies of the family. See, for example, Edward Shorter, *The Making of the Modern Family* (New York: Basic Books, 1975); Christopher Lasch, *Haven in a Heartless World* (New York: Basic Books, 1977); and Lawrence Stone, *The Family, Sex and Marriage: In England 1500-1800* (New York: Harper and Row, 1977). For a good sampling of American scholarship, see Michael Gordon, ed., *The American Family in Social-Historical Perspective* (New York: St. Martin's Press, 1978).

than what we have made them—reminding us once again that the exteriority and constraint exercised by Durkheimian "social facts," having been made by human beings, may be changed by them to suit their changing historical circumstances.

In treating the history of the concept of childhood, social scientists have emphasized the differences between, on the one hand, pre-industrial or agricultural or, sometimes, lower-class families, and on the other hand, industrial, post-industrial, or middle-class families. In the former, the status of children is seen as ascribed at birth and rooted in the kinship system, where they are regarded as simply small or inadequate versions of their parents, totally subject to traditional or otherwise arbitrary parental authority. The modern, industrial, middle-class view of children is also rooted in the kinship system, but in this case children are increasingly treated as members of a distinctive social category, their social participation is increasingly limited to age-homogeneous groups, and their welfare is increasingly regulated by government action.[7] Children have their own special psychology, their own distinctive needs set by patterned processes of growth, which are often elaborated by psychologists and psychiatrists into theories about developmental stages, each with its own set of crises and transitions, which may postpone advent to "full" adult status (and the privileges that go with it) well into a person's twenties, and sometimes still later.[8] The task of parents and other "socializers" of children in this latter view is to "raise" or "produce" the child according to more or less "scientifically" elaborated principles of child-

7. See Shmuel Eisenstadt, *From Generation to Generation: Age-Groups and Social Structure* (Glencoe: The Free Press, 1955), for a theoretically interesting treatment of the significance of "age-heterogeneous" and "age-homogeneous" groups in pre-industrial and industrial societies. See also, Lasch, *Haven in a Heartless World.*

8. In his "Introduction" to Edgar Friedenberg's *The Vanishing Adolescent* (Boston: Beacon Press, 1959), David Riesman comments that in some professions where "referral" systems determine the advancement of practitioners, getting ahead for young professionals depends upon being someone's "boy," perhaps until the age of forty.

rearing and child management, a process that depends upon the presence and the availability of occupationally specialized persons to perform some of the socializing and that in many modern families transforms a woman-with-child into a full-time child raiser.

COMMUNAL CHILDREN: MOTHERING AND FATHERING

The prevalent view of children at The Ranch (and other communes like it) fits neither of these models exactly. Rather than being members of an autonomous category of "children" or being inadequate versions of their parents, legitimately subject to their arbitrary authority, children and young people (or "small persons," as they are sometimes deliberately, perhaps preciously, called) are primarily regarded as "persons," members of the communal family, just like anyone else—not necessarily less wise, perhaps less competent, but recognized primarily, as my colleague Bruce Hackett put it, "by lowering one's line of vision rather than one's level of discourse." This status for children is part of a larger, communal, equalitarian ethos in which almost all the communards at The Ranch resist attempts to "define" or characterize family members in terms of any standard that indicates role differentiation even remotely conceivable as exploitive or binding or restrictive of one's broadly "human" characteristics. Even when a division of labor appears to be natural, for example when persons have special skills or aptitudes for gardening or construction or mechanics or teaching, they are likely to disavow being described as "the gardener," or "the carpenter," or "the mechanic," or "the teacher."[9] Thus, the characterization of

9. Despite their aversion to "roles," communards generally understand the language of social roles but regard roles (although not skills) as something mere, something that, if one is coerced into "playing" them, may threaten one's basic humanity. The resistance to occupational role identities in communes may, of course, be strengthened by the absence of any particular rewards for accepting such identity. And although their argument that one is more authentically a person than a role might be sociologically quarreled with, their resistance to the taken-for-granted character of social roles does provide some ideological leverage for an equalitarian point of view.

children as small persons parallels the claims of women that
they are not just gender or kinship roles but people first,[10]
and the "humanistic" claims of men that they are not just bus
drivers or timber fallers or communards or sociologists, but
"human beings" first. In this sense, children are persons first.

But as a practical matter, of course, age makes important
and understandable differences. Infants and "knee babies"
are almost always in the charge of their mothers, particularly
if they are nursing. Rural communards occasionally discuss
the possibility of communalizing even infants—as in the notion of placing infants at an available breast rather than an
exclusively maternal one—but we have actually seen no instances of this, nor of several men having sexual intercourse
with a woman during her fertile period to make paternity deliberately ambiguous, although we have heard it rumored in
other places. We have, though, made many observations of
communal child care, for example, communal feedings, bath-
ings, and even defecations. Casual conversation between
children sitting on a two-holed outhouse seat was common.
And returning to The Ranch one afternoon with a carful of
kids after a trip to the beach and store, I stopped the car when
two toddlers complained of "bellyaches." In the care of one
commune adult, the two toddlers, joined by a third, got out
of the car, squatted in the woods by the side of the road, chatted amiably about the color, smell, and texture of each other's
feces, and under the ecological guidance of their elder, buried
the shit and burned the paper and dry leaves with which they
cleaned themselves.[11]

Children aged two to four frequently "belong to the commune" in a stronger sense than infants and knee babies be-

10. Eight-year-old Grove corrected me when I referred to Vickie as "her
mother." "Don't call her 'my mother,' " said Grove. "Why not?" I said, "she
is, isn't she?" "Yes," said Grove, "but her name is Vickie."

11. Babies are typically without diapers at The Ranch, with the predictable
inconvenient results. More than once I saw a turd picked up off the living
room rug by an adult with a patient, long-suffering face. One mother muttered ironically (and repeatedly) "I must not be upset by this." Another
mother, exasperated, shouted "What I wanted was a baby, but a *kid*, that's
something else!" Yet the children get toilet trained early.

cause they are less dependent upon continuous monitoring. Nevertheless, even with children of this age the conventional pattern of sharing their care was primarily in the hands of the group of mothers-with-children, any one (or more) of whom would do collective baby-sitting to give the other mothers a break from child care. The obligations of such care could drain the energies of women with respect to their interest in men. I remember sitting one summer afternoon in a large tipi with Colleen and Anne, two nursing mothers, as a half-dozen young children played in and around the tipi. We talked about the burdens of mothering, and both women confessed to feeling so oppressed by little children hanging on to their bodies (both literally, while nursing, and metaphorically) that the very thought of sexual attention by men to their busy breasts was repulsive.

I do not mean to imply that small children did not get a lot of fathering. They always did at The Ranch, although it was not necessarily by their biological fathers or their mothers' current lover. Over the years the men have increasingly shared child care as they became adapted to and accepting of the increasingly strong currents of feminism among the women at The Ranch, which increasingly required the attentiveness of men. Adult male communards at The Ranch hold the children often, cuddle them, and may be attentive in other respects. Celt, for example, father of no one at The Ranch and not coupled with any of the women there, could sometimes be found with four or more children all over him, reading them stories. Paul was a spontaneous inventor of stories and could hold the children spellbound with his improvisations. Moreover, the men have a *right* to such behavior, and sometimes fathering functions would be performed even over the objection of a biological parent. Maxwell, particularly good, wise, and patient with the children, was holding the infant Kashfi on his lap at dinner, feeding him. When Kashfi's mother, sitting across the table, complained about the sloppiness of the process, Maxwell told her sharply not to interfere with his "doing a dinner thing" with Kashfi. The others present seemed to regard Maxwell's claim as legitimate, and Kashfi's mother did not interfere further, although she was probably the most influential woman at The Ranch.[12]

But such fathering behavior also depends to some extent on the personal predispositions of the men. In the first few years of my association with The Ranch, there did not seem to be strong norms *requiring* the attentiveness of men to the young children.[13] Some of the men are fond of children, are good with them, and gravitate naturally toward nurturing functions; some are not and do not, although even they may help with child care out of a felt obligation to relieve the burden of the woman with whom they are coupled. But in the first few years of my association with The Ranch, it could not be counted on. Returning from the store with Candice, who was then coupled with Flint (who had a child of his own, Freddy, by a previous liaison), I heard her say wistfully to her own daughter, Nicole (who was with us), "I do hope that Flint has spent some time with Freddy."[14] But her tone indicated that she didn't have any right to expect it.

12. Although he was not his father, Maxwell had an especially close relationship with Kashfi, who would sometimes sleep in Maxwell's house. Other men also developed special affinities with children who were not "their own." Very late one night at the main house, Maxwell and I were talking about female homosexuality while he and Kashfi (four years old at the time) were oiling several pairs of leather boots. Maxwell managed to pause every now and then in our conversation to instruct Kashfi in his work but reprimanded him both firmly and gently when he interrupted the conversation. Kashfi obviously adored him.

13. In the early years of the commune movement, hippie men were always free to leave when the spirit moved them. Hip norms negatively constrained women from forcing them legally to support their children, if any. And paternity would have been difficult to prove, in any case.

14. Freddy was unusual in being very withdrawn, at least far more so than the other children at The Ranch, who seemed to me to relate easily and openly to almost everyone, members and visitors alike. Candice, Flint, and Freddy did not stay at The Ranch for long. Over the years, adults have either willingly or as a result of pressure from others gradually left The Ranch as it became increasingly apparent that they were not fully committed to the increasingly *family* emphasis of the dominant group there—which means primarily the centering of their lives *at* The Ranch, dealing with the growth and education of their children and the personal relationships of the adult members. The latter is more fully discussed in Chapter 5.

For children older than four or five, the supervisory responsibilities of either parents or other adult communards are much attenuated. Children are regarded as intrinsically worthy of love and respect, but not necessarily of special restrictions or privileges or attentiveness or close monitoring. As they grow out of primitive physical dependence upon the care and supervision of adults, they are treated (and tend to behave) like other members of the communal family.

It is important to be very clear about this. I do not intend to imply that the degree of equalitarianism extended to children is a rationalization or an ideological disguise for "neglecting" them—although this is probably true to some extent in some communes.[15] But at The Ranch, being treated "like anyone else" implies for children that they participate in the intimacies and the mutual concern for each other's welfare that characterize the entire group. At the same time, although there is greater equalitarianism at The Ranch than in most middle-class families or in doctrinally based communes, the children are not fully autonomous persons or fully the equals of adults. They have to go to school and they have to be instructed in the skills of rural life and they have to be kept from being bored—which is why I speak of the *decline* of age-grading rather than its disappearance. Moreover, like "natural" or "God-given" rights, which are sustained only to the extent that governments support them, the "equal rights" of commune children are sustained only to the extent that the governing adults support them. Indeed, despite these views of children that I have described, controversy about child-rearing was common at The Ranch, with opinions ranging from total liberation to strict control. But in contrast, for example, to the noncommunal, rural hippie families observed by Sherri Cavan, in which children ranked just below women and just above dogs in the family hierarchy,[16] attempts are seriously made at The Ranch to allow children to grow "naturally," and to be optimally autonomous and "free."

15. On communal indifference to children's "needs," see Sonya Rudikoff, "O Pioneers!" *Commentary* (July 1972).

16. See Sherri Cavan, *Hippies of the Redwood Forest* (unpublished ms.).

CHILDREN'S RIGHTS

Free with respect to what? A decline in age-grading is evident
in rural hippie communes with respect to a wide variety of
behavior. Children over five or six years of age come and go
largely as they please; they eat or do not eat when and if they
please: they do not necessarily sleep in their mothers' houses.
After dinner, as people would wander off to their houses in
the woods, I would occasionally hear mothers at The Ranch
ask their children "Do you want to sleep in my house
tonight?"—implying thereby that they could sleep in the
house of a surrogate parent or other adult. Children are also
encouraged to express their views on communal affairs at
family meetings and to participate in useful labor. But the
sharpest breaks in age-grading (important because of their
contrast with what is conventional in most sectors of American society) are to be found in the handling of drug use, quarreling, and sexual behavior.

Drug Use

At many hip communes, if a joint is passed around a family
gathering, it will routinely pass to any of the children present
who show an interest in it. Interest is shown primarily by the
older children, those over five or six, but I have held on my
lap a two year old stoned on two hits, and (although this was
not at The Ranch) one visiting sociologist's five-year-old son
was initially "turned on" by a companion whose father (then
running a small "free school," now a Christian convert) regularly included two carefully rolled joints in the boy's kinder-
garten lunch pail. One day at The Ranch I was standing in the
kitchen talking with Abe, who was holding his two-year-old
son. The boy reached out and grabbed my tobacco pipe and
put it in his mouth. Abe put his hand on the pipe, but did not
yank it away from him because the boy did not want to give it
up. When he finally coughed on the smoke, he gave it up
willingly.

Small children are occasionally encouraged to smoke
marihuana for the amusement of adults, but such deliberate-

ness is rare. The spirit of it is comparable to blowing marihuana smoke at cats and dogs, or similar to the report by Aries in *Centuries of Childhood* of courtiers playing with the penis of three-year-old Louis XIII of France for the amusement of the assembled dignitaries, who would laugh uproariously at the little erection. (Sexuality was not imputed to small children at the time.) Marihuana use by children in these rural communal settings is part of a pattern in which it takes considerable ideological work to exclude children from any significant dimensions of group life that are not demonstrably harmful to them. The operative word is "demonstrably," and hippie commune parents are not usually persuaded that marihuana use is demonstrably harmful to children.

Children are not, as a matter of policy, forbidden to use even stronger psychedelics, like LSD-25, peyote, or mescaline. But these drugs are not often used frivolously. Their use is mostly ritualized, embedded in ceremony to solemnize special occasions: to welcome a season, to celebrate a birthday, to cope with some intracommunal problem perceived, perhaps, in terms of tensions or bad vibrations that the drug may help the participants transcend or understand more clearly. When children participate in such occasions, it is generally with the supervision that respect for ceremonies and powerful drug experiences requires for all. But despite the absence of any explicit or self-consciously developed policy or creed about drug use, it is nevertheless clear that marihuana use is regarded by many communards as a relatively normal and benign family activity from which there is no good reason systematically to exclude the children. Childhood, as one communard said, and many believe, "is a natural acid trip from which maturity brings you down." But communards at The Ranch are not missionaries about drug use (as was true of some in the early days of the hippie movement, when they aimed to turn on the world). In recent years The Ranch seems to have become increasingly traditional about drug use by children, acknowledging that it occurs routinely in nearby communes, but denying that it occurs among their own children— then qualifying the denial with a "well, maybe occasionally one or two tokes." Permissiveness in child-rearing has been under almost continual debate at The Ranch; nevertheless, in the absence of what they regard as good reason to impose age-graded restrictions on the participation of children, the readiness and willingness of children to participate are regarded as probably reasonable indicators of at least incipient competence.

Quarreling

Children are also notably "adult" in the degree to which it seems taken for granted at The Ranch that they will enter into agreements with each other without adult supervision and settle their quarrels, disputes, and disagreements without adult intervention. Over the years of our field research, we have observed a large number of quarrels or fights between children, but we have only rarely seen adults intervene to settle them, and then only when the possibility of severe injury was present or the adult was actively annoyed. Personal aggression, of course, is not generally approved in friendship-based communes like The Ranch,[17] but this disapproval is combined with an apparent acceptance of the inevitability of "hassling" as a permanent part of group life. Taken together, the two provide an apparent rationale for the civil inattention to quarreling children *if the practice of civil inattention should be questioned or challenged*: as family members, children will learn to live communally by learning to get through their hassles by themselves.

There are problems working this out of course. Adults do not feel that their belief in nonintervention is seriously compromised when they separate quarreling children if real injury seems likely: a little ideological work defines their intervention as a defense of *their own* interests in not being

17. There are, of course, communes where aggressiveness is more common. In a New Mexico commune she was a member of, Margaret Hollenbach describes the major source of leadership in that group as the willingness to hassle relatively passive others and to persist in hassling them until they submit. See "Relationships and Regulation in 'The Family' of Taos," in R.M. Kanter, ed., *Communes: Creating and Managing the Collective Life* (New York: Harper and Row, 1973).

annoyed. If smaller and weaker kids are occasionally vic-
timized by larger and stronger kids, they will learn to respect
size and strength; size and strength are respectable. Bullies
will learn that there are always others bigger and stronger
than themselves—adults, for example, who, like kids, being
persons too, will not hesitate to express their irritation with a
child (for example by throwing him out of the house) who
is hassling or nagging or otherwise annoying an adult who is
not in a tolerating mood. Like other aspects of child-rearing,
quarreling among children has been a continual source of
soul-searching and discussion among Ranch communards.
But the residual guilt that some of them feel at peremptory
action is compensated by the equalitarian ethos that permits
adults to treat an aggressive child as a troublemaking peer,
rather than constraining them to repress their own anger on
the grounds that the offender is, after all, "only a child."

But quarreling is an endemic problem that is not, of course,
always solved, not in communes or anywhere else. If the
habitual bully or hassler does not eventually modify his or her
behavior, avoidance or ostracism may sometimes follow, and,
if necessary, a family meeting in which "sensitivity" or encounter techniques may be invoked to explore the matter.
And if all this fails, children are particularly susceptible to
being labeled and understood astrologically, with their own
karma or fate, and their own special problems largely beyond
deliberate human control by others, which they must "work
out" for themselves over the very long run.

Sex

Sexual behavior in commune children is governed by principles similar to those that permit children to smoke dope on
the grounds that it is not demonstrably harmful to them: the
predisposition in anarchist communes generally is to believe
that the sexuality of children is not demonstrably harmful.
Psychologists have known about infant sexuality for a long
time, but such data as my collaborators and I came upon in
the commune research fail to indicate the existence of a "la-
tency stage" in childhood, during which (according to the

classic Freudian belief) interest in genital sexuality is supposed to disappear until it reappears in puberty.

The data are neither good nor plentiful. Neither I nor any of my co-researchers were actively looking for evidence of childhood sexuality. Even if we had been looking, access to it would have been extraordinarily difficult to get, not only because sexual activity, in the nature of the case, is usually private, but also because we researchers, as outsiders, had to be careful not to seem excessively prying or prurient in our interests, even after our on-site presence had been accepted.

I should emphasize that I myself came across no incidents of overt childhood sexuality at The Ranch, except for the following funny encounter: two six-year-old boys were playing in the mud by the side of the road as I walked toward my car after a spring afternoon spent at The Ranch. They were giggling and laughing and apparently having a wonderful time. As I approached them, I stopped and asked what they were doing. "Fucking," one of them said, both of them breaking up into laughter. "You know," the first one said, and then, moving his hips back and forth, he simulated the sounds of sexual intercourse. He then showed me the fleece lining of his jacket, which was lying on the ground, and explained that it was a "vagina" (pronounced correctly); then he took the index finger of one hand and pushed it rapidly back and forth between a circle made by the thumb and index finger of his other hand, again repeating the sounds of lovemaking, interspersed with more laughter. "Have fun," I said, and began to walk on, when the second boy asked me if I had ever "done it" (indicating with his index finger through the circle). I said, yes, I had. "How many times?" he asked. "Oh, lots of times," I replied. "A hundred?" he asked, eyes wide. "More," I said, "thousands, maybe." "I've never done it," he offered wistfully.

He may well do it before very long. We have the following bits of evidence from field reports at other communes regarding child-child sex: Gilbert Zicklin reported two documented cases (admission by the children and verification by the parents) of sexual intercourse between six-to-eight year olds, which occasioned no punitive response or even tortured discussion by commune adults. At a commune near The Ranch, there was one instance of a multiple rape of a small girl by several boys only slightly older than she. When I interviewed the girl's mother and father about the incident, they both expressed some anger (although not furious rage) about it, but they emphasized that their anger was not about the sexual episode itself (the girl, according to her mother, had been previously sexually active, willingly), but rather about the fact that the boys had forced her. In another commune, an eleven-year-old boy and a twelve-year-old girl were conducting a relatively conventional romance, and the local adults assumed that they were routinely having sexual intercourse. In still another commune, three twelve- to thirteen-year-old girls talked openly of their plans to seduce two teen-aged boys at a farm not far from the commune where the girls lived.

About child-adult sex, we have the following bits of data from Gilbert Zicklin's research: a sixty-year-old handyman-builder, well known to the group, was discovered in sexual play with a three-year-old girl. The response of adults was various, ranging from sympathy for the man through confusion and ambivalence to an outright punitive response from a few. The child's mother felt that nothing bad had been done; the child suffered no apparent harm, and the mother thought the two were genuinely fond of each other. At another commune, a twenty-five-year-old, "mind-blown," gentle young man was discovered making love to a four-year-old girl in his bed. There was reportedly an ambivalent response by some adults, but most felt that the young man loved the child and would do her no harm. The girl's mother felt it was nobody else's business. The child, she said, had been previously sexually active with boys her own age, and the mother did not think it strange. The most punitive response came from the mother's lover (not the father of the child), who wanted to kill the offender. Zicklin reports, however, that the mother's lover was highly untypical of adult male communards, being of working-class origin and having strong beliefs in traditional age and sex differentiation. Finally, we have a report of one five-year-old girl asking her mother if she (the child) could make love to her as the mother's lover did.

It's not much in the way of data, and it doesn't come from The Ranch, but given the emotional volatility of the subject,[18] the vulnerability to official harassment to which it exposes communes, and the fact that there is, in society generally, far more child-child and child-adult (for example, incestuous) sex than is either acknowledged or reported, I assume that there is more than we discovered inadvertently, since, as I said, we were not actively looking for evidence of the sexuality of children. Such data are not easy to come by. Direct interviews will not elicit the information reliably; children are very difficult to interview, and observation is nearly impossible. The evidence gets revealed mostly unexpectedly, through on-site ethnographic study in which the topic may come up in otherwise ordinary conversation, and communards will talk about events they have observed or which have come to their attention.

Nevertheless, despite the weakness of the data, it seems clear enough that (1) children are exposed to sexual awareness early, often by virtue of the very close quarters in which they live (note their presence at the birth ceremonies at The Ranch); (2) sexual language is used and sex discussed openly in the presence of children (I have never heard an adult communard repress *anything* he or she was about to say because children were present); (3) both child-child and child-adult sexual behavior occurs, although it is not possible to say how common it is; and (4) the dominant parental or other adult response to the sexuality of children is complex.

Parents and other adults in communes do seem to have some mixed feelings about the sexuality of their pre-

18. At a conference on the sexuality of children, sponsored by a branch of the British Psychological Society at Swansea in Wales in 1977, the topic provoked considerable local tension. Some nonacademic employees of the university at which the conference was held threatened a strike; admission to the sessions of the conference was closely monitored by officials to keep out undesirable persons; and I was asked by one official to promise *not* to speak to the press about any of the papers read at the sessions.

pubescent children. It is not surprising that, coming themselves from families where feelings about such matters are deeply socialized, commune adults are sometimes surprised, even disturbed and perhaps shocked to discover the sexuality of their children. But neither is it surprising that, given their favorable predisposition to "natural" morality, they would reflexively examine their own responses to "test" them for natural virtue. Communards are generally very busy "straightening out their heads" and trying to get free of feelings and impulses like greed and sexual possessiveness and competitiveness, which many of them believe to be neurotic residues of the mainstream culture they have rejected. Their libertarianism predisposes them to the view that what is not justifiably proscribed should be permitted (rather than what is not justifiably permitted should be proscribed), and sometimes they cannot find reasons with which to justify their initially disturbed or uneasy response to the sexuality of their children. If sexual behavior seems to do no visible harm to the children, the burden of proof tends to fall on those who wish to forbid sexual behavior to children rather than on those predisposed to be tolerant of it.

Like the rationale for drug use, the appeal seems to be to some natural sense of equalitarian propriety. If we (adults) believe that making love is a good thing, and if the children seem interested in participating in something that we have found rewarding or beautiful, and if there is no persuasive evidence (other than traditional mores, many of which communards have already rejected as repressive) to suggest that what's good for us is bad for them, then it will seem reasonable and ideologically consistent not to obstruct erotic equality, regardless of race, creed, color, national origin, sex, or age.

But it is also important that this point not be exaggerated. At The Ranch, discussions of the sexuality of children were always controversial. Even as far back as the birth of Swallow, there was some disagreement about the propriety of having the other children present. As The Ranch has become more civically prominent in its community, its postures toward controversial issues have become somewhat more conservative on the questions of drugs, sex, and children, and they have

done considerable ideological work to stabilize those postures. The view presently dominant at The Ranch, for example, is that active sexuality in children is not developmentally
wholesome because sexuality creates dependencies, whereas
the primary task of growing children is to establish independence; and that the apparent sexuality of children is not true
eroticism but rather part of their general *physicality*, which
some adults misunderstand.

Nevertheless, there are important respects in which it is
legitimate to speak of the decline of age-grading in rural hippie communes. The evidence of children's sexual interest and
behavior, their drug use, and their rights to autonomy in the
settlement of their disputes and disagreements all suggest a
greater equalitarianism with respect to age than seems to be
normal in either working-class or middle-class sectors of the
mainstream of American culture. We have made similar observations regarding work roles and the right to a political
voice in family/commune affairs, and to personal decisions
normally made by parents themselves—for example, the
kind of education a child will receive and the place in which
he or she will be exposed to it.

Again, it is important that this equalitarianism not be
exaggerated; nowhere in communal life are children as influential as adults in collective affairs; adults may be reluctant to
lend fragile or expensive tools to a child who is regarded as
too irresponsible or too incompetent to use them:[19] adults
sometimes exercise strong, or furtive, pressures to discourage
children from becoming addicted to bad habits, such as eating
sweets or watching television (if the latter is available, as it
was not at The Ranch). But in general, there is a widespread
predisposition by adult communards to assume that there is a
strong relationship between a child's expressed interest in
doing something and a probably incipient competence to engage in it.

19. But steps are taken to reduce incompetence very early. Bob, for example, instructs children as young as six or seven in automobile mechanics and
in toolmaking at the forge in the Quonset hut.

There is a sense in which it might be ideologically embarrassing for them to assume otherwise. Many communards are veterans of university conflicts in which they demanded from authorities a "right to participate in the decisions that shape [their own] lives." Met with rebuttals that they were too young or too inexperienced or too incompetent to shape university curricula, to assess the competence of professors, or to make other academic judgments, hip communards might well be receptive to the idea of children's rights. At the very least, they might be sensitive to the self-serving character of arguments by elders for age-graded exclusions of the young on the grounds of an imputed incompetence.

IDEOLOGY AND CIRCUMSTANCE

What is the ideological status of the practices described above regarding the decline of age-grading? The analytic question is whether they are expressions of (that is, *attempts* to manifest) the equalitarianism that the communards brought with them to their rural settings from the urban counterculture. If so, are they therefore definitive of the culture of the group, a culture fundamentally different (at least with respect to age-grading and child management) from the mainstream of American life? Although there are communes in which the freedoms of children are sharply restricted,[20] the decline of age-graded culture in many hippie communes seems real enough, and not simply the result of observer bias, sampling errors, or observer-induced "Hawthorne" effects. Surely the same pattern would not be found in *any* community that is closely watched.

20. For example, in Christian communes, whose fundamentalism appeals to the Bible as a sanction for the need to *train* (as distinguished from merely *teach*) one's children, who are born in sin and who may need the Rod. At a Wednesday night potluck dinner given by a Christian commune not far from The Ranch, I spoke with a young ex-hippie couple about child-rearing. The young father said to me "Since we've become Christians, I must have spanked little Jonathan a thousand times, and both of us are so much the better for it!" I have never seen a child hit by any of the adults at The Ranch.

Nevertheless, it is possible that the practices I have reported constitute more or less *ad hoc* behavior, induced by circumstances (therefore, perhaps, temporary) that, ironically, make the behavior seem routine and therefore hardly worth ennobling with the moral rhetoric of equalitarianism. Interpretive ethnography always runs the risk of overestimating the amount of normative culture that is *there*—imputed to the scene by ethnographers who see evidence of that normative culture expressed in the words they hear and actions they observe. The danger of interpreting words and deeds in this way is to exaggerate the established cultural character of the patterns one sees by exaggerating the consensus about them, by ignoring the possibility that much of the behavior may be more or less tentative, exploratory, or improvisational,[21] and that some of the "beliefs" conveyed by the words may be vaguely conceived or superficially felt.

It is, therefore, worth considering the possibility that the attenuation of age-grading reflects not a radically different set of moral beliefs in the communes but a different set of practical circumstances that, to be sure, have practical consequences for the *folkways* of these groups but that are not necessarily constitutional of a radically different ideology. The major theoretical basis of this interpretation is that no difference in culture need be invoked to explain apparently "deviant" behavior when the settings in which this deviance appears are socially *safe* for such behavior,[22] for instance, structured such that no vital interests are threatened by it, which structure then makes the behavior appear benign. The rural communes in question are, for example, relatively removed from the moral centers of the larger society, insulated from the potentially disapproving eyes of police, welfare officials, schoolteachers, hostile neighbors, psychiatrists, probation officers, grandmothers, and other social caretakers. Moreover, the communes themselves are on the whole socially

21. On the role of improvisation in the creation of subcultures, see Joseph Damrell, *Search for Identity* (Beverly Hills, Calif.: Sage Publications, 1978).
22. See, for example, David Matza's *Delinquency and Drift* (New York: John Wiley and Sons, 1964).

homogeneous "families"—a fact that promotes a substantial amount of toleration of unconventional behavior so long as it is "kept in the family," the unconventionalities of a family being, indeed, those features of it that remind its members of the distinctiveness of their membership.

Situational exigencies in the facts of rural communal living may go far to explain the inclusion of children in normally adult prerogatives without invoking ideologies or other beliefs. Leaving children to settle their disputes by themselves often involves spillage, breakage, and other damage to property. But if there are no expensive rugs on the floor, and if most of the endangered property is not costly enough or symbolically valuable enough to warrant aggressive protection from battling children, an indifferent posture toward the battle is viable (along with the moral gravy of some pride in not being excessively attached to the value of "things"). The virtual absence of any risk of pregnancy when pre-pubescent children engage in sexual intercourse, combined with favorable predispositions by commune adults toward sexual behavior to begin with, helps permit a tolerant posture toward it—as the widespread availability of contraceptive techniques has permitted an enormous growth in post-pubescent, premarital intercourse (and public toleration of it) even without mainstream ideological celebration of the moral virtue of sexuality. When life is rural and poor there is always important work to be done that children are competent to do. When an eleven-year-old boy becomes fascinated with an old wringer washing machine (as happened in one commune near The Ranch) and likes to play with it to the point where he begins to do the family laundry regularly, no important property is risked to probable incompetence, a boy does useful work, and a small blow is struck against the sexist division of labor.

The settings, moreover, are usually benign, in the view of some even therapeutic (birds, trees, flowers, gardens, woods, fresh air), so that children can be provided wide margins of freedom with little risk to their well-being. The men and women are usually nearby for children to work and play with, to imitate, learn from, and interact with. Not only the physical settings but also the internal social arrangements of

communal life make the inclusion of children in adult life a
relatively routine affair. The closeness of living quarters
means that commune kids, like ghetto kids, are exposed at an
early age to sex between their parents and other adults. The
parents and other adults are themselves relatively young on
the whole, and because stable nuclear couples are not modal,
courtship is regularly in process and children are present to
observe it. Under these circumstances, the status of children
begins to approximate other domestic animals, such as cats,
dogs, and goats; within a semi-isolated communal compound, all may be included, in the bedroom as well as at the
dinner table, even if relatively disattended in both places.

Given the routine character of this inclusion pattern, there
is little need to make an explicit moral virtue out of these arrangements or to defend them with ideological argument,
unless an explanation is requested or a question raised or a
problem encountered regarding such virtue as might be implicit in them.[23] Questions may disrupt the civil inattention
communards routinely accord to inclusion behavior, and
those questions sometimes make it necessary to generate deliberate rationales for it. Nevertheless, the presumption of
agreement that such practices are normal and need no explanation also helps ward off requests for explanation in the first
place.

But that there may be little need to make a virtue of these
arrangements until an explanation is required does not mean
that commune adults don't think the arrangements are virtuous. The presumption of normality itself suggests the presence of moral assumptions, as Harold Garfinkel's work has
made dramatically clear,[24] and, as should be well known by
now, communards are nothing if not moral entrepreneurs
who know perfectly well that the freedoms they extend to

23. This fact, of course, presents an important and frequently noted
methodological problem for sociologists, because in treating research subjects as informants, the questions we ask sometimes contribute to the genesis
of the culture we are trying to study—including explanations of how and
why things are as they are.

24. Harold Garfinkel, *Studies in Ethnomethodology* (Englewood Cliffs, N.J.:
Prentice-Hall, 1967).

their children are not "normal" in the world outside the commune. Like any other routine or taken-for-granted social pattern, the pattern of extending the usual rights of commune members to children reveals an ideology. That ideology may not be as thoroughly formulated or explicitly rendered as an applied philosophy of child-rearing, but it is more likely to be readily at hand in an intentional community (which does, after all, have moral intentions) than in a community whose values are "received" or traditional.

The decline of age-grading, then, is not simply an expression of an *ad hoc* accommodation to the circumstances of communal living among rural hippies; nor is it simply a direct manifestation of an explicit "policy" of child-rearing, although it does ultimately rest its claims to legitimacy on the equalitarianism of communards, which principle predisposes them to extend rights rather than restrict them as age-graded privileges. When that legitimacy needs ideological work, communards selectively utilize some of the ideas from the counterculture critique of modern urban life to provide a reasoned defense for their pattern of including children in adult life *when and if any defense of it is required.*[25]

Most of these ideas are familiar ones to sociologists, for example, an emphasis on the irrationality of the "straight" world, the poor fit between means and ends. Smoking dope is intrinsically harmless, a real danger to life and limb only by virtue of the consequences of being caught in the act by law enforcers. The dangers of sexual activity are similarly socially constructed by the punitive response to it and the secondary deviance generated by that response.[26] The distinction between straight and hip can be reasoned into a generational

25. See, for example, Paul Goodman, *Growing Up Absurd* (New York: Random House, 1960); also Theodore Roszak, *The Making of a Counterculture* (New York: Anchor Books, 1969). For a concise statement, see Fred Davis, *On Youth Subcultures: The Hippie Variant* (New York: General Learning Press, 1971).

26. On the labeling of deviants, see the statement by Howard S. Becker in *Outsiders* (New York: The Free Press, 1963). For the classic statement on secondary deviance see Edwin Lemert, *Social Pathology* (New York: McGraw-Hill, 1951).

argument as well: the association between the "innocence" of childhood and the (romantic) idea of childhood's elemental intelligence or wisdom is understood as connected by the fact that children have not yet had the opportunity to learn the taboos in terms of which an "adult" perspective is defined. This devaluation of the adult, straight world carries with it a devaluation of its association of competence with conventional "learning", thus strengthening the belief of communards that it is important to *un*learn much that they were taught to reacquire the "natural" competences to enjoy the "highs" of dope and sex and freedom and community.

These ideas draw to some extent upon Philippe Aries's influential (but still controversial) work on the history of childhood and the late Paul Goodman's also influential (and more popular) work in behalf of preserving the natural wildness of children, ideas that not only provide historical and philosophical support to the ideas of communards, but many of which have also passed into the popular culture. Aries wrote unsentimentally about the invention of modern childhood in the seventeeth and eighteenth centuries as a means of separating, even segregating, the experience of the young from their elders. And Goodman has added to the traditional romantic view of childhood as innocence or noble savagery the argument that helping to preserve what is best in the natural wildness of children involves *adults as children;* that is, it calls upon adults to reach for the residues of their own childhoods from which they may have only reluctantly "come down" into maturity.[27]

This idea, of course, can be (and has been) caricatured by more than a few graybeards who not only argue for but attempt to live by the tenets of perpetual childhood. But hippie ideas about children draw some intellectual respectability from a tradition that stretches from Rousseau and de Tocqueville to Aries, Goodman, A. S. Neill, and large numbers of contemporary "free school" theorists who have all, in one way or another, pointed to the potential and actual con-

27. Paul Goodman, "Reflections on Children's Rights," in Beatrice and Ronald Gross, *The Children's Rights Movement.*

flicts between raising children—especially, perhaps, ped-
agogically—and having them "grow up."[28]

Through such sources and by such more or less diligent
ideological work is the equalitarian pattern of inclusion-
disattention "rationally" legitimated, or made sensible, as an
approach to the management of children. This ideological
work sanctions a pattern of behavior produced neither by the
arguments themselves nor by *ad hoc* responses to immediate
circumstances, but by the interaction between the "beliefs"
that bring hippies to communal living in the first place and
the situational exigencies (some of them unanticipated) they
face in managing their daily lives and those of their children;
or, to put it another way, by the selective utilization of
ideological elements from the accessible tradition of the counterculture,[29] elements that are then interpreted, under the
pressures of circumstance, and applied to the management of
children, with consequences that are not entirely calculable.

ADULTS AND THE SELF-SERVING CHARACTER OF
IDEAS ABOUT CHILDREN

In this dialectical process a lot of things can happen to ideas.
Beliefs may be "sold out." Or they may be gradually undermined as groups exhaust or destroy themselves struggling
against insuperable obstacles in their efforts to attain utopian
aims. Arguments and ideas may be subtly modified to provide more effective legitimations for policies and beliefs in
trouble. But at The Ranch, communard ideas about children
seem to dovetail nicely with the pressures and interests dic-

28. Among the large numbers of books in the schoolhouse at The Ranch,
there is a shelf filled with the works of A.S. Neill, Maria Montessori, John
Holt, Jonathan Kozol, Herbert Kohl, James Herndon, and other educational
reformers.

29. There is a continuous counterculture tradition of "underground"
ideology, which goes back at least two hundred years. See Bennett M. Berger,
"Hippie Values: More Old than New," *Trans-Action* (December 1967); David
Matza, "Subterranean Traditions of Youth," *The Annals of the American
Academy of Political and Social Science* (November 1961); Cesar Grana, *Modernity
and its Discontents* (New York: Harper and Row, 1967).

tated by the circumstances in which communards live, in a way that enables the ideas and the circumstances to provide consistent reciprocal support and meaning to each other. Even where, as at The Ranch, generally skeptical or disapproving attitudes toward child sexuality have recently become salient, the ideas that sanction these attitudes and the circumstances in which they have developed (the increasing civic prominence and visibility of The Ranch) provide reciprocal support.

Like all ideas about children, hippie ideas about children imply a complementary conception of adulthood—which should be no surprise to sociologists, who are trained to think of role structures as reciprocal. The dominant, modern, middle-class conception of childhood (as a distinctive social category involving clear stages of development with characteristic crises and transitions requiring continual monitoring and elaborate principles and systems of rational child management) also implies a complementary, managerial conception of adulthood. Regardless of its cognitive merits, the modern middle-class conception of children and what they "need" requires full-time mothers and at least part-time fathers, or functional equivalents like nurseries, day-care centers, and schools, and the assembled and organized professionals to do the conscious work of socialization, to apply the principles and keep the system going. And it requires an appropriate ideology to dignify the hard work of parenting and to honor the efforts of child-care professionals to turn children into responsible citizens.

Hippie parents, on the other hand, have disavowed most of the dominant models of proper adulthood; they are not into "growing up" to meet middle-class standards of maturity and adult responsibility. These standards are symbolic of what they dropped out of and dropped out for. In rural communes, hippie parents are busy creating their physical settlements and their symbolic communities, experimenting with family forms, attempting to "survive." Like Shaw's dustman in *Pygmalion*, they can't afford middle-class morality and its application to the rearing of children. Like the little kids who are their children, the big kids who are the children's parents are busy "seeking their identities," repairing egos damaged (in their view) by their own crippling socialization, and looking for psychological frontiers to cross, all the while trying to get the food from the seed to the garden to the table, get the bills paid, and make ends meet, like anyone else. Communal living in rural locales reinforces the predisposition of hippie parents, reluctant from the start to perform full-time roles as socializers of children, to believe in the benignity of nature's unseen hand, to see normal children as essentially healthy plants needing only a little sun and water and breathing space to grow up straight and tall.

Moreover, in the dominant sectors of modern society, marriage and family are supposed to mean a "settling down" for spouses after a post-adolescent period of identity searching or sowing wild oats. This is not true for communards (it seems decreasingly true for "straight" couples too—which may help account for recent changes in ideas about "what is good for the children"). They are not "settled," and they routinely face the *Sturm und Drang* of courtship, coupling, uncoupling, and recoupling as frequently and intensely *after* they are raising children as before. The ordinary middle-class responsibilities of child-socialization do not mesh easily with such *Sturm und Drang*, to say nothing of their conflict with the quest for a broadly defined personal freedom in which many communards are engaged.

A conception of childhood and children, therefore, that diminishes the apparent need for, or even the desirability of, heavy, deliberate socialization, that emphasizes the natural intelligence or wisdom of children (rather than their dependence or incompetence), reduces thereby the degree to which the deliberate socialization of children may be said to be fateful or *self*-implicating for parents. It reduces, that is, the degree to which the reputation of parents is contingent upon how they manage their children—thus enhancing the freedom and mobility of adults even in the midst of fertility and poverty.

In rather clear contrast to most middle-class views, in which the behavior of children "reflects on" their parents, who are in some sense "responsible" for it, the communal view tends to resist characterizing parents in terms of the consequences of what they do with or to their children— although this, like the "burning out" of sexual jealousy (see Chapter 5) is harder to accomplish in fact than in utterance. Ideological resources prominent in the counterculture (karma, fate, astrological influences, God's will) lie about like slash on the forest floor to kindle explanations of the behavior of children that minimize the importance of parental influence by emphasizing the impact of nonhuman, nonmanipulable forces upon them. Surely, there is ideological work getting done here.

Do these arguments seem self-serving for hippie parents? They certainly do. Nevertheless, I think it is important to point out also that they are probably no *more* self-serving than the dominant middle-class conception of the needs of children, which, by requiring an enormous and intense expenditure of time and energy on socialization by parents and parent-substitutes, creates millions of meaningful jobs in child care, and dignifies the days and nights for millions of traditional women who devote a major part of their adult lives to mothering.

In either case, a distinctive conception of a *parental* role is involved in all ideas about children. And upon hard reflection, the conception of that role is based upon *very little reliable knowledge of what kinds of parenting produce what kinds of consequences in children.* Despite an abundance of theory and research and strong feeling, we are all still pretty much in the dark. Throughout modern society, parents raise children while having *only the dimmest consciousness* of the relationship between the causes and consequences of behavior; yet they are burdened by "responsibility" for that relation and therefore constrained to "have convictions" about child-rearing. Throughout modern society, parents raise children according to principles defining what is good for them (which may or may not be valid) and utilize techniques for producing these goods (which may or may not work), but their commitment to which has clearly self-serving functions for adults.

Although it can reveal the self-serving functions in these small ideas about the socialization of children, the explanatory tradition of the sociology of knowledge does not necessarily disparage or impugn the claims made by either conception of childhood in behalf of its view of child management. And although my own biases in this matter should be clear to a careful reader, neither does that tradition disparage the critiques each make of the other (each—for different reasons— is likely to accuse the other of one or another form of child neglect or abuse).

Nevertheless, the set of attitudes communards develop in the struggle to cope with the problems of living with children in rural communes can contribute to the critique of some of the more aggressive practices of middle-class parents seeking to produce successful adults from the raw material presented by their offspring.[30] Wouldn't the costs of *not* taking credit for, and vicarious pride in, the successes of one's children be more than compensated by the benefits of absolution from the shame and anxiety of being responsible for their failures? Moreover, this critique gains strength as schools, peer-groups, mass media, and other institutions take over a greater share of socialization. In addition, the self-serving functions of middle-class conceptions of child-rearing are undermined by an increasing divorce rate, by an increasing feminist rejection of the traditional child-nurturing female role, by the financial burden of schools and other caretaker institutions on taxpayers who increasingly resist their increasing costs, and by the "youth culture" problems generated by the prolongation of childhood and adolescence, which keeps the young off the labor market and exacerbates the "warehousing" problem for schools.[31]

THE PROBLEM OF SCHOOLING

One very important caution is in order at this point. As the commune movement has grown older, the children of com-

---

30. There is a line of such research and criticism stretching from Arnold Green, "The Middle-Class Male Child and Neurosis," *American Sociological Review*, 11 (1946), to Philip Slater's *The Pursuit of Loneliness* (Boston: Beacon Press, 1970), to the current criticism of educational reformers.

31. See Frank Musgrove, *Youth and the Social Order* (Indianapolis: Indiana University Press, 1964); and Bennett M. Berger, *Looking for America* (Englewood Cliffs, N. J.: Prentice-Hall, 1971), pt. 1.

munards grow to school age, and the "schooling problem" constitutes a powerful circumstantial pressure, potentially threatening both to the autonomy of communards and to their beliefs about the welfare of children. The Ranch has dealt with this problem by organizing an "alternative" school that, by 1978, has had a continuous existence for more than five years, some of that time located in the village community center, but more recently in three small buildings built at The Ranch in a clearing in the woods, down a path from the Quonset, in whose workshops some of the school's practical instruction occurs.[32]

One of these buildings is the proverbial, rural, one-room schoolhouse, complete with maps, globes, tables, chairs, books and shelves, paper masks, metal sculptures, toys and games, children's drawings, a typewriter and a mimeograph machine, and hippie touches like a fiberglass skylight, a homemade wood stove, and an open loft lined with pillows. There is no picture of George Washington or any other President. The school teaches some twenty-six children (in 1977–78) between the ages of six and fourteen, only eight of whom live at The Ranch. Some of the adults at The Ranch teach at the school, but they have outside help also, and usually four or five teachers are present on any school day. The formal reality of the school, of course, is a response to the fact of compulsory education in California, but the substantive reality of the school, particularly for the younger children in it (under ten years old), reveals a lot of the equalitarianism I have described.

Although curriculum is determined in part by what parents and teachers think it worthwhile or beneficial to learn (reading, writing, arithmetic, arts and crafts, and practical skills like blacksmithing and bicycle repair), it is also determined by bargaining and discussion in which the subjects that available adults are competent to teach are balanced against what stu-

32. The good reputation of the alternative school at The Ranch has induced the local public school board to offer it a contract for the instruction of local children for the school year 1979–80. In the summer of 1979, a fourth school building was under construction at The Ranch.

dents ask to learn. About half the school time of the older children is scheduled with required subjects. But both the older and the younger children tend to have individual arrangments with teachers, with whom they make "contracts" to carry out long- or short-term lessons and projects. Some of these are conventionally "academic" and others are practical, workshop experiences, for example, when Bob instructs children in mechanics or the use of the forge. A lot of it is informal too: one rainy afternoon I was talking with Bob and Linda (who was reupholstering automobile seats, using a manual sewing machine to shape the vinyl, and pliers and big staples to secure it to the seats) when school let out and a nine-year-old boy with a broken umbrella wandered into the workshop. Bob very carefully showed him what was wrong: the thin wire had broken that held the umbrella's ribs in the notches on the ring of metal that slid up and down the shaft. With a sour comment on the flimsiness of the material, Bob showed the boy how to renotch the ribs, threaded them through the ring with a heavier piece of wire, tied the ends of the wire with a pliers, and presto! the umbrella was fixed.

The school is governed by those who participate in it, teachers, parents, and children, any one of whom may call or participate in a meeting. Each school day is begun with a meeting to plan the day, which according to Patricia, the primary coordinator of the school and a founding communard of The Ranch, "helps children to realize from a young age that they have something to do with the society that they live in . . . and that they have some control over it." Despite the fact that the children's parents are supposed to pay $50 a month toward the support of the school (many do not but nobody is thrown out for inability to pay), which contribution provides The Ranch with a small cash income, the coordinator is worried; she needs more regular help with the school, which in 1978 was claiming virtually all of her energy, a toll she resents somewhat.

Listen to her educational philosophy:

> The importance of learning is not in its product; learning and teaching are valuable because they create a good

focus for living . . . with staying aware of the place where the soul meets the body, the place of aliveness. . . . It's exciting for them [the children] to begin to see the difference between feelings and thoughts. They're also learning about liking to do something and not liking to do it, but wanting to do it anyway, for a different reason than just because you like to. . . . They also need to accept that it is OK to make mistakes. They can either take on a project and finish it, or give it up, knowing why they gave it up and then discuss this with their teacher. Staying tuned in to their own interests, the children develop decision making . . . skills, and begin to understand why they want to learn things and why they don't. They begin to see whose influence is behind their motivation. . . . We can't help but teach the values that we hold. When we put children into a particular social order, they'll learn that order. I think the job of education is to teach people to be conscious of the fact that they're creating their environment. I don't want to teach propaganda, even the propaganda I believe in. The crux of the educational process is giving children the tools . . . to keep in touch with the learning process throughout their lives . . . [to] keep touching in at that place where illumination happens. I want an environment that gives you the freedom to question continually.

Here we see a long-term communard, mother of two children herself, developing an educational philosophy, even a child psychology, faced, as she is, with the necessity of keeping an alternative school together—a difficult task under the best of circumstances, one which has seen many such efforts dissolve into chaos. I don't know why the school at The Ranch has been able to survive successfully this long—except that there is impressive expertise, formally educated and otherwise, available among the adults at The Ranch, the environing community has large numbers of sympathetic and hip residents ("The Ranch is the only *real* commune," one of them told me), and the nearest public school is sixteen miles away. But the success of the school is not at issue; what is, is the empirical difficulty of playing off the inevitably dominant role of adults in the education of their children against the belief of *these* adults in extending as much responsibility as they can to the children for their own education, and optimum equality in the determination of its substance.

Ultimately, of course, the adults are in control, and such control requires the legitimation of ideological work, such as that contained in Patricia's philosophy of education, developed in consultation with others at The Ranch. But note that the philosophy puts a lot of the responsibility for education on the children themselves and minimizes the almost inevitably age-graded dimensions of formal education by emphasizing the importance of "touching in at the place where illumination happens" *throughout* the life cycle.

The growth of The Ranch's children and the establishment of the school there have had profound consequences for the commune. They have promoted closer ties both between the commune and the larger rural community, and among the members of the commune as a "family" unit—even to the extent of gradually inducing those former members who put their personal or nuclear-couple interests ahead of communal purposes to leave The Ranch. The increasing corporate prominence of The Ranch in its community and the focus of its collective energies around an established and growing school have, perhaps inevitably, moderated its originally strong "counterculture" quality. As I said earlier, they now (1979) look unfavorably on dope smoking among children and on childhood sexual activity. Their early "hippie" interest in exploring exotic religions has apparently been supplemented or replaced by more familiar modes of ritual celebration. One of my most recent visits to The Ranch was on the occasion of a double *Bas Mitzvah* for two of their children who had just turned thirteen. A ritual dinner and the formal confirmation ceremonies were conducted by a visiting rabbi for the commune and more than fifty guests, including the fathers of the two girls and the paternal grandmother of one of them, all three of whom had come from the east coast to attend. The increasingly established character of The Ranch, then, has had its ideological effects.

I have seen some children in my wanderings through communes who could be called neglected (though not at The

Ranch), but commune society is like other societies in the sense that it is stratified: there are "good families" and not-so-good families, "together" ones and fragmented ones. And in regions of commune concentration, local people tend to know which are which, in the same sense that ordinary residents of small towns or rural areas know who the good and bad families are, or that residents of poor urban neighborhoods will know which children from what families are recurrently in trouble. But I have not seen a lot of neglect, and what I have witnessed is often benign enough, at least by comparison with some of the more pressure-ridden practices of middle-class child-rearing.

It is not always benign. Just as much of the anxiety of middle-class parents may be understood as an unanticipated outcome of being "responsible" for how their children turn out, while most parents most of the time are in fact largely ignorant of the relationship between what they do to their children and the developmental consequences of the doing,[33] the easygoing inclusion of children in adult communal life can have its own unanticipated consequences. Communards are not always unconventional in their view of the care required by children, but may be pushed by the dialectics of argument in that direction out of a need to defend their integrity against demands that they explain their behavior. Such defensiveness may promote a kind of self-censorship on the expression of the kinds of worries and uncertainties about the welfare of their children that any parents might reasonably have, given their (and our) ignorance and whatever their philosophy of child care, thus creating interpersonal tensions or anxieties whose origins are not perceived. Sociologists may, indeed, occasionally and uneasily redeem themselves in these precarious circumstances by asking the kinds of difficult questions that, despite their tendency to call forth defensive or remedial ideological work, may also serve to remind their respondents of what it was that was worth defending in the first place.

33. Not only anxiety, but anger too, as the "responsibility" of parents continues to be ideologically affirmed, while actual power and influence over their children shifts to public schools, peer groups, and mass media.

What was worth defending was the image of family solidarity, of rural community based upon optimal equality of membership, and of following through the devaluation of modern society's dominant institutional culture by an attempt to substitute a set of practices of their own that insulate them and their children from the influences they regard as damaging. Such pastoral pioneering induces child-care practices that bring the young away from dependence and toward equality as early as possible; it also requires ideological work, a set of legitimations, *arguments* that are worked out in the interpretive process of *applying* the things they believe they believe they believe to the conditions in which their practices must be carried out.

There is an image in our popular culture of mothers attempting to prolong the childhood of their daughters to keep themselves young by contrast. The image is ironic because prolonging the childhood of the young tends to emphasize the continuing authority (hence the "elder" status) of parents and other caretakers of dependent children—contributing, therefore to distance, separation, even "generation gaps." The fraternal (or sororal) treatment of children, on the other hand, seems to help them grow up fast. By exposing them to the possible delights of adult-peer relations early, such treatment seems to motivate them to achieve adulthood as soon as possible. By minimizing the extent and duration of authority relations among parents and children, a good commune brings the generations closer together by virtue of the decline of age-graded differentiations between them.

Commune children look to me much like other children, except that their tongues are saltier, there are very few shy or withdrawn ones (the younger ones tend to be very loud and boisterous), and the older children (say, between eight and twelve) seem far more self-possessed and confident than comparable middle-class children.[34] Early on the boys ape the

34. In *The Children of the Counterculture* (New York: Doubleday, 1975), John Rothchild and Susan Wolf recurrently comment on how grave, "mature," and well behaved commune children seemed to them, especially by contrast with their own two children (whom they took along on their commune research), who were whining, nagging, and manipulative.

cool and hip masculine postures of their male models, and the girls do so similarly. I have seen very few "adolescents" in the communes, but if my understanding is correct, adolescence should be very brief (if it exists as an age status at all) because children will have had several years of experience as all-but-fully participating members of a commune by the time they turn the corner into puberty.[35]

35. There is an ambiguity of status in the adolescents we have seen. If a teen-aged person happens to be in a commune *because* his or her mother is there, the teenager takes on "child" status. But if a person of the same age appears in the commune autonomously, unrelated to any adult, he or she will be regarded simply as a member.

CHAPTER 4

AMERICAN PASTORALISM
AND THE
COMMUNE MOVEMENT

Deke Jones is old by communal standards. Probably around sixty years of age, he has been in or around the fringes of the counterculture far longer than the word has existed. We first encountered him at Gertrud's Land, a commune near The Ranch that, during the period of our research, went through a change from "open" hippie settlement to a generally "religious" commune and finally to an exclusively Christian evangelical ("Jesus Freak") one. Deke was a very prominent person in the community, and his skills were much in demand because he was a genius in the garden; and since the communal garden was typically one of the first major projects mounted by new communards (most of whom were urban-bred and, at least initially, decidedly not green-thumbed), Deke was an important neighborhood resource, whose skills were frequently called upon by novices attempting to make their gardens grow—and without which they could not survive.

Deke was grizzled and mystical, his leathery head preoccupied with the mysteries of nature and primitive survival in it. Pastoral or "nature" themes have been prominent in the armory of counterculture ideas from the beginning,[1] whether as a passionate interest in ecology, the purity of one's diet or

---

1. Although their salience has waxed and waned over relatively short time spans. See Daniel A. Foss and Ralph W. Larkin, "From 'The Gates of Eden' to 'The Day of the Locust,' " *Humboldt Journal of Social Relations* (Fall/Winter 1975).

the quality of one's health or in the simple conviction that the more *natural* one's life (the closer to nature it was) the more wholesome it was likely to be—an idea, of course, with deep roots in romanticism and in the anti-urban animus it bred.[2]

Deke Jones partook of this spirit. One of his beliefs was in the theory of "companionate planting," an idea that regarded plants as thriving best when they grew alongside other complementary or ecologically compatible plants. Showing us through his gardens, he would sometimes comment on how well (or how poorly) plant A got along with plant B. But Deke was not merely a theoretical gardener, he was a pastoral seeker as well. His mind was blown one day, he told me, when he suddenly realized that, regardless of his skilled and learned efforts, the major difference between his garden and the natural "garden" beyond it was the fence he had built. For him, his garden *became* the fence, for he grew convinced that, whatever his efforts on his side of the fence, nature did it better on its side of the fence. The insight was a genuine crisis for him, and it apparently so devastated him, that he talked of plans to abandon his work and withdraw into nature (in his imagery almost to merge with it) to learn its secrets and live with (as well as off) them.[3]

This is perhaps an extreme view of counterculture pastoralism, but it catches something of the religious dedication many communards reveal toward the natural. So prevalent is this dedication that some communards become almost competitive in their desire to demonstrate their commitment to the natural and the unvarnished. Like other spiritually am-

2. For an historical consideration of some of the rural or pastoral themes in the communal tradition, see Laurence Veysey, *The Communal Experience: Anarchist and Mystical Countercultures in America* (New York: Harper and Row, 1973).

3. It is not irrelevant to point out that, at the time Deke expressed these ideas to me, he had recently been cast out of the Jesus commune for not accepting Christ as his Savior. Deke, of course, had to decide what to do next, and such decisions, especially for spiritually motivated people, need ideological sanction. Deke's being cast out itself reveals one form of resolving a conflict between ideas and circumstances: he was in possession of valuable skills the commune needed but in this case was apparently willing to do without for doctrinal reasons.

bitious persons describable as attempting to be "holier than thou" or "hipper than thou," some communards could be described as attempting to be "more primitive than thou." Indeed, that competitiveness is itself an indication of the high esteem in which the natural is held. However rural, pastoral, or bucolic their milieu, at least some communards are likely to respond to the incursion of civilized or urban amenities with an impulse to flee to more remote surroundings. Raymond Mungo catches this impulse well when he observes that "even fabulous Mendocino and glorious Vermont are not good enough for us anymore, no a new generation of city dropouts is coming along and it is for them that Mendocino remains; for us who flatter ourselves with the notion that we are always a coupla years ahead of the real stampedes . . . , for us there must be higher and further out places: B.C. [British Columbia], Ireland, Greenland, whatever."[4]

THE PASTORAL MYTH AND THE MYTH OF SUBURBIA

Counterculture pastoralism has deep roots in American history. American culture can be understood as a plurality of competing traditions, and even as the countryside was being emptied out and the cities filling up, pastoralism has been a perennial part of that plurality. Rural communes are contemporary bearers of the pastoral tradition, and before I get to the analysis of the pastoralism at The Ranch, I think it is worth a long digression to set that analysis in an historical context.

Like the relationship of recent events to cultural traditions, the thought of individual scholars usually reveals continuities with their own past thinking. One of my own intellectual habits is periodically to ask myself whether within the apparently disparate subjects I have written on over the years there are patterns of continuity suggesting some binding theme that connects them. In thinking about the relationship of my commune research to my earlier work on suburbia in the late

4. Raymond Mungo, *Total Loss Farm* (New York: E.P. Dutton, 1970), p. 107. At last report Mungo was not in Greenland, but was working as Religion Editor of the magazine *Mother Jones*, based in San Francisco.

1950s and early 1960s, it occurred to me that the rural commune movement contained some of the same themes that had characterized the migration of many of the parents of communards to suburbia a generation earlier.

Instead of seeing the commune movement as a "revolt" by the children of the affluent against the more stereotypic "suburban values" (careerism, consumerism, striving for status, "plasticness," etc.) of their parents (which, of course, to some extent it is, as just about every sympathetically partisan commentator on the movement has pointed out), I want to suggest that it can also be understood in part as continuous with the suburban exodus from central cities over the past thirty years (and earlier still), and the ideology of "togetherness" (much publicized and celebrated in the late 1940s and 1950s) it was represented as expressing: the suburban family, warm and secure in its domestic enclave full of plenty.[5] The rural commune movement, in short, can be understood in part as an attempt to extend some of these "suburban" values but to set them in contexts more promising for their realization.

Having no sooner thought this, and said it, I found my intellectually reflexive processes set in motion an internal dialogue that pointed out to me that one of the typical forms that interpretive controversy takes is for one party to argue that a pattern of recent events constitutes a "revolt against" or a "reaction to" the established past, whereas an opposing party argues that these events are but the most recent expression of a long tradition continuously extending itself into the future. Each of these arguments may be made in a spirit of ideolog-

5. See Bennett M. Berger, *Working-Class Suburb* (Berkeley: University of California Press, 1960), for some of the evidence. See also William H. Whyte, *The Organization Man* (New York: Doubleday, 1956), for a summary of the literature constituting the "popular" myth of suburbia. The trends reported there continued into the 60s as relatively homogeneous communities (of the retired, the young-marrieds, "swinging singles," and so on) developed, which come together on the basis of common problems they have (by virtue of age, family status, or some other status attribute) that may be solved collectively but not singly. In this perspective communes are continuous with parallel developments in other sectors of the society.

ical approval or disapproval—depending upon what one thinks of the established tradition to which the recent events are related. The "revolt against" argument may function as a *legitimation* of the events it describes *if* the tradition against which it reacts is a despised tradition. The "continuity" argument may do the same *if* the tradition is one the arguer intends to honor. Similarly, both arguments may de-legitimate the past, depending on one's approval or disapproval of the specific past one is talking about.

Nevertheless, the "continuity argument" is often taken by radicals as a derogation of the "radical" character of the recent events in question—even though the asserted continuity is with a *radical* tradition and can therefore function as a certification that the events belong to that tradition. When, in 1967, I published an article on the hippies, connecting some features of their culture with a two-hundred-year-old bohemian tradition, it was interpreted by some as a put-down of the radical character of the phenomenon, in spite of the fact that I characterized it as part of a culturally radical tradition, and, indeed, spent the last part of the article describing what was in fact new in their contribution to that tradition.[6]

Another recent example of this type of controversy (and most relevant to the topic at hand) occurred over the meaning of the political activism of radical students in the 1960s. Lewis Feuer and other opponents of the movement derogated the motives of radical students by arguing that they were "revolting against" their parents by acting out unresolved Oedipal problems through hostility in the public forum, rather than in the privacy of the family room.[7] But survey data showed that student militants came disproportionately from families that tended to be liberal to left-of-liberal in political sentiment. These data were used by scholars, such as Richard Flacks and Kenneth Keniston and others sympathetic to the movement, to defend the authenticity of its political dimensions by asserting that radical students were not rebelling against but

6. Bennett M. Berger, "Hippie Morality: More Old than New," *Trans-Action* (December 1967).

7. Lewis Feuer, *The Conflict of Generations* (New York: Basic Books, 1969).

extending and realizing the political persuasions of their parents.[8]

Well, neither view probably tells the whole story. It seems very likely that a lot of radical students had grievances against their parents. Many of the communards we spoke to routinely complained of the emptiness of their familial upbringing and were adamant about their intent to raise their children differently from the ways in which they themselves were raised. But that this is so does not necessarily diminish the importance of the political issues they raised. On the other hand, the survey data that Flacks and Keniston cite are not inconsistent with felt grievances in the movement against middle-class family life. Despite the affluence and the liberal political sentiment in these families, dad was likely to be busy with his career and psychologically absent a good bit of the time; mom may well have been busy with a full-time job called child-rearing-in-the-suburbs, puzzled and maybe more than a little resentful that this is what her liberal education prepared her for. Add to the image of a busy, harried father and a frustrated mother the not entirely satisfactory sexual or emotional relationships between them, and it suggests a tense and anxiety-filled domestic scene that, although liberal, enlightened, and "cultured," its heirs might not have been strongly motivated to reproduce.

Nor does this hypothetical logic even nearly tell the whole story. I tell the part of it I do to suggest that, for the rural communards at The Ranch and other communes like it, the pastoral tradition is the cultural analogue of the political liberalism connecting suburban parents of student activists to their children. The pastoral myth—the vision of a simple and self-sufficient rural life in harmony with nature—connects the rural communards of the counterculture with the suburbanites of the 1950s and with the more distant American past.

Even a casual glance at rural communards reveals obvious continuities with the still-honored rural past of America. Rural communards *look like* down-home country folks, with

8. See Kenneth Keniston, *Young Radicals* (New York: Harcourt, Brace and World, 1968); and Richard Flacks, "The Liberated Generation, an Exploration of the Roots of Student Protest," *The Journal of Social Issues*, 23 (July 1967).

their rubber boots, overalls, dirty jeans, and work shoes caked with mud; and they would not dress and adorn themselves differently if they could. There is a country tavern in rural California that on Saturday nights during the period of our research was regularly jammed not with disco fever but with whole family (commune) groups, children included, from Chicago and Brooklyn, and L.A. and the Haight, mostly college-educated, in gingham and denim (not the $25 kind from jeans boutiques, but the 50¢ kind from rummage sales), mixed with local loggers, fishermen, and farm hands, drinking, dancing, and singing to country music played on instruments they brought and played (and in some cases made) themselves—in a scene that might have been out of some folklorist's image of Appalachia. During a screening of the movie *McCabe and Mrs. Miller*, ostensibly about life in a frontier community in the state of Washington around the turn of the century, I remember saying to myself, in the middle of the movie, "this is a hippie movie!"—not fully understanding what I meant until later, when I met someone connected with the production of the film who told me that they had used local communards in their native costume for some of the minor roles.

There are other continuities as well. Frederick Jackson Turner saw the availability of free land beyond the frontier as a safety valve, sparing the centers of civilization from some of the potential ravages of urban poverty and discontent. Turner's safety-valve hypothesis is given added credence by the fact that, despite widespread hostility to hippies and counterculture life styles (and despite the only metaphorical character of their "frontier" status), the rural communes we studied have *not* been harassed by public officials nearly as much as one might expect, given this hostility and their vulnerability to harassment over such issues as drugs, sex, building and health codes, child welfare, and (for a while) draft evasion. Legal harassment of this population, according to safety-valve thinking, could well have turned out to be more trouble than it was worth.

Indeed, the rural commune movement in The Ranch's region of California has achieved some striking successes in being permitted to run its own schools, and in a political campaign (mounted in alliance with other rural residents) to prevent the enforcement of county building code regulations on some of the homemade structures that violate these regulations.[9] And the communards have been able to take advantage of the traditional rural respect for private property to conduct their private lives pretty much as they please, so long as it is confined to their own acres.

It is true that traditional rural realities include far more than is covered by the myth. I know that rural life has been and still can be harsh and severe. I know too that the demographic trends from rural to urban over most of the past hundred years reflect not only the "push" from the land to the cities created by urban factories and the industrialization of agriculture but also the "pull" of the city itself, which represented freedom and privacy and economic opportunity, as well as indoor plumbing, paved streets, electricity, and hot baths, and the corresponding liberations from rain and snow and cold and mud and the tyranny of tradition and the watchful eyes of neighbors.[10]

Nevertheless, the pastoral myth has remained continually strong in spite of such facts,[11] and in spite of the unresolved tensions suggested by the discrepancy between fact and myth. In his influential book, *The Machine in the Garden*, a study of the pastoral myth in American literature, Leo Marx

9. Unlike, for example, Morningstar Ranch or Wheeler's, which were eventually defeated by harassment from Sonoma County (California) officials on the grounds of code violations. See Hugh Gardner's account in *The Children of Prosperity* (New York: St. Martin's Press, 1978).

10. To say nothing of epidemic disease, insanity, and suicide. See, for example, Michael Lesy, *Wisconsin Death Trip* (New York: Pantheon Books, 1973), for some of the pictorial (as well as other) evidence against pastoralism. Renato Poggioli's *The Oaten Flute* (Cambridge: Harvard University Press, 1975) is a series of essays on the pastoral myth in literature, going back to the Greeks. Like Lesy (but on a grand, historical scale), Poggioli seems sour about the pastoral myth because pastoral reality is closer to Hobbes's brutal image of "nature" than to Rousseau's.

11. The most recent best sellers invoking images of pastoralism are Jane Kramer, *The Last Cowboy* (New York: Harper and Row, 1977); and John McPhee, *Coming into the Country* (New York: Farrar, Straus, and Giroux, 1977).

says that "American writers seldom, if ever, have designed satisfactory resolutions of their pastoral fables." The power of the fable rests, he says, in the gradual domination of nature by technology, symbolized by the roar of the locomotive (the machine) violating the quiet of the Thoreauvian glade (the garden), revealing that "our inherited symbols of order and beauty have been divested of meaning," so that in the end, as he puts it, "the American hero is either dead or alienated from society."[12]

If the heroes of American literature end up dead or alienated from society, that bodes ill for the rest of us (at least those of us affected by literary myth), less heroic beings, who must live in that world divested of meaning in which, as Scott Fitzgerald's narrator (himself a great pastoral nostalgist) in *The Great Gatsby* says, "we beat on, boats against the current, borne back ceaselessly into the past." If American heroes just don't make it, if the best and the brightest wind up betrayed and betraying, and if Mick Jagger himself can't get no satisfaction, what will the unheroic rest of us do?

Most of us most of the time try in one or another way to accommodate our "beliefs" to our practical actions, constrained by our day-to-day circumstances, to lend dignity to action and behavioral substance to belief in a mutually reinforcing dialectic. The attempt is not always successful. I remember the late Laurence Harvey, in the film *The Manchurian Candidate*, chanting over and over to himself, "I am not lovable," wistfully repeating it as if the only comfort to be drawn from the fact was his ability to recognize it, reflect upon it, and perhaps to make himself a little more lovable by virtue of his acceptance of what he was, unlovable, and maybe to neutralize his potential critics by confessing a vice before they had a chance to discover it and maliciously point it out—the sort of cagily self-deprecatory candor that disarms critics in advance of their criticism.

Can a whole society be unlovable? There is a sense in which the collective analogue of a person's self-image is the myth or

12. Leo Marx, *The Machine in the Garden* (New York: Oxford University Press, 1964).

myths that a culture invents about itself. When a myth is living or vital, it enriches the daily lives of individuals by justify-
ing their actions, by dignifying their motives, by rendering
their lives (and their deaths) "meaningful." In my more generous moods, for example, I like to think that the people who
decorate their vehicles with "America, love it or leave it," or
"I'm proud to be an American," are, in fact, in possession of
such a myth. (Do they know something that I don't know?)
But I don't believe it (which is not to say that I don't believe
that they believe they believe it), for it is no longer exactly a
secret that the old myths (in whatever incarnation: as Leo
Marx's "pastoral," as Henry Nash Smith's idea of America as
"the garden,"[13] as Fitzgerald's image of "the fresh green
breast of America," as "rural values," or as Frederick Jackson
Turner's idea of free land beyond the frontier as the source of
virtue and prosperity) no longer dignify the motives, justify
the action, or otherwise inform the daily lives of over 200 mil-
lion post-industrial Americans, most of them crowded into
dense metropolitan areas in a culture that has little good to
say about megalopolis, struggling to get ahead in a culture
whose intellectuals teach disdain for status seeking, working
at Chaplinesque assembly lines whose engineers somehow
forgot to build into them the promise of self-fulfillment
through work. Or they find themselves in enormous
bureaucracies—while they are taught contempt for Organization Men, pencil pushers, and paper shufflers—or shoulder-
to-shoulder in a thousand football stadiums on autumnal
weekends, apparently preferring vicarious experience to
what they have been taught to believe is the real thing.

Well, what of it? Myths don't lie down and die just because
the facts are at odds with them or because they are embedded
in historical "contradictions," or because social and economic
changes weaken their viability, or because they're no longer
"relevant" (they may be a little like college curricula in that
respect); and if the culture of advanced industrial capitalism
has somehow failed to make America lovable by failing to
create an industrial or technological equivalent of the myth

13. Henry Nash Smith, *Virgin Land* (New York: Random House, 1950).

of rural virtue and self-sufficiency and mutual aid, and if the available stock of institutionalized fantasy doesn't enrich one's daily life, isn't an irrelevant fantasy life better than none at all? Isn't a "false consciousness" better than an empty or barren or cynical one? In the age of television, the answer seems to be yes for a considerable majority of the American population.

But that leaves large numbers of people, uneasy at the absence of an available transcendent myth to ennoble their own daily lives, who can afford to attempt a life enriched by the traditional pastoral. In an essay published around the time I was doing the research for my book on suburbia, David Riesman pointed to some of the pastoral elements from America's first suburban migration (at the turn of the century), still visible when he was writing late in the 1950s. The desire for that "little place in the country" with its own piece of green was for him a re-evocation of the image of Jeffersonian independence and British gentry patterns. Riesman also saw in the suburban migration after World War II the desire of the new suburbanites to protect their children against the possibility of downward social mobility, symbolized even then by the increasingly dark ethnicities of the urban cores— in the same way that the earlier generation of wealthy suburbanites fled the central cities, corrupted in their view by the crowds of immigrant Irish, Italians, Jews, and Poles pouring into them. In the suburbanites of the 1950s, Riesman saw, in addition, a desire to recreate the sense of local community through primary-group ties and face-to-face relatedness in a roomy suburban house, a domestic establishment spacious enough to permit the family to grow together, and in a suburb demographically homogeneous enough to permit the possibility of friendship developing into a kind of quasi-kinship.[14]

The recreation of community had a more practical meaning as well because most new suburbs (the Levittowns were striking exceptions) had been mass-produced without much pre-planning attention to the needs for local services and facilities

14. William H. Whyte, too, emphasizes this point in his discussion of suburbia in *The Organization Man* (New York: Doubleday, 1956).

and institutions such as schools, churches, community centers, parks, playgrounds, newspapers, public transportation and the like, leaving to the new residents the work of creating these features of community from scratch. Finally, the anti-urban and anti-technological animus of much of this migration encouraged Riesman to say that "sometimes it seems to me that what people are seeking in the suburbs is a kind of pre-industrial incompetence and inefficiency."[15]

On an economic level higher than the average middle-class suburbs Riesman was talking about, the pastoral ideal is still more visible in the desire for a country house on land sufficient to sustain gardens, a stable, and a few horses, and maybe some live-in retainers. It is now visible in a new wave with the boom in vacation and retirement homes—at a secluded beach, in the country, on a mountain, as the cities get more polluted and less safe. Advertising for such real estate almost always emphasizes pastoral themes. Recent promotions for "La Costa," an expensive San Diego suburb, *cum* retirement, *cum* vacation, second-home community, refer to polluted and problem-ridden cities and the "respite and refuge" provided by their community, "where life is healthier and less pressurized." These survivals of the pastoral ideal are, of course, corrupted; they are mixed, that is, with dependence on industrial civilization. Leo Marx calls it "complex pastoralism." La Costa is perhaps an especially good and ironic symbol because it is reputed to have been built with Mafia money channeled through the Teamsters' Union.

Suburbia, like the Teamsters, has always depended on transportation. The first suburban migration depended upon the extension of rail and trolley lines,[16] and contemporary suburbia depends upon the automobile and the superhighway. Its very success sowed the dialectical seeds of its

15. David Riesman, "The Suburban Dislocation," *Annals of the American Academy of Political and Social Science* (November 1957).

16. Carl Bridenbaugh, in *Cities in Revolt* (New York: Alfred A. Knopf, 1955), traces suburbanization back to the eighteenth century, when it occurred for much the same reasons it occurred in the nineteenth and twentieth centuries. See also Sam Bass Warner, *Streetcar Suburbs* (Cambridge: Harvard University Press, 1962).

downfall as pastoral ideal. Riesman's house in the country became millions of houses in what is no longer the country. The quiet piece of green was invaded by a thousand power mowers, that other machine in the garden. The image of Jeffersonian independence became bondage to the long commute and the crushing enervation of fingers-drumming-on-the-wheel, bumper-to-bumper, rush-hour traffic. The fresh air got smoggy, and the image of recreating community yielded to "suburban" images of harried husbands, bored *and* harried wives, and teen-aged children who would almost always prefer to be somewhere other than at home, where the action wasn't. The reportedly high rates of transience in middle class suburbs didn't help the image of stable community either. The suburban idyll of the little community restored became, in short, increasingly urban, increasingly massive, and increasingly privatized.

Eventually defeated by its dependence on the economic forces of capitalist civilization outside it, this corrupted ideal of "complex pastoralism" evokes Frederick Jackson Turner's own ambivalence between "nature" and "civilization." Although Turner affirmed the myth of the garden with his frontier hypothesis, he also persisted in his belief that "civilization" was a higher stage of development. Turner's ambivalence on this point should be no surprise, because the viability of pastoralism has always been limited by political and economic constraints, as the experience of suburbia illustrates, as Leo Marx's book shows, and as Michael Lesy's work reproduces photographically.

But the pastoral *myth* has eluded simple political formulation or characterization because of the complex, even contradictory, ideological sources from which it has drawn. New Left philosophers (Herbert Marcuse, among many others) regard rural communes with dismay because they drain off a lot of the potential political energy that might be devoted to urban radical movements.[17] Rosabeth Kanter, whose sympathy seems to be with rationally organized urban com-

17. Herbert Marcuse, *Counterrevolution and Revolt* (Boston: Beacon Press, 1973).

munes, refers to rural communes like The Ranch as "retreat" communes (although they see themselves as attempting to make a "revolution by example").[18] Sonia Rudikoff and Lewis Yablonsky are among those who are most impressed by the squalor and disorganization of rural communes,[19] whereas Raymond Mungo and Stephen Diamond are representative of those writer-communards who portray their pastoral efforts in primarily elegiac terms.[20]

Nevertheless, contemporary pastoralism cannot be easily pigeonholed as "reactionary" or "progressive" or in terms of simple political categories anywhere in-between, because it has drawn not only (as Riesman suggested) from the anti-industrialism of the nineteenth-century British aristocracy, but also partly from the socialist critique of the wretched urban squalor created by the early stages of English industrialism that, despite Karl Marx's remark about the idiocy of rural life, might well have made the community life of peasants and artisans seem idyllic in retrospect. And as the German youth movement made clear, pastoralism is also consistent with German conservatism (even fascism) and its emphasis on ties of blood, soil, and *Volk*;[21] but it has drawn also from the bohemian tradition, mostly French, which, although urban, strongly emphasized Rousseau's primitivism, wilderness, exoticism, sexual expressiveness, and even mind-expanding drugs.

Given this mixed bag of ideological heritages, it is no wonder that the contemporary pastoralism of rural communes can project so wide a range of political imagery. Now, late in the 1970s, when the ubiquity of words like "ecology" and "environment" and "pollution" suggests an intensifica-

18. Rosabeth Kanter, *Commitment and Community* (Cambridge: Harvard University Press, 1972), chap. 7.

19. Sonia Rudikoff, "O Pioneers!" *Commentary* (July 1972); Lewis Yablonsky, *The Hippie Trip* (New York: Pegasus, 1968).

20. Raymond Mungo, *Total Loss Farm* (New York: E.P. Dutton, 1970); Stephen Diamond, *What the Trees Said* (New York: Delacorte Press, 1972).

21. Howard Becker, *German Youth: Bond or Free?* (London: Kegan Paul, Trench, Trubner, 1946).

tion of the ill-repute of uncontrolled technological development, when the woods are filled with campers and bikers,
the hills with hikers and the mountains with climbers, when
college students walk the vinyl floors of academe in shoes
made for rough country and carry their books in backpacks
rather than briefcases or Harvard bags, when, indeed, census figures show the first net increases in rural population
since the nineteenth century, it seems a likely historical moment for a renaissance of pastoralism. And this brings me,
finally, to rural hippie communes and the extent to which
they have selected from this mixed bag of available ideology
to make sense of, to legitimate and justify and honor the way
they live.

COMMUNAL IDEALS AND THE PASTORAL MYTH

Survival

The first element of the pastoral myth among communards
that I want to examine is the celebration of self-sufficiency
and survival. "Survival" is a word that rural communards
weight with heavy emotive meaning, for it carries with it the
connotation of a victorious "look, we have come through!" To
have survived a first winter in the country, or a failure in the
garden, or the first major intracommunal dispute, or a flu
epidemic, or a dry well, or the departure of a welfare mother
whose monthly check was an important part of communal
income, or the tensions induced by a member losing his or
her lover to another member are all triumphs to be savored
and celebrated; for each of these (and many other even-
tualities) constitutes a real threat to the survival of a group.
"Survival" for rural communards conveys the *pride* they take
in the development of the requisite skills and techniques that
enable them to overcome such real threats to their collective
continuity.

Why should "survival" carry with it the strong sense of
self-esteem it does for these people who live in a society in
which survival is no longer a problem for most people, who
are less concerned with survival than they are with affluence?
There is a simple issue of *competence* here that is evocative of

Edgar Friedenberg writing on why he admired high school athletes more than he did those students who found it easy to get A's in civics and social studies. Unlike civics and social studies, basketball and track required skills that couldn't be faked. On the field and in the game, you could either cut it or you couldn't, depending on your command of the skills that were clearly central to the task at hand. In the classroom, good grades went to those who had developed a certain verbal facility for expressing appropriate pieties that had only the most tenuous relation to the actual learning of substantive curricular materials.[22]

Something of this spirit is clearly evident in the communards who, in the place of "bullshitting" skills, substitute an emphasis on fundamental survival skills: putting in a healthy garden, constructing a dwelling with a roof that doesn't leak, disposing of their shit in useful or otherwise benign ways, scavenging the county dump for usable items (for example horsehair from an abandoned mattress to use as mulch for the beets in the garden), keeping the moss off the apple trees and their ancient vehicles in running order, making cheese and yogurt ("this little piggy had yogurt," one mother crooned to her baby) and sturdy fences, becoming good woodsmen, weavers, fishermen—resourceful rural folk.

The evidence of their pride in the development of survival skills is almost endless. One young man working on a construction project to repair an old shed had to remove a bunch of nails from his mouth to tell me that a year earlier he was unable to drive a nail straight. Another serene and visibly "spiritual" fellow, busy splitting redwood shakes in his workshop, confessed that not long before he had been so oppressed by his sense of uselessness and incompetence that

22. See Edgar Friedenberg's review of James Coleman's *The Adolescent Society*, "Hot Rods and Questionnaires," in *Commentary* (November 1961). Not that bullshitting skills are unambiguously derogated. Communes, like the counterculture generally, are full of "rap artists," and philosophical, rhetorical, prophetic, and argumentative-interpretive skills are appreciated, but not usually if they are the *only* skills a member possesses, unless he (or she) is the acknowledged ideological leader of the group and the verbal magic is exercised in behalf of the solidarity of the group.

he had been suicidal.[23] The first time I was shown through the original garden at The Ranch, my guide seemed to me much like a new mother letting a friend peek into the nursery at her sleeping infant: I was asked to be quiet and to tread lightly because "too many vibes freak out the plants." On the afternoon that I arrived at The Ranch to find a group of communards gathered around the not-yet-completed composter-shitter on which they had been working, the discussion was full of evident satisfaction at their accomplishments so far and anticipated satisfaction still to come—almost like suburban neighbors commenting on and admiring the backyard brick patio that one of them is putting in on a weekend do-it-yourself project. One Sunday I participated in a barn-raising project that involved traditional rural mutual aid on a massive scale, with probably more than a hundred women, men, and children wielding hammers, nails, axes, ropes, levers, and wedges; and when the hand-hewn timber was eased into place as the ridgepole of the roof-to-be, there was spontaneous applause and a festive potluck dinner to follow.[24] At The Ranch, Patricia spent much of a whole day scraping the skin of a freshly slaughtered goat, nailed to the side of a shed, and she would not be distracted by the small-talk I tried to engage her in because, as she said, she was interested in learning how to do it. Tim Gull, who lived in a geodesic dome at a commune not far from The Ranch, developed locally celebrated skills as a fisherman after dropping out of a successful career as a clothing salesman. A bizarre accident, in which he fell on his fishing spear and was almost killed, he interpreted as a warning from God that his success was *too* great—that he had taken too many fish from the sea.

One could go on piling example upon example of the importance with which rural communards endow the develop-

23. "Jesus Freaks" often reveal the same kind of pride in being "reborn," the spiritual rebirth redeeming them from meaninglessness and despair. The rebirth is usually a powerful event, but it is generally only an initial step in becoming a Christian. A major *problem* for these people is in routinizing the charisma of their transformation.

24. See Judson Jerome, *Families of Eden* (New York: Seabury Press, 1974), for another, more detailed description of a similar event.

ment of practical skills and the dignity they attribute to them, but it seems to me that the point is not at issue, for its influence has diffused far beyond the commune movement; for example, down to the universities, where, among many of my more countercultureish students, I find greater respect for carpentry (or skilled surfing and skateboarding, for that matter) than for verbal, bureaucratic skills.

It is true that many of these skills may not amount to much. I have heard serious and accomplished artists and craftsmen deplore the quality of the crafts practiced by California hippies (leather, woodworking, pottery, jewelry, weaving, etc.), and when I took a friend of mine, an eccentric seventy-five-year-old master craftsman of fine furniture, to visit a commune to see its homemade architecture and woodworking, he was polite but patronizing, saying, "Well, it's very nice, but not really fine work." To some hippie builders who were constructing a small house out of an enormous wine barrel, he gave a spontaneous lecture on comparative cabinetry, reminding them that English, though simple, was the best work. "Italian work can be elegant, but the drawers tend to stick."

Nevertheless, and regardless of expert judgments, communards take great pride in such survival skills as they have been able to develop. Like the suburbanite twenty-five years ago, freshly installed in a new tract house, the communards are very much into doing it themselves, proud of every step in their progress toward self-sufficiency. That these skills may be primitive by expert or sophisticated standards is less important analytically than that they do in fact support and ennoble the communal enterprise by providing much of the grounding that enables them to sustain the ideological vision of what they are about: the creation of community, the resistance to alienated work, the revolution by example. A small idea such as the legitimation of pride in manual skills helps to sustain the small social structure of communes, whereas in a middle-class family a child's gift for carpentry or tinkering might be discouraged on the grounds that cultivating the gift would lead to a working-class life and preclude a more financially rewarding career.

Apocalypse

But unlike the suburbanites, who depended upon the central city for income and commercial entertainment, the communards take pride in surviving by doing it themselves, which pride they usually invoke *in connection with* another and complementary belief: in the imminent collapse of urban industrial civilization; the image of apocalypse-around-the-corner undergirds their pride in survival skills.

One of the favorite topics of conversation at The Ranch was the apocalyptic significance that could be read into the latest news items: wars, revolts, fuel shortages, racial disturbances, power outages, double-digit inflation, unemployment, strikes by employees in essential industries, alarms over pollution levels, nuclear hazards, urban bankruptcies, "senseless" multiple murders, suicides, and various and sundry other disasters. Such items were typically received and discussed with a sort of bemused and mock-helpless shaking of heads, suggesting the inevitably self-destructive course on which the urban industrial world was set, and suggesting also a confirmation of their own decision to insulate themselves from that world bent on self-destruction and to live as simply and self-sufficiently as they could in their pastoral style. When Bob and Linda drove The Ranch's old school bus down to southern California with my household goods aboard, they stayed for a few days after the bus was unloaded. One evening we went to a movie in a big shopping center in San Diego. When we came out it was late, the broad expanse of parking lot was nearly deserted, and the big department stores loomed through the fog like the superstructures of battleships. Bob looked at their immensity and remarked thoughtfully that when there were no more goods left to sell in those stores they would make terrific communal living spaces. The apocalyptic vision was almost casual.

It was also unshakeable. Like the faith in Judgment Day, the prospect of apocalypse could not be weakened by good news or by any short-run evidence that capitalist industrial society might find some lasting resolution of its crises. In this respect, communards regard the prospect of apocalypse as inevitable in however long the long run takes. Like the faith of orthodox Marxists in an inevitable class war, or the unalterable conviction of some about the eventual California disaster in which the whole state will simply break off and fall in the Pacific Ocean, a belief in the prospect of apocalypse serves the interests of the faithful and motivates them to continue their efforts in behalf of them.

Now urban industrial civilization (to say nothing of California) may or may not sink into oblivion under the weight of its garbage, its pollution, its racial conflict, its imperialist wars, and its individual estrangement and loneliness; I do not know. And such opinions as I have are modest and tentative and full of contingencies. But I am relatively certain that it is patently more viable and self-serving to believe in the prospect of urban apocalypse if one is in possession (and committed to the further possession) of the necessities for surviving it; more viable, that is, than if one is incompetent to change a light bulb or unplug a clogged toilet or understand electricity. Like the surgical skills that may give a physician interests in doubting the therapeutic efficacy of prayer, the possession of survival skills by rural communards reinforces their belief in the imminent doom of industrial civilization (from which they initially dropped out at least in part because of their revulsion for it), confirms their sense of the wholesomeness of their enterprise and enhances their motivation to increase their resources for sustaining it by developing still further skills in a self-strengthening cycle of ideological work that generates and reproduces "meaning."

In a peculiarly perverse sense, these skills may even give them a sort of vested interest in the prospect of apocalypse: after it happens (if it happens), their skills (and hence they themselves) will be more highly valued by the world than they are now. In short, the pride of communards in survival dignifies their daily life, and the belief in the prospect of apocalypse lends further dignity to the humble work of survival and self-sufficiency "on the land" (reverently uttered), just as it could not for the suburbanite forever bound to his career in the city. And that pastoralism-based and self-generated dignity transforms rural communal life from something absurd and reactionary (is *that* what the revolution was about? reversion to a nineteenth-century subsistence agriculture?) into something "meaningful" for the children of industrial affluence.

Technology and Ecological Ideals

In spite of the fact that there has been considerable sympathy in at least some parts of the counterculture for some kinds of technologies (as is evident in the elevation of Buckminster Fuller into a sort of folk hero, the prominent place *The Whole Earth Catalog* earned on counterculture bookshelves and coffee tables, and the fascination with dome construction and systems of solar power), the counterculture, and particularly that part of it involved in the rural commune movement, inherited much of the traditional romantic bias against and distrust of "technology."

I use quotation marks around the word to indicate that its reference has never been entirely clear; its rhetorical uses have evoked images of everything from machines to science to expertise to factories and other large enterprises organized in a "functionally rational" manner and dedicated to bureaucratically efficient goals. As Theodore Roszak pointed out in *The Making of a Counterculture*, "technology" evokes this image of implacable and impersonal systems governed by system-generated rules administered by invisible experts— an image that fired the counterculture's reaction to "establishments," and that was the dominant, Luddite-like metaphor in Mario Savio's celebrated Berkeley speech that proclaimed there comes a time when it is necessary to throw one's body on the "machine" to bring it to a halt.

Rural communards adopt this negative attitude toward "technology" (despite the fact that they have, use, and need a wide variety of tools) *in association with* a reverence for "the ecology" of the land and a refusal of bureaucratic or "alienated" work. At The Ranch, for example, the communards faced a recurrent problem with flies in the kitchen. The kitchen there was liberally hung with strips of yellow, gluey, old-fashioned flypaper, and almost every time I would notice the crowds of fly corpses on them, I would be reminded of James Thurber's famous fable about the fly and the paper—whose moral was that there was no security in numbers or anything else. One morning somebody hung a Shell "No-Pest Strip" in the kitchen, and the ideological protest was immediate because there had been widespread publicity to the effect that the insect-killing chemicals in the Shell product were ecologically dangerous. A family meeting was called to discuss the issue, and the merits of a fly-free kitchen versus sound ecological principles was debated. The Shell product lost the debate—a victory in this case for principled belief over ideologically thoughtless problem solving.

Similarly, in spite of the recurrent need of The Ranch for cash income (and their perennial shortage of it), they have consistently refused opportunities for the commercial exploitation of the rich timber resources on their 140 acres. Even without touching their living trees, they have enough redwood stumps on their land (from cutting many years ago) to make at least feasible their use for the manufacture of fashionable burl tables. Celt proposed this idea to the family at The Ranch but was rebuffed on the grounds that it would commit the family to alienated, factory-like work and otherwise interfere with their primary commitments—apparently another victory for principled belief over the prospect of ideologically thoughtless problem solving (although not in Celt's opinion, for he eventually left The Ranch).

There is other evidence of a consistent ideological refusal to make technological "improvements" at The Ranch when such improvements contradict a belief or when their costs outweigh their putative benefits. There are no flush toilets at The Ranch because human feces are useful in the making of compost. The Ranch lost one of its most loved and admired members because he was a serious and dedicated photographer who needed a darkroom and electricity to do his work. The Ranch refused to put in electricity, even for him. The costs were too great for the benefits. Similarly, the limits of animal husbandry at The Ranch and other communes like it seem to be set by the ideological limits they place on "rational" organization in the division of labor: goats, yes; cattle, no.

REMEDIAL IDEOLOGICAL WORK

The consistent realization of none of these ideals comes easily, particularly the ideal of self-sufficiency. None of the rural communes studied by any member of my research team has achieved the self-sufficiency ideal of consuming only what is produced on the land. None has come close, despite its emphasis on and pride in the development of survival skills, and this fact places its beliefs under a good deal of strain.

Although unlike the suburbanites of the 1950s, in that they are not bound to urban careers, communards have been for the most part dependent upon a variety of benefits from the world they devalue. Food stamps and the Department of Agriculture's surplus food program have been important sources of sustenance for rural communards. Other "unearned" income has also been important for most of the communes we studied, urban as well as rural. "Welfare," in the form of Aid to Dependent Children, has been an important source of income on which many communes have depended, a fact that enhances the attractiveness of single mothers as commune members—in much the same way that in the working-class districts of industrializing England, women with several illegitimate children were regarded as desirable wives because the children were more significant as wage earners than as mouths to feed.

Welfare also comes in the form of "disability" payments to communards whom the state regards as psychologically unfit. Also important as a source of dependence on the outside world are "windfalls," which include such blessings as occasional inheritances, birthday checks from parents and grandparents, and other unsolicited gifts from relatives or other benefactors—perhaps including my own occasional bearings. In a commune of a dozen or two dozen members, an average monthly birthday and other gift income of $100 to $200 is not uncommon (communards tend to come from relatively prosperous families), and this can go a long way toward meeting their cash-flow needs.

Circumstances like these can, of course, pose a threat to the credibility of their own beliefs and can be used (indeed *have* been used) by unsympathetic commentators on the commune movement to "unmask" the emptiness of their pastoral and self-sufficiency rhetoric. That would be about par for the usual course of ideological conflict. But my analytic aim here is not to expose discrepancies or contradictions between practice and preachment, which (as I said earlier) I take to be more or less endemic in all human attempts to live with ideas. My aim is to show how human groups attempt to cope with such dissonances by *remedial ideological work* aimed at bridging gaps, sweetening dissonances, and restoring (perhaps only temporarily) a measure of harmony and consistency.

Communards, for example, will interpret self-sufficiency in *developmental* terms, as an ideal *toward which* they aspire and work, with inevitably less-than-full success—not unlike the ideal of "objectivity" for many social scientists. Their failure to live up fully to this ideal reflects the newness of the enterprise, the present priority of survival, and the inherent difficulties of the obstacles they face; but it still remains an aim to be achieved at an indefinite, future time. At one of my most recent visits to The Ranch, I was told with considerable pride that they no longer depend on "welfare." Like most other welfare recipients, communards tend to share the dominant view of welfare as a temporary but necessary evil. They know that they cannot depend upon it permanently, and they know that it makes them vulnerable to the state when and if it should decide to make trouble for them.

At the same time, less common (though far from rare) is a certain cynicism toward living on public largesse. Some communards regard it as a sort of legitimate rip-off, analogous to price supports for mainstream farmers or the absence of price competition in oligopolistic or federally regulated industries (like airlines), or the tax deductability of corporate advertising as a business expense (which means that the public pays for it), which the state permits or encourages because the stability of the entire economic system is said to depend upon these corporations, even if they are difficult to reconcile with classical economic theory, whose free-market rhetoric will still be invoked, despite the contradictions, when it serves the proximate aims of farmers, or airline executives and other advertisers.

With this logic, the more sophisticated rural communards cope with the discrepancies between their ideals and their practice by doing the remedial ideological work that imparts a *context* to the discrepancies, makes them comparable to other more widely tolerated discrepancies and hence renders them *relatively* innocuous. With this logic too, communards can (to some extent cynically) define some of the welfare payments they receive as functioning not unlike universities do for students who are not particularly interested in higher education: it keeps them off the labor market and off the streets, and in places where government can, if not literally "keep an eye on them," at least know where they are.

Also interesting and ideologically revealing of the interchanges between beliefs and circumstantial exigencies was an issue that developed in one commune over the use of a chain saw. The winters can get cold in California, particularly a few miles inland from the coast, and a gasoline-powered chain saw can cut more firewood in one day than can be cut by manual labor power in a week, and with considerably less effort. But chain saws were "technology." Moreover, they were associated by rural communards with the large lumber companies, which own most of the land (and provide most of the nonhippie employment), which clear cut thousands of acres of redwood and fir, leaving the gorgeous landscape of California stumped and scarred and "slashed" and bald, and whose major symbol was the harsh and ugly sound of chain saws reverberating off the hillsides and echoing through the canyons as if in announcement (the machine in the garden again) of more corpses of trees ready for the trucks to carry them out of the woods to the mills where they would be transformed into studs and beams and joists and rafters and plywood for more suburban houses.

Chain saws, then. Like the Shell "No-Pest Strip," the chain saw was objected to by some communards. The discussion went forward. The argument in favor of the chain saw was based on its efficiency and the situational requirements for fuel for the winter; the argument against its use invoked a more abstract ideological feeling against technology: the ugliness of the sound, the need for more gasoline, making them more dependent on outside sources, the psychological association of the saw with the hated lumber companies. The clinching argument in behalf of the chain saw was the one that denied that the use of the chain saw constituted giving in to "technology." A chain saw was *not* technology; it was a "tool."

A fine distinction, that, but a very important one. Like giving discrepancy a context, the making of "fine distinctions" is one of the major means by which ideologies are accommodated to circumstantial interests. The chain saw, which apparently contradicted the bias of communards against "technology," was saved by remedial ideological work—by a redefinition that excluded it from the category of things-to-be-despised. The outcome, I think, also reveals that the hippie predisposition against "technology" is not a negative attitude toward machines as such (they have all sorts of machines and take pride in their abilities to use them, repair them, and even recycle their parts), but toward means and relations of production that alienate labor. So long as a direct connection could be established between the tool and the collective welfare of the group, the ideological accommodation could be made by an interpretive act that rendered an apparently inconsistent practice ideologically consistent.

Although The Ranch has so far maintained the purity of its romantic pastoralism by refusing to log its land, it may not be able to resist for much longer the interaction of circumstantial pressure that pushes it in that direction and the potentially available justifications enabling it to do the ideological work to sanction it. At this point, the ideological work is conjectural, but in behalf of its plausibility I want to quote from comments on a reading of the first draft of this book by my colleague Bruce Hackett, who now spends occasional weekends at his farm near The Ranch. The comments on logging are so subtle and so apt that they are worth quoting nearly in full:

> They logged the place across the road from Reznick's, on the ridge. Charlie Guidi [a neighbor] goes over to where they are logging, since it abuts his land, to keep an eye on them. They talk. Charlie finds out how much

money this guy is making by taking out the trees.
Charlie looks at his own trees. Later I go to visit, and
by the time I have arrived on the scene Charlie has decided to log *his* land too. But he carries the community
around in his breast and he decides to log very selectively, taking mainly trees that are broken, leaving all the
big trees along the road. I express dismay and joke
about EIRs and such. In the evening he comes to my
place to visit. He is concerned about my reaction. He
starts to talk about "thinning" the trees, about "dying"
trees, and about "culls," and I say to him . . . "Charlie
don't make up all these half-assed justifications. I know
the price of redwood has doubled in the past year . . .
and that you're hurting. I've been through all this
ideological work before. Just tell it like it is." And we
talk. And he says yes, he walked up and down the road
and sat at the edge of the woods and invented all kinds
of good reasons about proper woodlot management,
and said ok I'll do it. And I'm right, he needs the money.
And here an interesting thing happens: once you have
decided to log, there is a hierarchy of virture to which
one attends: you can do a good job or a bad job, you can
take out a few trees and they'll charge you $120 per 1000
board feet; if you take out a lot of trees, you pay $60 per
1000. You decide on the former and you reclaim a lot of
lost respectability. You become a member of a new
hierarchy, as it were, with its own gradations, its own
saints and malefactors. And then another thing of interest happens: *I* say to myself, Hmm, I need some wood if
I'm going to do some building here. Perhaps I can buy a
few of these trees, and mill them myself, on the spot; no
forest damage, or very little, cheaper wood for me, more
virtue for Charlie. (I don't know if this will happen, I'm
just giving you the phenomenological blow-by-blow.) I
am inventing solutions to an otherwise difficult situation, I say . . . The next day I go down to the Grants to
attend a gathering on how to raise fir and redwood seed-
lings for purposes of reforestation, and I see [Maxwell
and Sheila] [from The Ranch—BB] there. Later I talk to

you. You note that Maxwell rarely leaves The Ranch. I say, Hmmm. I did joke a bit with Sheila about "woodlot management," and she responded as if I'd taken the words out of her mouth, and so this: perhaps the appearance of the practical solution (practical, private reforestation) might be a virtue that would overcome The Ranch's resistance to logging, and that's why Maxwell has ventured out! Sociologist begins to froth and bloom with hypothetico-deductive engines revved up. But now back to Charlie for a moment, and an even thicker plot: it is my firm suspicion that my encounter with Charlie may have missed the point, or part of it, namely, that if you have a lot of trees, and you can log them, it means something about you, that your holdings are impressive, and that, in addition, you are not a sentimentalist, a Sierra Club intellectual or some such pillow-like substance. And something like that seems to be happening here: small woodlot owners are logging all over the place. Dancey's mill is going day and night. I talked to Dancey on the phone and he starts telling me stories right away about "ideological work," about how people got their heads turned around by the rise in prices (or so the story goes). But is it just the rise in prices? Or is it the invention of solutions, new strategies, new technologies that allow you to have your cake and eat it too? And is it really a turning of heads, or a fulfillment of secret dreams in which you appear as a logger, or a fisherman, or a farmer rather than as a "hippie" or a communard or some other kind of romantic?

There are many fine distinctions here, for fine distinctions, along with providing contexts and what could be called "temporalizing" (as in the conception of self-sufficiency as an ideal *toward* which communards continue to strive) are some of the major techniques through which ideological accommodations are made.

Fine distinctions are evident inside communes not only in the chain saw issue and, conjecturally, with the logging problem quoted above, but also in the problems generated by the counterculture's belief in "brotherhood." The rhetoric of universal hip brotherhood was interpreted early in the commune movement as a principle that opened communes to everyone. In many communes some of these individuals turned out to be rip-off artists or drains on the limited collective resources, resulting for some communes in their eventual dissolution but for other communes in the modification of their understanding of the meaning of "brotherhood." For some it led to a policy of selective recruitment; at The Ranch it led to a "closed" policy and eventually to a modification of the group's belief in "brotherhood"—more precisely to a *redefinition* of brotherhood, one which excluded undesirables for *ad hoc* (but retrospectively principled) reasons. A fine distinction separates brothers (and sisters) from nonbrothers (and nonsisters) in a way that yet retains some semblance of commitment to the original rhetoric.[25]

Outside communes but in their immediate area, a corresponding ideological accommodation to practical circumstances can be noted. Just as experience with the troublesome consequences of a broad interpretation of the "brotherhood" idea can lead communards to a narrower interpretation of it, nonhippie and noncommunard old locals in the regions of communal concentration can *differentiate* their anti-hippie prejudices when it serves their interests to do so. This does not happen to everybody, of course. One local grocery store owner, a National Rifle Association member, and well known for his antipathy to "dirty, filthy hippies" was eventually forced out of business when, without conducting a formal boycott, local communards and other hippies took their trade to another grocery store. The owner of the second store, also a traditional village merchant and initially hostile to the counterculture invasion, was able to accommodate his prejudices to the prospect of the continued presence of his landholding,

25. Groups often exclude their enemies, of course, from the categories of human beings who deserve decent treatment. Many years ago I asked an official of the New York State Communist Party what the party's position was on civil liberty. He replied with a slogan: "The Communist Party defends the civil liberty of all peoples." "What about Fascists?" I asked. He did not hesitate: "Fascists are not people," he said, "they are dogs."

taxpaying, cash-on-the-barrel neighbors (and customers) by distinguishing (paternalistically, to be sure) between what he called "*our* hippies" (i.e., good, hard-working, land-holding, cash-paying ones) and the dirty filthies out hitchhiking on the highway: another fine distinction, paralleled by a distinction that serious, stable communards themselves make in distinguishing between brothers and nonbrothers—the latter, for example, including transient hippies looking for a place to crash. One communard, fresh from an unsuccessful group that had fallen apart, described his new, about-to-be-undertaken communal venture as one that would not tolerate people looking for a place to hang out. "No more goddam hippie hangouts," he said with the strong feeling of someone who knew what it was like.

Communards, then, sometimes modify their beliefs through the interpretive processes of ideological work that accommodate them to circumstantial interests, and sometimes their beliefs are sustained by or in spite of the constraints of situational pressures. In this respect they are like all human groups. My contention is only that the meaning of these relations must be understood as a process if we are to avoid vulgar and structurally fixed (reified) characterizations of them as a cynical "selling out" of original faiths or as a "fanatical" adherence to "principle" against the efforts of revisionists.

Either of these characterizations, of course, is *available* as an ideological weapon in the conduct of political conflict; either may even be an apt and accurate characterization in many instances. But the understanding of such conflicts, even at the level of macropolitical struggles, is likely to be deepened and strengthened by their linkage to this microsociology of knowledge.

IDEOLOGICAL WORK AND DOWNWARD SOCIAL MOBILITY

Like any other human group faced with apparent and embarrassing inconsistencies between its ideological professions and its attempts to develop specific practices and routine strategies to cope with concrete situations, communards do the requisite ideological work to bring the two more closely together when the discrepancies are argumentatively pointed out and if such remedial work can be made to seem plausible.

With respect to the relationship between its pastoral ideals and the day-to-day circumstances it must face, The Ranch has done its ideological work relatively well. Despite this small success, rural communards clearly belong to the category of "rural poor." Although it renders them "downwardly mobile" (compared with their own relatively prosperous parents), rural communal life provides an "alternative" to *conventional* downward social mobility for these children of the middle classes who have been unable or unwilling to meet the certification requirements imposed by institutions of higher education for access to high prestige occupations. (Or, having met these requirements, they may have rejected the putative benefits as ultimately unrewarding.) These people may be poor and without saleable skills in a post-industrial labor market, and their rejection of higher education (or their rejection by it) may have cut them off from the prospects of middle-class affluence. But their involvement in groups committed to visionary ideals (frequently with a religious or other traditionally "noble" character) and experimental living cushions the impact of these facts and insulates them to some extent against the "disgrace" of downward mobility in America.

When Peter and Brigitte Berger spoke of "the Blueing of America"—the eventual transformation of hippie dropouts into a new blue-collar class, leaving vacant places in the middle strata for ambitious blacks, chicanos, and Puerto Ricans to rise into—they may have been right to imply that the decisive generational event for these people was downward social mobility.[26] But that prospect begs most of the interesting questions the image suggests. That image suggests the prospect of something relatively unprecedented in this country and whose consequences are difficult to imagine: a small but strategic stratum of rural poor people who have nevertheless

26. Peter Berger and Brigitte Berger, "The Blueing of America" (1969); rpt. in Peter L. Berger, *Facing Up to Modernity* (New York: Basic Books, 1977).

been sufficiently exposed to higher education and the sophistication of urban culture and middle-class heritage to be able to *celebrate* their style of life as something other than an inevitable result of downward social mobility.[27] Is a person with a master's degree in political science or education or philosophy or history adequately described sociologically as "working class" or "lower class" because he scratches a living out of the soil or scavenges building supplies from lumber trucks overturned on the curves of mountain roads or barters vegetables from the garden for the catch-of-the-day from local fishermen?[28]

The question is rhetorical because "class" membership is largely a matter of definition. Whatever the definition, however, it usually carries with it explicit or implicit cultural correlates that do not describe the life style of communards. Despite the scratching and the scavenging, the barter and the poverty, rural communards will say things like "domes and tipis are good to live in because rectangular rooms unnaturally constrict the spirit," or "eating honey is very good for sperm production because bees are very heavy into sex." They will hitchhike a hundred miles to attend a Yoga workshop, advertise for lessons in belly dancing, organize the showing of antique films and provide tinkly piano accompaniment, mount petition campaigns against lumber company plans to clear cut forests near bird sanctuaries, publish a magazine celebrating the joys of rural independence, maintain a library of two thousand books. "Cultural revolutionaries," as many such communards fashion themselves, are not likely to

27. There are relatively few clear *images* of downward social mobility in American culture, and most of them are *southern*, for example, Tennessee Williams' work, which invokes a fall from genteel status, or Faulkner's contrast of the Snopes's and the Sartorus's standing. Until the past generation, American immigration patterns lent a distinctly *ethnic* cast to lower- or working-class culture. Indeed, when I used the term "working-class culture" in my Ph.D dissertation, one reader objected, saying that there was no such thing in the U.S., where the most important feature of working-class life was the opportunity to rise out of it.

28. One of the best dinners I've ever had was a dinner at The Ranch of freshly caught red snapper swimming in surplus Department of Agriculture butter, together with fresh vegetables out of the garden. (They do not, of course, always eat so well.)

feel that a social scientist's definition of them as "working class" or "lower class" (with the conventional baggage of cultural implication those terms convey) adequately suggests an image of their style of life.

An "alternative life style," in short, suggests alternatives; alternatives suggest choice; choice suggests preference; and preference either implies some ideological basis for it or will *generate* that basis if the preference is challenged. There may, of course, be a latent irony in the phrase "alternative life style" when it is opted for by people who do not have real alternatives. Like other social movements that have touched a resonating chord in the larger culture, the commune movement attracted not only ideological visionaries searching for a more hospitable ambience in which to attempt to realize their images and ideas about the creation of community; it also attracted drifters and sociopaths and camp followers and the strung out as well—people perhaps without any strong ideological vision or motive, or who had lost it early as casualties of the drug culture.

But the *availability* of the pastoral myth as ideological currency constitutes a negotiable resource for *both* groups. For the ideological visionaries it motivates the rural communal enterprise, sanctifies the efforts of that enterprise, and legitimates the continuing struggle to cope with the difficulties of realizing it. For the drifters, the casualties et al., it can at the very least clothe naked Necessity in the fine garments of moral choice by providing some sense of moral coherence for wherever they happen to be, and then may, in that process, dialectically motivate them to continue with it.[29]

29. In a rural commune in central California, we ran into a young man who was clearly hospitalizably insane. He conducted dialogues with plants and animals. He would occasionally drop his pants and shit on the floor of the communal house, or, if he could be induced to go to the toilet, would sit on the stool for hours. But he was a gifted gardener and very good with the farm animals. The group banished him from the house to a shed in the field he cultivated and close to the animals he looked after. The group took care of him, protecting him from the world he was incompetent to live in, in exchange for the useful services he performed for them. In the days before Gertrud's Land became a Christian commune, it was still "open land" providing refuge for hippie drifters. One night there I watched a bearded young man who wore a robe, carried a staff, and who held his head in a tilted

In this chapter, I have been describing and interpreting some of the specific ways in which rural hippie communards have selectively utilized ideological elements from the pastoral tradition, which were present in the original image of suburbia, to enrich the day-to-day reality of communal living in a way that proved to be not viable for suburban living. Although I am less interested in the history of ideas than in the sociology of ideas, even the latter reveals historical continuities. Greek philosophers (and aristocrats since)[30] defended slavery as a necessary condition without which the high achievements of Greek culture would have been impossible; eighteenth-century spokesmen for capitalism invoked Social Darwinism (before Darwin) to provide "scientific" and philosophical support for their moral indifference to poverty in an economy governed by the pitiless logic of competition;[31] contemporary Hell's Angels (and other urban gangs) invoke an eye-for-an-eye sense of the dignity and justice of *personal* retribution under conditions in which they cannot rely on law enforcement personnel to do their "police" work, and in doing so Hell's Angels express contempt for the bourgeois reliance on hired police to do their dirty work for them;[32] and white convicts in San Quentin invoke a quasi-Nazi, "Aryan" ideology to justify racial conflict in the prison. From ancient Greece to contemporary San Quentin, the business of myth has always been legitimation, the attempt to create moral capital out of available ideological resources (meager or abundant) to justify action, to dignify motive, to transform interests into justice, privilege into right, fate into virtue, power into authority.

---

fashion, à la medieval paintings of Christ. He sidled up to several women and stared at them longingly and lovingly. At dinner, he sat next to a woman, and after staring in this way, kissed her gently on the cheek and rested his head on her shoulder, as if seeking solace. He used to walk around Berkeley with a sign on him offering "free fucks" to girls.

30. See Clive Bell, *Civilization* (London: Chatto and Windus, 1928).

31. Malthus, among others, for example. Donald MacRae points out, in *Ideology and Society* (New York: The Free Press, 1961), that Darwinist ideas are perhaps the *only* theory borrowed by the biological sciences from the social sciences.

32. Hunter Thompson, *Hell's Angels* (New York: Random House, 1967).

Volatile ideological beliefs like these (in slavery, in the survival of the fit, in posse justice, or in racial superiority and inferiority), of course, generate a lot of heat. And argument often focuses on whether these ideas represent "genuine" convictions that motivate their adherents to establish and sustain social orders and social policies devoted to their realization, or whether they are (mere) "rationalizations," the self-serving search for ideological weapons with which groups attempt to justify the pursuit or maintenance of interests, privileges, and powers dictated by their social placement.

One answer is cynical and retrospective: if the beliefs are successful, the former will turn out to be the case; if unsuccessful, the latter (successful revolutionaries are heroes; unsuccessful ones, criminals). Another response is to conceive the questions as empirical ones in which, say, like the investigation of the relationship between correlation and cause, answers could be sought by attempting to find out whether groups espoused such ideas *before* their circumstantial relevance to interests was clear, or whether they seized upon the ideas opportunistically, *after* the fact, to sanction powers and privileges initially inherited or usurped—or even to dignify the circumstances that they are in fact historically stuck with.

Neither of these answers is likely to catch the ways in which groups actually *use* ideas to impose some coherence on their lives and hence to create meaning. Each answer has a fixed and static quality about it; one of them conveys an image of people driven by the convictions that possess them; the other suggests an utterly nihilistic image of people who select such ideas as are convenient for them at a given historical moment.[33] It seems likely that both types of people do exist, but it also seems likely that they represent the extremes

33. The ideas I have used as examples have clear, volatile, and general political relevance, so much so, perhaps, that relatively few people would have interests in regarding them dispassionately. One of the merits of using the pastoral ideas of communards as data for the microsociology of knowledge, then, is that they are *not* so volatile that the vital interests of large numbers of people are directly threatened by a disinterested consideration of them. Their relative innocuousness constitutes a positive cognitive inducement for looking at them dispassionately.

in a range of variation in which most people, rural communards included, fall toward the center of the distribution, a
center in which we find concentrated the great bulk of us who
"have" convictions (perhaps shot through with internal contradictions) that we do not entirely live up to, and caught in
circumstances that we have neither sufficient power to
change nor unlimited desire to alter in a way that would bring
them into closer ideological accord with what we believe we
believe we believe. . . .

CHAPTER **5**

INTIMACY: COUPLING, UNCOUPLING, RECOUPLING

We love each other
It's plain to see
There's just one answer
That comes to me
Sister-lovers, water-brothers
And in time maybe others
So you see, what we can do
Is to try something new
If you're crazy too
I don't really see
Why can't we go on as three?

From a song, "Triad," by David Crosby,
© Guerrila Music, Inc., 1970.
Sung by Grace Slick, of
The Jefferson Airplane.

In Stephen Diamond's book on the New England rural commune to which he belonged, there is a whole chapter on the events that ensue when he leaves his woman, Kathy, and goes to San Francisco because their relationship has become "routine." Kathy then gets together with Laz, another member of the commune, but she soon follows Diamond to San Francisco to see if there is still anything between them. There is. Next day, Laz shows up in San Francisco and Kathy returns east with him because "her life is at the farm." Then Diamond returns to the farm to reclaim Kathy, and Laz leaves. Guilty and remorseful for the pain they have caused Laz, they call him back, and eventually Kathy gets pregnant by Laz.[1] But amid all this pain and their talk about cultural revolution, it apparently never occurs to any of them that they might have gone on loving each other "as three." Group marriage experiments notwithstanding, coupling still hangs on even in culturally revolutionary "anarchist" communes.

But it is a fragile kind of coupling, which is only too reminiscent of the situation evoked by a *New Yorker* cartoon a few years ago: the scene is obviously a wedding reception, and the bride introduces the groom to one of the guests. "I'd like you to meet my first husband," she says to the guest.

It's hard not to be interested in sex and intimacy, but it's almost impossible if one has a serious interest in communal living. But sex and intimacy were far from our primary concern when my research group undertook its study of child-rearing in counterculture communes. Along with economic issues, sex and other aspects of intimate interpersonal relations are major causes of membership turnover and communal failure. Communes often founder either because of insufficient money, labor skills, or other economic resources to sustain the enterprise, or because interpersonal tensions and hostilities from more intimate sources grow to the point where routine cooperative actions become difficult or impossible to sustain.

The economic problems, of course, are frequently expressed *as* interpersonal tensions.[2] Over the years, several people left The Ranch because they were unwilling to yield to the increasing pressures to create financial interdependence or to subordinate their private "trips" to the increasing demands for labor dedicated to the *collective* effort. But in my attempts

1. Stephen Diamond, *What the Trees Said* (New York: Delacorte Press, 1972).

2. One male communard at The Ranch eventually left, for several reasons, perhaps, but prominent among which was the negative response by the group to his economic proposals for increasing the commune's income, which response made him feel rejected and uninfluential, and that, in turn, increased the tensions between him and other members of the group.

to sort out the most significant dimensions of the research, the sexual and other intimate aspects of communal living loom as increasingly important because they are directly connected with some of the features of communes that made them sociologically interesting in the first place.[3] It seems clear enough that communes with an articulated religious creed, devout believers, disciplined organization, and clear commitment to formally stated goals are more likely to survive successfully than a group of ex-hippies who want to live together in cooperative fellowship and mutual concern for the *differences* in each other's paths to self-knowledge and self-fulfillment.[4] I take it that no sociologist who has heard of Emile Durkheim will find this conclusion surprising. A commune like The Ranch is sociologically interesting because it attempts to sustain its commitments to both family solidarity and individual freedom *without* the formal structures, the doctrinal rigidity, or the myriad rules that characterize most "successful" communal efforts.

The solidarity and commitment of terrorist cults or revolutionary undergrounds that live communally or as "collectives," and the power of religious creeds and charismatic gurus to transform the lives of psychologically needy individuals are no mystery to sociologists. We already know (or think we know) a good bit about how the political vision of revolutionary doctrines and the sacred word of gods and sages can transform formerly meaningless or despairing or *ressentiment*-filled lives into models of dedication and commitment through processes of ideological indoctrination, ritual discipline, reinforcement through dense structures of interaction in isolated communal settings, and symbolic

---

3. I say *sociologically* interesting because there are many respects in which communal enterprises are not sociologically interesting beyond the dimensions of their obvious topical appeal as utopian zealotry, colorful deviance, cynical parasitism, or other headline-worthy emphases that shock, please, surprise, outrage, or otherwise entertain newspaper readers over their morning coffee.

4. See, for example, Yablonsky (1968), Zablocki (1971), and Kanter (1972).

enactments[5] that objectively commit individuals to the group and that experientially validate the meaning of the ideology, the ritual discipline, and the reinforcements of interaction.[6]

But that communes like The Ranch survive at all is a kind of miracle. Without sacred doctrine or a charismatic leader, without ritual discipline to solemnify membership, without a formal political vision to inspire dedication, without organized fund raising, living with constant poverty, they (in addition to relying on common labor and financial interdependence) depend upon a history of friendship, a sense of family, and their weekly meetings (which may go on for a whole day) as resources with which to transform their diffuse set of "humanistic" beliefs into policies to guide them through their social experiments. The bizarre or pathetic or tragic attempts at solidarity expressed in the Manson cult or the Symbionese Liberation Army, or in the Unification Church ("Moonies"), the Children of God, or some Christian communes (in one of which I was solemnly told that Jesus was more favorably disposed to fish than to mammals) do not seem to bear much relevance for the problems of mainstream adults. But the experience of communes like The Ranch, particularly their experience of spousal-like relations, may have some relevance for those individuals who, like them, live largely without intense dedication to formal religious creeds or political doctrines. Many Americans live in fragile nuclear units with high divorce rates (approximately 40 percent now in the United States) and are searching for substitutes to the traditional sources of primary human solidarity (family, church, village, neighborhood, occupation) whose traditional competence or authority can no longer be taken for granted, and which, however strong they remain in some sectors of society, are increasingly burdened by the moral debris of the twentieth century.

5. For example, assassinations, bombings, highjackings, obliged participation in sexual acts, or symbolic renunciations of a past life through, for example, celibacy, or rebirths-through-renamings, or redefinitions of former friends and relatives as devils of one kind or another. (This was written before the mind-boggling events in Jonestown, Guyana, in November 1978.)

6. See Rosabeth Kanter's work on commitment mechanisms (1972).

INTIMATE RELATIONS AT THE RANCH

Coupling

At The Ranch, the relationship of nuclear couples is structurally fragile. It has few if any of the traditional institutional supports that sustain the bonds between couples or reinforce shaky relationships under tensions and pressures that threaten them. Unlike the commune couples studied by Dennis Jaffe,[7] couples at The Ranch are neither legally married, nor affluent, nor regularly employed outside of the commune; they do not own personal property jointly; paternity, even if acknowledged by the father, may be denied by the mother for reasons ranging from custody problems to welfare checks. In most cases, common residence (sleeping quarters) is not even prevalent. And most important, *exclusive sexual access is ideologically disavowed:* coupling does not carry with it exclusive property rights for one to the other's body. All members of the communal family are expected to "love" each other and show intimate regard for each other's welfare, and I think that on the whole they do. But a sexual relationship continues only as long as it is mutually gratifying in erotic terms or related psychological terms, for example, when two people have some special emotional complementarity that binds them.

Under such conditions, a great deal of uncoupling and recoupling is to be expected, and this in fact has been the case. Over the years of my association with The Ranch, not a single couple has survived unambiguously intact over the entire period. I say "unambiguously" intact because, given the conditions of coupling, it is not entirely clear what *constitutes* a couple. Therefore it is not entirely clear in all cases what constitutes the breakup or the separation of a couple. Bob and Linda, Abe and Bonnie, Maxwell and Sheila, Paul and Vickie, for example, were for one period or another "couples," but exactly *how* I know this is difficult to say. Coupling is "taken

7. Dennis Jaffe, "Couples in Communes," (Yale University, Ph.D. dissertation, 1975). Jaffe's study was of urban commune couples in Boston; it involved couples whose marriage was already in some trouble and who sought the commune as a way of coping with it.

for granted." Sometimes they had children together, sometimes not. I suppose coupling could be sociometrically
documented simply by the amount of *time* they spend with
each other, or the frequency with which others refer to the
members of a couple jointly. Couples do spend more time
working with each other than they do with others, but they do
not necessarily "live" in the same private residence together.
They may sleep together fairly regularly, probably more often
than they do alone and surely more often than they sleep
with others, but they gradually drifted toward having separate houses. Each member of a couple may or may not sleep
with others, but there are no *rules* about this—as there were
at the Oneida community in the nineteenth century, or at The
Family of Taos in the recent period of the commune movement, or in other group marriage communes. [8]

Group Marriage

A word is necessary here about group marriage. There are
and have been such things as group marriage communes in
which all the adult members regard themselves in some formal or ritual sense as "married" to each other. In these cases
the commune itself is a conscious and formal expression of a
deliberate ideological intention to create a "group marriage."
In such groups not only is exclusive coupling explicitly disavowed, but sexual preferences are formally discouraged:
"dyadic withdrawal" (or the seclusion of couples) is regarded
as a threat to communal solidarity. Sanctions may be invoked
against excessive pairing. Some group marriages have tried
schedules for serial sleeping together; at Oneida in the
nineteenth century, couples who showed too much pair-

---

8. On group marriage, see Larry and Joan Constantine, *Group Marriage*
(New York: The Macmillan Co., 1973). See also Margaret Hollenbach, "Commune or Cult?: The Family of Taos, N.M." (M.A. thesis, University of Washington, 1971). See James Ramey, *Intimate Friendships* (Englewood Cliffs, N.J.:
Prentice-Hall, 1976), for discussion of group marriage and other plural forms
of marriage. There is a lengthy literature on Oneida, but for its present significance see R. M. Kanter, *Commitment and Community* (Cambridge: Harvard
University Press, 1972). See also Raymond Lee Muncy, *Sex and Marriage in
Utopian Communities* (Bloomington: Indiana University Press, 1973).

bonding were asked by authorities to sleep with others; in other group marriages people with an actively negative attraction to each other may be encouraged to sleep together to overcome it.

The Ranch is not a group marriage in this sense. It did not begin with a formal ideological intention to create a group marriage. It did, however, begin as an intentional extended family composed of nuclear subunits. But in any commune of this sort, given the process of coupling, uncoupling, and recoupling that occurs, it is likely that over a period of years most of the adult members will have had sexual relations (briefly, occasionally, or regularly) with some or many of the other adult members. One woman decided systematically to sleep with each of the men at her commune, "just to get it over with." Over time, then, what is produced is not exactly a group marriage, but something in effect not entirely unlike it, for which there is no precise, convenient, and morally neutral descriptive term.

Ironically, this sort of thing seems to indicate The Ranch's *success* as a family commune, rather than its disorder or instability. A "good" commune (of the type represented by The Ranch) is one whose members affirm a sense of solidarity and identification with each other because they live together, depend upon each other for their very survival, and are committed to the collective purposes of the commune: equality, rural or pastoral self-sufficiency, a reverence for the land, and a variety of "spiritual searchings" for transcendence and self-understanding. It should not, then, be surprising that people who eat together, drink together, work and play together, educate their children together, and depend upon each other not only for survival but also for their various spiritual searchings, should "love" each other and find each other sexually attractive from time to time and therefore sleep together— particularly since their definition of "family" includes no incest taboo.

The irony is that if The Ranch were not so "good" a commune, it would probably have "failed," crushed under the weight of pressures generated by the turmoil that sometimes accompanies uncoupling. For the uncoupling process, at The

Ranch as everywhere else, usually occurs more at the initiative of one member (of a couple) than the other, and therefore can leave a good deal of suffering in its wake.

Even though the emotional costs of uncoupling are not nearly as high in communes as they are in conventional nuclear families,[9] individuals still often suffer from a sense of rejection, guilt, loss, or ambivalence. Moreover, the uncoupling and recoupling processes in communes (but not in conventional marriage) usually go on in full view of (and frequently with the participation of) other members of the group, which openness subjects the entire commune to a lot of stress; so much so, in fact, that group marriage experiments usually fail before they have had a chance to be fully studied.[10] And even in the urban communes studied by Dennis Jaffe, which did not have group marriage but which apparently did have a rule proscribing sexual possessiveness, it was eventually necessary to establish an in-commune incest taboo because the turmoil generated by extramarital affairs inside the commune was too intense to tolerate.

COUPLING AND SOLIDARITY

Dyadic Withdrawal

There are theories that attempt to make sense of the relationship between intimate coupling and communal solidarity. Philip Slater has written on the relevance of "dyadic withdrawal" to group solidarity, and Rosabeth Kanter, using her knowledge of both nineteenth-century utopian communities and contemporary communes, remarks upon the functional equivalence of celibacy and promiscuity vis-à-vis communal solidarity. Both have drawn upon the ideas of Lewis Coser. The exclusiveness of couples, so this theory goes, short-circuits the libidinal network, threatens the solidarity of the larger group by creating areas of private experience and special or sectarian interests that weaken the ties of the coupled

9. See Roy Wallis, "Sex, Marriage, and The Children of God" (unpublished ms.).

10. Marcia Seligson, *Options* (Ashland, Md.: Lexington Books, 1978).

individuals to the larger collectivity. Celibacy acts as a brake upon the development of such intimate differentiation; but promiscuity can do the same thing, for if everyone shares everyone else sexually, the group is still protected from the potentially divisive consequences of stable and exclusive coupling.[11] The woman who systematically slept with all the men at her commune also told me that she has been celibate for several years.

Given the risks of pregnancy or disease, and the power of Victorian morality, celibacy was the usual choice in the nineteenth century (although Oneida is a prominent exception); in the current period, given the power of the sexual revolution and availability of contraceptives, promiscuity is usually the favored option. But the stubborn fact remains that free love (or promiscuity)[12] has apparently proved to be too heavy an emotional burden for most communes, even for most of those formally dedicated to group marriage. Where free love or promiscuity has been successful (for example, at Oneida and perhaps a few contemporary communes) it has, according to Kanter, usually been circumscribed by rules and sanctions that carefully regulated the time, place, and other conditions of sexual encounters. On the other hand, she regards the "permissive" sexuality of communes like The Ranch as symptomatic of their anarchy and expressive of their reluctance to establish and enforce the rules and practices that constitute social controls on the volatility of sexual relations, and hence help create the "commitment mechanisms" that increase the probabilities that a commune will survive these predictable problems.

11. Kanter, pp. 85–87. See also Lewis Coser, "The Sexual Requisites of Utopia," in *Greedy Institutions* (New York: The Free Press, 1974).

12. "Free love" is the term that Kanter uses. Despite its harshness of connotation, I prefer "promiscuity," because love, like lunch, is hardly ever free. "Promiscuous" is an adjective that refers to *indiscriminate* mixing. The term loses much of its pejorative connotation if it is remembered that in communes like Oneida the promiscuity is limited to members of the group and its functions are *for* the group. Even with this restricted definition, The Ranch is not a promiscuous commune, because (unlike Oneida) positive pressures are not exercised to *prevent* coupling.

It is an impressive analysis. Yet The Ranch continues to
survive as the pride of its region, without either stable, conventional coupling or the rules that govern group marriages.
Although it is like Oneida and contemporary group marriage
communes in ideologically disavowing sexual possessiveness, it is unlike them because negative sanctions are not invoked against *self-selected* coupling. At the same time, the
nonpossessiveness rule, combined with the fragile supports
under which coupling occurs, encourages a *drift toward* group
marriage. But The Ranch is still not a group marriage, even
after ten years of existence, because (1) coupling is a fact of
commune life, recognized by the partners and acknowledged
by others, and (2) the drift toward group marriage is uneven:
there has been wide variation in the commune regarding *how
many* others any one individual has been sexually involved
with, from only one or two others, to almost everybody.

Jealousy and Social Control
Nevertheless, The Ranch has the same basic problem of coping with the consequences of its belief in sexual nonpossessiveness as other communes that share this belief, from
Oneida to the Boston communes described by Dennis Jaffe.
For Jaffe's communes, the consequences were sufficiently
volatile that an incest taboo was established; Oneida and
other group marriage communes exercise social control over
the potential volatility by strict regulations to prevent dyadic
exclusivity; most other groups, faced with this problem, eventually go under, casualties to the powerful emotions generated
by—dare we say it?—*jealousy*.

The Ranch has not gone under. It has had (and continues
to have) its problems of jealousy (and the suffering that goes
with it), but it has not attempted to "solve" this problem by
recourse to an incest taboo or to strict regulatory practices.
Indeed, however impressive is the theory relating the social
control of sexual coupling to communal solidarity, there is
very little evidence to suggest that *any* structure of control
"solves" the problem of jealousy and its consequences. In
violation of theory's dictates, The Ranch muddles through,
unwilling to pay for the possibility of communal solidarity

with mandatory sexual regulations, and unwilling to sacrifice its belief in individual choice to an arbitrary incest taboo; unwilling, that is, to sacrifice its anarchist hope for a "natural" order to the always-present temptation to impose unhappy and tight-lipped rules that violate the libertarian spirit of the counterculture.

Nevertheless, the Coser-Slater-Kanter functionalist interpretation of the problem posed by coupling for communal solidarity continues to make a lot of sense; the functional requisite of communal solidarity is threatened *to some extent* by the tendency toward exclusive coupling. But Jaffe's data show that communal survival is also threatened by sexual relationships beyond the couple, which also generate jealousy and the volatile interpersonal tensions that accompany it. Oneida and the urban Boston communes coped with this dilemma in different ways. Oneida, recognizing exclusive coupling as a threat to group solidarity, and "believing in" group marriage as one aspect of its comprehensive interpretation of Christian doctrine, initiated strict sexual regulations that discouraged exclusive coupling. The priority of group solidarity and sectarian doctrine led them to attempt to overcome the problem of individual jealousy by *practices* that, "consistent with" their beliefs, rendered individual *feelings* (like jealousy and special sexual preferences) secondary and constrained individuals to sacrifice their feelings to the welfare of the group and the truth of doctrine in the faith that, over time, their feelings would be educated into greater accord with the group's beliefs. The Boston communes, peopled with legally married, affluent individuals involved in middle-class careers (which probably provided plenty of opportunity for out-of-commune sexual relations), and interested primarily in liberations from the constraints of traditional sex roles in conventional marriages, opted for an in-commune incest taboo, thus sacrificing or accommodating their "belief in" nonpossessiveness to the volatile feelings of jealousy generated by in-commune extra liaisons. In both cases, the "rules" (as applied interpretations of the belief in nonpossessiveness) seem self-serving for communes that exist under quite different sets of conditions.

It is these conditions and their relationship to beliefs (and to the consequences of beliefs) that constitute the central problem of this book. Oneida, a rural utopian community with about two hundred members guided by a sectarian interpretation of Christian doctrine administered by a charismatic leader and with a well-organized division of labor and ritual discipline to integrate its members, contained the resources and the circumstances to "live up to" its belief in nonexclusive coupling by adopting the sanctions and other practices (in spite of the costs in feeling, which their faith told them was temporary) to sustain its rule of not respecting persons.[13] The Boston communes had different circumstances, fewer community resources, and members who seem (from Jaffe's report) less interested in sustaining the collective effort than in using the presence of others for largely transitional efforts to "work through" some of the typical problems of contemporary marriage among urban, well-educated, and "progressive" people, toward a contemporary form of more "open" marriage. Under these conditions, "feelings" take precedence over belief, and ideological work gets done to modify belief (the no-incest rule) in light of the inability of communal circumstances and resources to enable the Boston communards to cope successfully with the problem of jealousy.*

13. Oneidans were forbidden to be "respecters of persons" in much the same sense that the law is supposed to not respect persons.

*In his wise, learned, and comprehensive study of 120 communes (which was published while this book was in galleys), Benjamin Zablocki reports an intriguing and apparently puzzling set of findings regarding what he calls the "love-density effect." The more love a commune member experiences, the more likely he is to remain a member of his commune. But, comparing communes as wholes, the greater the amount of love-linkages reported, the more likely it is that a commune will disintegrate. To complicate the matter further, the strong association between dyadic love and communal instability seems to disappear when a commune has a charismatic leader.

Zablocki opts for a structural analysis of "relational networks" in explaining this intriguing finding about the "corrosive effects of emotional cathexis upon communal stability." But in his nearly 400 pages of text there is no discussion of jealousy (although there is a question about it in the questionnaire he used). It seems likely that a lot of the corrosiveness of the "love-density

The Ranch, though similar to both of the preceding examples in some respects, is like neither of them in other respects. They brought with them from the counterculture the general belief that individuals have the right to sleep with whom they wish when they wish, so long as the desire is mutual. "Natural" preferences lead to recognizable coupling, but the coupling is fragile and unstable. The uncoupling process produces jealousy and suffering, which fact constitutes a functional problem for group solidarity. But they have not dealt with this problem by opting for either an incest taboo or rules that discourage coupling and promote group marriage. Why they haven't and how they have been able not to can be found in the interaction between what they "believe" and the circumstances in which the problem occurs.

COUPLING AND UNCOUPLING AT THE RANCH

Early in the history of The Ranch, almost all of its members were coupled, and with perhaps one exception, this was largely by mutual choice. So long as couples seemed to be getting along OK, The Ranch had no interests in discouraging the coupling since (ignorant of or unbothered by the theory of dyadic withdrawal) neither its ideology nor its solidarity were perceived as threatened. Unlike Oneida or other doctrinal group marriages, it did not regard special attractions or bonds between coupled individuals as in themselves immoral or sinful or threatening. Hence no remedial action was necessary, so long as the coupling was relatively smooth, because it was either *exclusive* coupling by mutual choice or nonexclusive by mutual choice. Despite the "private" culture that exclusive coupling sometimes generates, coupling typically presents a problem for the group only when a couple is coming apart,

---

effect" may be attributed to the jealousy (and the consequent suffering and turmoil) generated by dense sexual ties in a commune. The power of a charismatic leader to counteract the love-density effect could well lie in his ideological ability to render the jealousy tolerable, to reduce the suffering from it by an appeal to a doctrinal conviction, as John Humphrey Noyes was apparently able to do with the Oneida community. See Benjamin Zablocki, *Alienation and Charisma* (New York: The Free Press, 1980), especially chapters 4 and 8.

when one member of a couple is suffering from jealousy or loss[14] at the other's sexual involvement with a third party, and when the turmoil involves the rest of the family.

Under these conditions, it would be tempting to say that negative sanctions are applied to (or support withheld from) the person suffering from jealousy—reminding him or her that jealousy (like greed) is not an emotion deserving of sympathy. This surely occurs (see the case of Paul and Vickie, below). But it does not occur *consistently* because other circumstances affect the way in which the problem is coped with.

The first couple-related crisis to which I was exposed occurred early in the research when Colleen, coupled with George, and mother of their son, fell in love with a musician in a rock band that lived nearby. Colleen's coupling with George had never been smooth, and, "swept off her feet" (as she put it) by the musician, she went off with him on a short tour the band was making, leaving George and the baby at The Ranch. Although George's suffering was relatively silent and contained, there was some criticism of Colleen for her flightiness and for adding to the burdens of the group, which had to fill in with child care. When Colleen returned from the tour, a family meeting was called to discuss the crisis, and some pressure was exercised on Colleen to sort out her feelings and her relationship to the commune. She eventually conceived her problem as a choice between what she called "love and duty," or between her romantic involvement with the musician and her sense of obligation to George, the baby, and The Ranch. Colleen opted for "duty," and she, George, and the baby stayed together for about another year (which included a trip to Mexico for the three of them) before they broke up, Colleen taking the baby to the city and George leaving The Ranch for a new life in the Pacific Northwest. George and Colleen are both still on good terms with The Ranch, George returning for visits occasionally and Colleen receiving visits from communards at her place in the city.

14. See the interesting treatment (and diverse application) of the concept of loss in Peter Marris, *Loss and Change* (New York: Pantheon Books, 1974).

The coupling crisis between Colleen and George reveals that her behavior was negatively sanctioned by the group because she had gone *outside* the commune for her new lover, thereby weakening her ties to the group, creating an added burden for the family by leaving the baby and by leaving George uncoupled and with a sense of loss. On the other hand, when Patricia, who was not coupled, took up a relatively brief sexual relationship with a married (although separated from his wife) man outside the commune (and eventually bore a child by him), she was not negatively sanctioned. Her ties to the group were not weakened; he came to The Ranch for his visits with her (although he did not become a member). And she, not being coupled with anyone at The Ranch, left no one with a sense of loss at her sexual involvement with a nonmember.[15]

But in the case of Vickie and Paul, the coupling crisis is more classic and pure. They are both in their thirties and were a closely involved couple for several years. Vickie has two children by previous couplings, and Paul has another child by Sheila, with whom he came to The Ranch and who still lives there coupled with Maxwell. At a visit to The Ranch in 1978, I wandered out to the porch overlooking the apple orchard to have a smoke, and Vickie and Paul were in the midst of a private lovers' discussion-quarrel-reconciliation. When I happened into their discussion, I felt at first as if I were intruding because they were being "intimate" with each other: touching, nuzzling, whispering, smokily gazing into each other's eyes. They were apparently arranging to have a private dinner down at her cabin, but when Paul expressed some uncertainty about whether he could be there, Vickie's mood changed and a heated discussion started. She had just returned from a short visit to the city, and while she had been gone Paul had made love to Seena, another woman in the family. Vickie was hurt, upset, and threatened by this.

15. Informal status may be important in this case because Patricia is probably the most prestigious woman at The Ranch and the man with whom she became involved was highly prestigious in the community outside The Ranch.

She accuses Paul of not caring enough about her to try not to hurt her. Paul is defensive; he invokes his right to freedom in relationships, to his "personal space," and to his need to work through feelings of possessiveness and guilt that oppress his spirit; he counteraccuses Vickie of sleeping with other men; she parries by saying it only happened a few times in the years they've been together and only because Paul had other lovers; and *hers were not in the family* (although the fathers of her two children were).

I am suddenly aware that I am in the presence of something very familiar, but it is an argument that only very rarely (outside the counterculture or a therapist's office) goes on in the presence of a neutral third party. During a pause in their discussion, I say that I have a feeling that I'm not supposed to be hearing this. They say stay; I stay. Paul says that Seena is a member of their family and he wants to be close with her; he says there's nothing between him and Seena nearly to the extent that there is between him and Vickie. Seena doesn't even particularly want him sexually, he says. Vickie says yes she does. Vickie, a member of the family much longer than Seena, says she never even liked Seena very much and was against her becoming a member of the family, but yielded to the consensus of the group in letting her in. Now, she says, turning to me bitterly, Seena is a threat to her relationship with Paul. Vickie is very angry and says she's close to leaving The Ranch. Paul is sympathetic but unyielding; he says he's committed to "going with the trip" (nonpossessiveness, anti-jealousy) and cites Vickie's having asked him to babysit her kids (which he did) while she made love to somebody else. Vickie says she resents being "sexually available" all the time and would not have been if Paul had not been fucking other women (he has been involved with at least two other women at The Ranch in addition to Vickie and Seena). Vickie says she's more "sexually mature" than Paul because he has to express intimacy sexually, while she can be intimate with others without sex. Paul says he "wants it all" (his coupling with Vickie *and* his rights to intimate relations with other members of the family). Vickie is frustrated, turns to me, and says, "She [Seena] wears this damn scent, some oil,

which stays on him after he's been with her. I can't even be
alone with him after he's been with her." Vickie says she gets
no support for her suffering from the family because the dominant sentiment is against sexual possessiveness.

SUFFERING AND SOCIAL CHANGE:
MICRO AND MACRO

Vickie gets no support for her suffering because Paul has the
right to do what he did, and the only threat to the group is
Vickie's jealousy, anger, and frustration. Instead of doing the
ideological work that would be necessary to cope with this
threat (for example, compromising the legitimacy of the nonpossessiveness rule by introducing a no-incest proviso), The
Ranch chooses to stand on its ideological grounds by defining
Vickie's feelings of sexual property in Paul as inappropriate
and by encouraging her to be willing to do the requisite "feeling work" to bring her feelings into closer accord with collective belief in the hope of gaining greater understanding of self
and others and of transcending the emotional pain of un-
honored feelings of lost sexual property. The relationship of
feeling work to beliefs, then, is analogous to the relationship
between ideological work and circumstances.

At the level of microinteraction (and even at the level of
psychic *intra*action), this process involves "struggle" that
may be as intense and as personally demanding as class
struggle at the level of macropolitics, where, say, your belief
in a person's status as your "class enemy" may conflict with
your personal fondness for him, thus requiring some *judgment* regarding whether "feeling is first" (as e.e. cummings put
it) or whether belief should take priority. Such discrepancies
between beliefs and out-of-phase or inappropriate feelings
are a form of contradiction between theory and practice.[16]

16. The contradiction may also be understood as paralleling the discrepancy between actual feelings (which are a kind of inner *practice*) and the *rules
about feelings*, which are theoretical or ideological assertions defining the
appropriateness of feelings to circumstances. Where discrepancies occur,
"feeling work" may be necessary to bring feelings into greater accord with
"feeling rules." The ideas of "feeling work" and "feeling rules" are Arlie

But whereas The Ranch treats Vickie's suffering stiffly but sympathetically, such contradictions are not often sympathetically regarded by outsiders. Outsiders who are opposed in the first place to the ethic of nonpossessive sex on moral, religious, pragmatic ("it won't work"), emotional ("I just couldn't take it"), or other grounds are often predisposed to interpret the evidence of failure to live up to it (for example, Vickie's failure) in a spirit of "I told you so," which affirms the moral, religious, pragmatic, or other pathology of the ethic of nonpossessiveness itself and deplores the immorality, the absurdity, the pretentiousness, or the "phoniness" of those who presume to profess it. That this debunking interpretation is commonplace indicates primarily the understandably widespread aversion to or anxiety about the ethic itself (which, of course, threatens traditional ego feelings about sexual property), rather than a thoughtful response to the problem of discrepancies between beliefs about, behavior in, and feelings regarding intimate relations. If communards were more consistently *successful* in closing the *emotional lag* between their belief in nonpossessiveness and their feelings about it, these critics might well regard such nonpossessiveness as even *more* grotesque than they do the evidence of failure by communards to bring their feelings into perfect accord with their beliefs.[17]

But when groups *share* values, the interpretation of such discrepancies is likely to be quite different, particularly with

---

Hochschild's, and I am grateful to her for their relevance in this context. Hochschild cites an interview with a woman who said she felt guilty *about* the fact that she felt jealous under circumstances where feeling rules defined jealousy as inappropriate. Reflexivity can make this phenomenon even more complex because the woman's expressed guilt may have contained a half-buried note of self-congratulation that she was still *able* to feel jealousy even under rules which forbade it. "Feeling work" includes such practices as "psyching oneself up" and a wide variety of group therapies (such as encounter, Synanon's "stews," and Oneida's sessions of "criticism")—all of them to some extent concerned with making individuals more conscious of the relations of their feelings to circumstances, behavior, and belief. See Arlie Hochschild, "Emotion Work, Feeling-Rules, and Social Structure," *American Journal of Sociology,* 85 (November 1979).

17. Notice that I'm doing a little ideological work here myself.

widely shared dominant values. It seems probable that many people much of the time don't live up to some of the Ten Commandments in which they profess belief (nor even feel guilt when they violate them). But their failure to do so is not usually understood as evidence for the absurdity or pretentiousness or unfeasibility of that ethical code. People who steal or cheat on their spouses or their income tax or who fail to respect their parents or who worship money before God are likely to be regarded as errant souls potentially redeemable by sanctions, counseling, guidance, support, rehabilitation, or other "help."

Similarly, in communes where, like anywhere else, there is less-than-perfect correspondence between belief and behavior (or "feeling rules" and feelings), *sympathetic* consideration of the problem occurs, in an attempt to devise means or create conditions (i.e., "struggling against circumstances") to achieve greater correspondence, or to review the beliefs and the "feeling rules" with an eye to modifying them toward greater workability, that is "accommodating," as Jaffe's communes did with their no-incest rule or by engaging in "feeling work."[18]

The predisposition of some to regard communards contemptuously or patronizingly as "phony" because they sometimes suffer from an emotional lag between the sexual ethics they profess and the jealousy or guilt they may feel is not only unsympathetic; it has a political dimension as well, which is evocative of the cliché that "you can't legislate feelings." It is, of course, true that you can't "legislate" feelings; legislation doesn't try to do that. It tries to alter circumstances by defining behavior as licit or illicit in the expectation that such definition (and its associated sanctions) will alter behavior and in the hope that altered behavior will eventually alter feelings. Political opposition to such change will often invoke a cogni-

---

18. At a more macroinstitutional level similar processes occur, as, for example, belief in the idea of equality of opportunity is eventually modified (not without objective conflict, ambivalent belief, and mixed feeling) to accommodate demands for "affirmative action" arising out of actual inequalities of circumstance.

tive bias in favor of the priority of feeling over belief, as if it were unquestionable that visceral emotional responses are somehow more authentic, more "real," than moral or ideological commitment. Thus, like war, which may be attributed to innate human aggressiveness, jealousy may be regarded as irremediable because it reflects an innate tendency to sexual property, which transcends social circumstances or ideology. Where these ideas function as bulwarks against social change, their adherents may be led to forget that those who endure suffering in the name of a presumably "higher" moral ideal (in this case liberation from what communards regard as the emotional tyranny of the idea of sexual property) are sometimes regarded as heroes and heroines rather than as "phonies."

Significant social change very often carries with it a good deal of personal suffering, regardless of whether it is macropolitical change (through wars, revolutions, industrializations, or other major institutional upheavals), or microchanges at the level of interpersonal relations (for example in the distribution of authority in the family or in the rules governing age relations, gender relations, or interracial etiquette). Large-scale institutional changes often involve the uprooting of populations, alterations in class and other relations of dominance-submission, and these status transformations disrupt established emotional patterns in small social units. Suffering, in any case, is always personal (*merely* personal, as Scott Fitzgerald once sarcastically remarked), and it occurs under conditions of stability as well as change (the routinely oppressed suffer routinely). That personal suffering, therefore, tends to be a particularly visible accompaniment to social change is not necessarily a persuasive argument against social change.

It is an elementary axiom of social psychology that patterns of emotional response are socialized, learned in relationship to established social contexts. When those contexts change, established affective patterns may become distorted, anomic; people may become confused, disoriented by the dissociation between their still-functioning (and apparently autonomous) feelings and the relevance of those feelings to changed cir-

cumstances out there in the world.[19] The point is that an attitude toward the relationship between social change and
personal suffering (or other emotions) requires cognitive and
moral judgments: about the value of the change, about
whether the suffering will pass, to be replaced eventually by
socialized feelings more in accord with structural realities and
behavioral probabilities, and about whether enduring the suffering through that process is ultimately worth the struggle it
requires.

"FEELING WORK" AS IDEOLOGICAL WORK: BURNING OUT JEALOUSY

But the character of these judgments is strongly affected by
the circumstances of the judgers and the resources available
to them. Oneida and the communes studied by Dennis Jaffe
represent different judgments and different sets of circumstances and resources. At The Ranch, Vickie received no
support or comfort from the group because she was apparently not yet ready to commit herself wholly to the struggle to
overcome her jealousy. Her apparent judgment was that Paul
owed her fidelity (at least inside the commune) as an expression of his love and regard for her feelings, while her at least
quasi-acceptance of the nonpossessiveness rule is indicated
by her feeling free to have other sexual encounters, and not
only (as she said) so long as they were outside the commune;
her involvement with Paul began while she was coupled with
another man at The Ranch (by whom she had her second
child), and she has had homosexual experiences with other
women at The Ranch.

---

19. A homely example: when Betty Ford, in an unguarded moment, told a
journalist that she would not be outraged if she discovered that her unmar-
ried daughter was having an "affair" with a man, some voters were very
upset; others cheered; still others were in genuine conflict about it. All these
reactions represent different stages of emotional accommodation to a historically recent normative change: that fornication is no longer criminal for
females, even presidential daughters.

When and if the trouble between her and Paul becomes critical, a family meeting will no doubt be called to air the trouble, and Vickie will be encouraged to "burn out" her jealousy. "Burning it out" was a recurrent phrase through much of the discussions at The Ranch about jealousy and sexual possessiveness. I first heard it used by Abe, early in the research, when he was suffering a great deal after Bonnie began a liaison with another man at The Ranch but before she left to live at the nearby Christian commune and took their son with her. "Burning it out" refers to a process of group-reinforced "feeling work" in which one tries to get through the fire of sexual jealousy to a condition of family love, which accepts the legitimacy of the nonpossessiveness rule.[20]

If Vickie is willing to "burn out" her jealousy, she will get a lot of support and comfort; that is what "families" are for when one of their members is enduring *worthwhile* or honorable suffering. Communards tell of sitting with a brother or sister while his or her former lover is making love with his or her new partner nearby: holding, rocking, succouring through the tears, the trembling, the nausea, the sweat, and the waves of goosepimples on the skin.[21] There is a strong element of ideological comfort as well: lovers come and go, but brothers and sisters (kinship) are forever. If a brother or sister is your former lover's new lover, you are still constrained to love both of them as kin. Although one or both members of a couple may leave a commune after they break up (and/or become recoupled with others), over the years at The Ranch several individuals, formerly coupled and even jointly parents of children, have elected to remain in residence at The Ranch, sharing child-care and other co-operative labors with former lovers while involved in new sexual couplings with others.

20. In this respect, The Ranch is similar to Oneida.
21. Compare the situation with a perhaps typical uncoupling in most strata of American society: families will regard the breakup as a "failure"; friends may feel that they have to choose between the separated spouses; there may be public quasi-humiliations at infidelity or "cuckoldry"; and even one's good friends may take some furtive pleasure in one's misfortunes.

But if Vickie persists in cultivating her jealousy and frustration, she will receive no comfort from the group. She will probably not be shunned or otherwise severely punished, but it will be made clear to her that she ought to shape up. She may, of course, leave The Ranch as a way of solving her problem; and she said, in fact, that she is "close" to doing so. But it will be hard for her because she has lived at The Ranch for more than eight years and loves it. Moreover, she has two children for whom The Ranch provides a good home, and she does not have much in the way of attractive alternatives. It is the very limitations of her circumstances that increase the probabilities that she will opt to burn out her jealousy rather than leave The Ranch.[22] If a "good" commune is good because it is in general a good place to live, a suffering communard with the impulse to flee the scene of such suffering may discover that there is no place else that is in general more attractive. Bereaved lovers may eventually discover that their commitment was primarily to the *commune* (or the extended family) rather than to their spouse-lover. Necessity, it is said, is the mother of invention; if necessity is nowhere else to go, the invention it may mother is new ways of doing the ideological work to burn out the suffering from lost sexual property and to find some moral comfort in that fact.

But it doesn't work for everybody. Leaving the communal life is, of course, a sort of solution not only to the inability to burn out jealousy and sexual possessiveness but to other problems as well. Over the years, some individuals have left The Ranch because they were unable to find there suitable others with whom to couple. *Singles* can be a problem for the commune because if they are seeking sexual gratification outside the group, their energies are diverted from the group. And if they find a mate outside, there is a problem of bringing such "strangers" into the bosom of the family, a process that requires the consensual OK of the group, which is not always given. Others have left The Ranch as they gradually dis-

22. Jealousy is sometimes stronger than "rational" probabilities. Vickie in fact left The Ranch early in 1979 to live with a new lover in the city.

covered that what they "really" wanted was less a communal family than a perhaps modified form of the conventional nuclear family. Some couples have left The Ranch *as couples* (once as a trio) as it became clear to them that they had greater commitments to the nuclear unit than to the extended family as a whole. Some have gone to other communes or communities (Gaby, Anne-Hawk-Jack); others have sought more conventional relationships and careers in other contexts (Celt, Abe, the photographer and his woman). Over the years, this process has led to a fluctuating but gradual decline in the numbers of adults residing at The Ranch, as the communal character of its major purposes became increasingly clear and as the education of its children moved to the forefront of its preoccupations.

FEMINISM

By the spring of 1978 the resident population at The Ranch had declined to nine adults and their eight children. Six of the nine adults were women, and each of them had at least one child. This fall in the adult population at The Ranch may be interpreted by some as an ominous indication of its impending failure: it is possible to argue that the refusal by The Ranch fully to go either the way of Oneida or that of the Boston communes described by Dennis Jaffe leaves The Ranch in a limbo of commitment, impaled on the horns of a theoretical dilemma that will drain the lifeblood of its solidarity and further reduce its membership to the point where the communal enterprise is no longer viable.

Although it is possible to make this argument, I think that on the balance of the evidence it is mistaken. For one thing, since the founding of The Ranch, membership has fluctuated up and down; that its dominant trend has been down is not especially ominous, because the reputation of The Ranch as a "good" commune is widespread in its vicinity, and there are many people in that vicinity who would prefer living at The Ranch to their present living arrangements. The recent size of the membership at The Ranch, therefore, is to a large extent a matter of their own choice. Moreover, my own most recent visits to The Ranch suggest that its solidarity is stronger than ever: the school is thriving, the gardens are healthy and productive, the group increasingly participates as a family in local political affairs, recent construction projects have been carried out successfully, and the children seem happy and free. In addition, its economic situation is probably better than ever: the school provides some income and so does the feminist magazine that The Ranch helps distribute. And the boom in California land prices means that they are now in possession of a very valuable piece of real estate.

Part of the reason for the gradual decline in the adult population (particularly the male population) at The Ranch over the past four or five years (and part of the reason for the solidarity of those who remain) has been the increasing strength of the women's movement in this post-hippie region of rural California. It is surely no secret by now that much of the counterculture was blatantly "sexist" in its early period[23] (despite its profession of equality), and the rural commune movement made many middle-class young women even more vulnerable to macho hippie cowboys than they were in the cities.[24] The sexual ethics and the outlaw spirit rendered men free to "split" whenever they felt like it ("A man's gotta do what he's gotta do"), and their obligations to their women were largely unenforceable because outlaw ethics in the counterculture forbade calling the cops to settle intracounterculture disputes.[25]

Early in our research it became clear that, despite the occasional presence of female leaders and other "strong" women

23. On this point, see the poignant portrayal of counterculture couples in Sara Davidson's *Loose Change* (New York: Doubleday and Co., 1977).

24. It is my distinct impression that the sexual exploitation of vulnerable young women, sometimes leaving them pregnant, abandoned, and without skills or other visible means of support, was partially responsible for the strong appeal of "Jesus" communes to young women. The Christian communes put women in a formally traditional and submissive role, but they also protected them against sexual exploitation.

25. Raymond Mungo, *Famous Long Ago* (Boston: Beacon Press, 1970).

in the commune movement, the communal division of labor tended to be traditional, with men doing the heavy work (or the heavy rapping) and women tending to the kitchen and child care. The Ranch was not *actively* sexist; it has always had its complement of strong women, and I was never aware of any positive constraints *against* women taking leadership roles or engaging in heavy work.[26] But in the early period of a rural commune's life, much of its efforts must necessarily be devoted to establishing the settlement itself, which involves a lot of heavy labor (like construction work), and the sexes gravitated toward their traditional roles. Communes couldn't *afford* affirmative action, the women didn't insist upon it, and young urban-bred women, without other usable skills, drifted toward *Kinder* and *Küche*, if not *Kirche*.

When the feminist movement hit the region in 1972–73, it hit with a vengeance. There were not only consciousness-raising groups but also retreats in which the women would isolate themselves for days at a time to discuss their common problems as females and as women *vis-à-vis* hippie men. Other results were the establishment of a few lesbian communes and a now nationally distributed magazine oriented to the problems of rural women, in which a few of the women at The Ranch have played an important role. Sisterhood is powerful indeed, and it had a number of important consequences. The men did more child care, and they did *all* the child care when the women were raising their consciousnesses. It made clear to the women (if it had not been made clear already) that hippie men do not generally provide many of the things that men "normally" provide in contexts where their dominance is routine: men provided neither regular income nor status nor security nor reliable emotional support. It reminded the women-with-children (who constitute most of the female population in rural communes) that their welfare checks gave them considerable leverage to increase their power *vis-à-vis*

26. One of the vivid memories of this research is an image of a woman six or seven months pregnant and stark naked, wielding a heavy scythe on the tall brown grass in a meadow on a hot summer day, her engorged breasts swinging in rhythm with the strokes of the scythe.

the men. Eventually, a substantial number of women in the area began to realize that they didn't even need the men for sexual gratification. One of the powers of sisterhood is the lesbian argument that women (understanding female sexuality better than men and not sexually exhausted or indifferent after a couple of orgasms) can be better lovers for women than men can be. In sum, the women's movement has had a powerful impact on communal life at The Ranch and on the problems generated by the rule of nonpossessiveness in intimate relations, by providing the women with the knowledge, the incentive, and the support to pursue their lives without counting upon a dependent or lasting association with a man.

That it is not easy to accomplish all this is indicated by Vickie's struggle with her circumstances; after more than a decade of experience with the fragility of intimate, interpersonal relations in the counterculture, she apparently still retains a residue of a "romantic" hope for an ideal lover or a permanent mate, despite the inevitable weakening of her *expectations* that it will actually happen. But that the *dominant* sentiment at The Ranch is on *communal* solidarity, rather than on couple solidarity, is indicated by the group's judgment that it is Vickie, not Paul, who is behaving badly.

What, then, are hippie men good for? Well, for the practical rural virtues they may possess, such as technical or other useful skills and a willingness to work hard, and for the "humanistic" virtues of the counterculture they may possess, like a gift for tenderness and intimacy, a readiness to perform fathering functions for the children, and a desire to cooperate with the women in their pursuit of "liberation."[27] There is a sense in which The Ranch has become a "feminist" commune: it handles subscriptions and distribution for the magazine, which, in addition to its practical articles on country living (problems of gardens, animal husbandry, farm technology, etc.) has a somewhat lesbian ideological cast. One of the

---

27. The three men left at The Ranch possess these qualities in abundance, although one of them is especially gifted with technical skills, another with simple goodness and tenderness, and a third especially sympathetic to sexual experiment.

men at The Ranch was recently appointed to its editorial
board (to which he commented ironically that the magazine
had broken through its sexism). In addition, some of the
women at The Ranch are bisexual or have experimented with
bisexuality (although the men have not), and both leadership
and the division of labor seem randomly distributed among
the sexes.

The increasing feminism at The Ranch, combined with the
gradual clarification that its commitments were to *communal*
life (expressed, for example, in the energy they have collectively poured into the school, and in the only secondary place
they assign to stable coupling) eventually induced those who
were less-than-fully committed to the centrality of the communal style in their lives (with equalitarian relations between
the sexes) to leave The Ranch. The women who were dependent or fragile or clinging or incompetent to handle a wide
range of the nonsexist division of labor have gone. The men
who could not accommodate to feminism or to bisexuality
among some of the women or who could not burn out their
sexual possessiveness or whose interests consistently led
their attention and energies outside the family (to boogie at
local dances, drink at local bars, pursue local women, or work
for wages with local employers) have similarly gone.

That The Ranch has succumbed neither to the temptation
to institute a no-incest rule nor to the temptation to initiate
strict regulation of sexual intimacy in coping with its problems of residual jealousy and sexual possessiveness (indeed,
that it has not succumbed at all) suggests that we look at the
special circumstances of the life at The Ranch that have enabled it to sustain its belief in "free" sexual choice.

Prominent among these circumstances is The Ranch's
feminism, which militates against female dependency and
thus acts to discourage the cultivation of jealous possessiveness regarding men. Moreover, the bisexuality of some of the
women provides females with an alternate sexual outlet, and
it further reduces the potential threat to the solidarity of the
group that is posed by coupling under conditions of sexual
imbalance in the adult membership (there are no female
homosexual *couples*). On the male side, the failure of hippie
men (middle class in origin) to provide the income, status,

and security that men "normally" provide (as grounds for their domination) undercuts the legitimacy of any residual claim they may still feel to sexual possessiveness.[28]

A DIGRESSION ON GENDER CULTURE

Vickie's backsliding is thus a double embarrassment to the group, for it violates both the belief in nonpossessiveness and the feminist spirit. But the response to her backsliding also reveals the powerful impact of feminism on the *culture* of relations between the sexes, and it exposes the relationship of that culture to circumstantial realities. Think, for example, of the traditional (or "sexist") culture of the relations between men and women as having a "material basis" in, say, the "substructure" of sexual property, or the institutionalized division of labor by sex, or the varieties of legally sanctioned political and economic male domination. Think, then, of a cultural "superstructure" that includes modes of courtship, conceptions of sexual attractiveness (e.g., machismo or its alluring female equivalent), norms of sexual and gender behavior, and the rules of feeling appropriate to involvement in such matters. Think further of this culture as a set of ideas whose "meaning" resides primarily in its relationship to the substructure of sexual property. Think, finally, of the character of that relationship: is it "functional"? adaptive? Are there "elective affinities"? Are gender norms "merely" reflective of substructural realities, or does phenomenal "experience" (as some sociologists say) "construct" the social reality of the material base? What about interactions, dialectics, feedbacks between the two?

These are the kinds of theoretical questions being implicitly raised when "advanced" people say that they don't understand the rules of sexual relating any more, that sexual cues are ambiguous, that feeling itself is problematic. Take jealousy, for example. Where men own women, and women

---

28. Despite his protestations of "going with the trip," and although he is more committed to struggling against jealousy than Vickie is, Paul did confess to slapping her once in a fit of jealousy. A "liberated" couple, they seem very familiarly "in love." They have a great passion for each other.

are in fact dependent on men for their very survival, meaning
in jealousy is not hard to find: men will be jealous of their
exclusive rights to the use of their female property; women
will be jealous when the security of their status as wife-
property or daughter-property or betrothed-property (in es-
crow, as it were) is threatened. Finding the meaning in
jealousy under "liberated" conditions in the substructure of
relations between women and men is harder. Is it a "survival" in the old functional anthropologist's sense, like the
buttons that don't button on the sleeve of a man's sport coat?
A "cultural lag"? Does it reflect innate tendencies to sexual
property that transcend substructural differences? Is it part of
the egoism and narcissism that post-industrial capitalism has
spawned? Does it reflect fears for the adequacy of one's own
sexuality that have been exacerbated or intensified by the
publication of materials obliging people to reach for previously unimagined heights of orgasmic delight?

That there are no definitive answers to these questions
means only that there are lots of answers and that much
ideological work remains to be done. But when cultural rules
are successfully contested (and social movements mounted in
their behalf) *without* reference to the substructure of those
rules—or, on the other hand, when socialized feelings (like
jealousy) are maintained and culturally reproduced *in spite of*
changes in the material substructure, the result is a peculiarly
unanchored and anomic set of feelings, which characterizes
those people who confess to their confusion about the rules of
sexual and gender "relating" and about what it is or is not
appropriate to feel.

One can understand that confusion sociologically (without,
alas, necessarily being able to reduce its awkward manifesta-
tions) by attempting to find the meaning (or absurdity) of
sexual possessiveness and jealousy (or other features of gender culture) in their contextual relevance to a substructure of
historically specific (though perhaps ambiguous) gender relations. The meaning of jealousy becomes problematic as the
traditional substructure of sexual property relations weakens
or disappears. Vickie's jealousy is "obsolete" or anachronistic
because it exists in a small social substructure that renders it

absurd. Yet jealousy remains, apparently oblivious to functional dictates. Similarly, machismo makes sense where physical strength and courage are required of men to dominate a recalcitrant environment and sustain their social groups, but it becomes laughable and absurd if they work in offices where the heaviest labor they do is hefting a pencil, or if they live beside swimming pools surrounded by servants continually offering more to drink. Yet machismo remains, apparently oblivious to functional dictates.

There may be some cultural lag operating here; surely desocialization and resocialization can be damnably slow processes. But I don't think that lag is the main element. More likely, we are seeing a result in gender culture that mirrors contradictory influences from the substructure. The Ranch now is relatively free of traditional sexism in the basic structure of the relations among its members. But The Ranch exists in a larger environment of communal pioneering that emphasized traditional male skills, and in a still larger environment where the modal male figure is a lumberjack, than whom there is no one more macho in local legend. And in this environment of mixed pressures and circumstances, women and men must go on trying to make it with each other using whatever resources of gender culture that are available to them.

I prefer this contextual view of gender culture to the ideologically unanchored one I see prevalent in my own intellectual environment, which *reifies* culture by pronouncing absolute moral judgments on phenomena (not things) like jealousy and machismo. When women tell me that they want to be my "friend," I sometimes think: "how unambitious!"—not for titillating, sexual reasons, but because I think they reify friendship, forgetting how trivial and transitory "friendship" can be under the actual conditions in which most of us live.

This long digression on gender culture was provoked by an attempt to explicate the role of feminism at The Ranch in generating a variety of special circumstances that have enabled The Ranch to sustain its belief in "free" sexual choice against the pressures to alter it. Underlying all of these cir-

cumstances is the fact that none of the people remaining at
The Ranch has more attractive alternative choices of living
arrangements available. The Ranch's acres are stunningly
beautiful, and whatever the difficulties under which The
Ranch labors, it remains a relatively wholesome place to live
for those who have rejected urban middle-class life and the
family structures typical of it (traditional marriage, cohabita-
tion, and/or serial monogamy); more wholesome, at any rate,
than other available options. That this is so is indicated by the
good reputation of The Ranch in its immediate vicinity, where
I have been told by several residents of more marginal and
less successful communes that they wish that they could be
accepted into the family at The Ranch; a further indication is
the frequency with which ex-members of the family return for
visits.

Closing the circle of explanation is the still-strong anarchist
impulse to freedom, natural order, and *ad hoc* solutions to
problems, which impulse helps them resist the structural
"necessities" that social theorizing tends to impose. They are
neither terrorists of the mind, ready for the sake of sacred
doctrine to *force* people into actions that violate their feelings
or conscience; nor are they materialists with the faith that altered political circumstances will necessarily soon bring in its
wake feelings and beliefs appropriate to the circumstances
they wish to maintain. They are above all thoughtful and sensitive people, *feeling workers* (as Arlie Hochschild might say)
for whom discrepancies between their life circumstances and
their beliefs, and between their beliefs and their feelings,
have been a prominent part of their consciousness for much
of their lives. And they are *experts* at making these discrepancies deliberately problematic and the discussion of them utterly out-front. Nothing less would be sufficient for those
whose intent was to make a good society in microcosm, the
revolution by example.

GROUP STRUCTURE AND EXPRESSIVE CANDOR

This ideological emphasis of hip communards on the virtue of
intimacy or the value of expressive candor about beliefs and

feelings is perhaps the most palpable and the most striking (at least to me) thing about them. They live in groups that they define as "family," and they commonly use kinship terms ("sister," "brother") to refer to each other. Some adopt a common surname. They elevate "out-frontness" to a major human virtue, in which the revelation of subtle feeling and the expression of complex emotions are highly valued as properties of personality that are exercised at weekly family meetings, and which, early on, made communes attractive to many by providing a kind of continual therapy group.

The aggressive assertion of honesty, candor, bluntness, and emotional out-frontness as major virtues in human relations (as distinguished, say, from the guarded or close-to-the-chest virtues like tact, discretion, politeness, and circumlocution) is likely to thrive where social circumstances make it difficult to hide or disguise or euphemize things.[29] Intimacy was also affirmed in the suburban myth of middle-class family life (remember "togetherness"?), but its larger context was a society in which social mobility was stressed, in which bureaucratic impersonality was ascendent (and apparently inevitable), in which the nuclear family was isolated as a unit, and in which intimacy as a *value* was therefore subject to a great deal of strain because of its variable viability from context to context. In rural communes, family *is* community; the closeness of living quarters and the density of interaction make it objectively difficult to dissemble; people's lives are more or less fully exposed to their brothers and sisters, and any *attempt* to disguise feelings or emotions is likely to be vain and *therefore* disapproved (why bother?). Under these conditions, "open-

---

29. But not *always*. I once lived in an oceanfront beach house on a street in which many such houses were packed closely together on narrow 25-foot lots. Each house had a patio facing the ocean, and each patio was separated from the one on either side of it by a *waist-high* fence. The fence was only a symbolic gesture at privacy since it was difficult *not* to see over into one's neighbor's patio if one was standing up. Yet the people on that block (including myself) all seemed to develop wondrous skills at *civil inattention* (the phrase, I believe, is Goffman's), which consistently enabled them to direct their attention elsewhere when a neighbor was busy lying in the sun on a chaise.

ness 'n honesty," an expression dropped into our culture by the human potential movement, is a self- and group-serving idea; in circumstances wherein emotional compatibility is a major feature of what holds a group (or a couple) together, "openness 'n honesty" constrains members to *pay attention* to their subtlest feelings:[30] it enhances and deepens their mutual dependence, instead of evoking guilt and anxiety (as it may in contexts where there are strong bureaucratic counterpressures) or betrayal and manipulation, as it may in casually organized groups without much real solidarity.

I think that this idea has important bearings upon the future of intimate relations. In American culture, traditional mate selection on the grounds of romantic love usually occurs from a pool of "suitable" others. Suitability here means mostly social and cultural match-ups in which mate-seekers may deliberately or intuitively go over an invisible check list in which the other's age, race, religion, family, education, social class, and so on will be scrutinized for their suitability; and from there, perhaps to another invisible (but more personal) check list of criteria like demeanor, dress, manners, and good looks. If the "score" is high enough, and if the courtship and the protosexual intimacies go smoothly enough, the mate-seekers may find themselves "in love." But the categorical structure of this process may disincline the parties to it from paying much attention to "little things" in the other that annoy or irritate or otherwise impede feelings of comfortable emotional complementarity.

The roster of such "little things" is almost endless and includes such habits as leaving the cap off the toothpaste or not folding the tube from the bottom; it also includes habits like nail-biting, nose-picking, speaking with one's mouth full of food, interrupting when the other is talking or, on an automobile trip, not bothering to look when the other with great urgency says "Oh! Look at that!" regarding some roadside

---

30. In much the same sense that Willy Loman's wife in *Death of a Salesman* insisted with great passion that *"attention* must be paid" to this ordinary man, her husband.

sight of passing tourist interest.[31] Because they are defined as "little things" *vis-à-vis* the "major" items on the check lists that render someone eminently suitable as a mate, they are likely to be regarded as unimportant, as inappropriate to make a major issue over, and are therefore likely to be suppressed as not deserving of discussion or expression until the accumulated anger has been built into a desire to hurt the other. It may take spouses years to discover (and years too late to repair) that they simply don't like each other for reasons they were trained to ignore.

Now there was a time not far in the past (it is still true for many today) when, far from having to love each other, spouses did not even have to like each other much to find good reasons for holding a nuclear family together.[32] Today, when many of these reasons have weakened or disappeared, the durability of spousal ties rests increasingly on affectional relations and mutual sensitivity to subtle and elusive feelings. Under these conditions it is surely not inadvertent or merely "fashionable" or mere "narcissism" to find high proportions of a generation of young (and not-so-young) people entranced by an ideological injunction to *pay attention* to their feelings, to be reflexive about them, to talk about them with others, and to listen to others talk about their own. Like Georg Simmel's insight into the relevance of the development of urbane, "blasé" psychological postures to the exces-

31. Another example from real life: at breakfast a pair of new lovers are buttering their toast. She slices neat pats of butter off the end of the cube; he is a butter-gouger, digging into the sides or the top of the cube, leaving gaping and irregular wounds in the corpus of the quarter-pound cube. She stiffens slightly, deeply annoyed, and at the same time perhaps surprised and a little guilty about the depth of her annoyance. She may be tempted to speak to him about it but is also a little abashed at the prospect of making an issue over something so "trivial." He notices only a slight change in her mood, wonders about it momentarily, but lets it pass. Their relationship is never quite the same again.

32. There were ties of property, kinship to locally rooted extended families, the convenience of an established household, and, of course, there were "the children." Moreover, in a more puritanical time, the consequences of divorce or separation were more stigmatizing and less filled (at least for men) with the imagined prospects of sexual adventure and delight.

sive neural stimuli of dense urban contexts,[33] "sensitivity training" has clearly adaptive functions for mate selection and family life under conditions that make their durability increasingly dependent upon satisfying emotional intimacy. And this functional relevance is as applicable to the solidarity of communal families as it is to nuclear families, particularly under conditions in which the rest of social life is increasingly dominated by the emotionally guarded and impersonal virtues of bureaucratic modes of organization, whose "rationality" Max Weber characterized as moving Western culture toward a "polar night of icy darkness," and whose dominant figures would be "specialists without spirit or vision and voluptuaries without heart."

But to point out the adaptive relevance of "sensitivity training" to intimate family life is not to say that the adaptation is always successful. There may be strong counterpressures at work. Bureaucracies can accommodate voluptuaries without heart; despite the ideological appeal of "togetherness," many suburban families have been unable to survive the pressures exercised on husbands by urban careers and on housewives by suburban isolation; Simmel's urbane blaséness may yield to a merely jejune sophistication that undermines the adaptive character of the former; and sensitivity training may degenerate into narcissism, psychological molestation, or manipulation when it is practiced in groups by individuals with little or no interests in the survival of the collectivity or dependence on the welfare of the other.

I had the opportunity one summer to observe (from behind a one-way mirror) a Harvard University undergraduate class being run as an encounter group. Early in the course of its meetings, I was particularly intrigued by one young man in the class. He was tall, skinny, ill-coordinated, with a promi-

33. In "The Metropolis and the Mental Life," in *The Sociology of Georg Simmel*, edited by Kurt Wolff (Glencoe: The Free Press, 1950), Simmel argues that if the organism found it necessary to respond to all the stimuli offered to the senses by an urban environment, it would become exhausted. A sort of selective inattention then develops (which he called "blaséness") as a psychologically Darwinian adaptation.

nent Adam's apple and a bad case of acne. He was also wonderfully bright, witty, and verbal. Could that boy talk! He
seemed to me to be the kind of young man who effectively
used what equipment he had, more than making up for what
he lacked in physical attractiveness by his extravagant intellectual skills. The group as a whole seemed to dislike him
because he did not abide by the norms of the group, which
dictated that its members pour out their sorrows, angers,
guilts, fears, weaknesses, and insecurities to each other, to be
received with expressions of support, comfort, reassurance,
and sympathetic understanding. He seemed to be full of the
sense of his own strength rather than his weakness. He was
consistently cheerful, funny, full of insight and relevant
analytic and psychological comment; and far from seeming
excessively aggressive or offensive to *me* (behind the mirror),
he manifested a lively and attractive presence. I liked him.
The group hated him; he revealed no demons; he confessed
to no psychological wounds that tortured him, thus depriving
them of their opportunity to comfort him. They dumped on
him whenever they could, but he remained consistently
cheerful and friendly.

Grades in the course were partly determined by sociometric rankings the students made of each other. Three weeks
into the course, it was time for mid-term rankings, and I was
surprised to discover that he was ranked near the top. As is
not uncommon in such groups, intimate relations developed
outside the class between some of the males and females in it.
This young man became involved with one of the young
women in the class, and I was told that at a class picnic during
the fourth week (at which I was not present), there was an
argument between the two of them, in which she publicly
humiliated him. He came to class the next day chastened and
grim in demeanor; and in the last two weeks of the class, he
came around to conforming to the group's norms: he confessed how stigmatized he felt by his acne, how no girl could
ever love him because he was so physically clumsy and unattractive, and how he merely tried to cover all this up by using
his intellectual skills and his wit and his personal charm. The

group loved it and was dutifully supportive. At the final sociometric ratings, he was ranked somewhere below the middle of the distribution.

I know that there are a variety of possible ways of interpreting these events, but what most impressed me was what I took to be the group's lack of genuine regard for the young man's strengths and their frivolity as a group for punishing him (the low final rating) when he finally yielded to what they apparently wanted from him. I think he was bright enough to have done his conforming calculatingly, deliberately giving them what they apparently wanted in exchange for an expected reward. But he was not sophisticated enough to anticipate their betrayal.

Under these conditions (a transient summer-school class; an *ad hoc* "rap group" of people who hardly know each other) one can, it is true, get some usable experience in expressing, confronting, and handling volatile emotionality. But unlike a family or a rural commune, these groups have no corporate continuity over a long period, and their members have no vested interest in the welfare or survival of the collectivity. The behavior of their members, therapeutically *self*-oriented, is not constrained by vital mutual interests in each other's strengths. Therefore, such groups are especially prone to ego-serving psychological manipulation and molestation because their members are tied by little other than a mutual emotional exposure, and because emotional skills to exploit this fragile bond to one's own advantage are very likely to be unequally distributed.

But the folks at The Ranch are tied to each other in deep and lasting ways for the reasons I have tried to make clear. Their commitment to intimacy and to "feeling work" functions for them without committing them to unalterable sacred doctrine. If drift and circumstance eventually indicate to them that their nonpossessiveness rule is not viable (though there is no indication of that at this writing), they will accommodate an *ad hoc* alteration in the rule and move on from there.

I do not know what will eventually happen to The Ranch. They may or may not carefully recruit a few more men to equalize the sexual balance. They have the room, and there are many men in the region who would be happy to join them. They have in fact recently placed ads seeking teachers for the school and have offered residence at The Ranch as an inducement. Paying the taxes will be a continual problem they will face. Growing their food will be easier as they increase their rural skills. Maintaining the school will be harder as the children grow older and need more specialized instruction. As the children grow into adolescence, the group will be confronted by *their* problems of coupling. As they themselves grow older, they will have to adapt to middle age, and they may eventually decide to divide the land, as the people grow beyond the point where other individuals (or the family) serve them anymore. In the meantime, it survives with ideological work.

CHAPTER 6

IDEOLOGICAL CONFLICT AND THE MICROSOCIOLOGY OF KNOWLEDGE

Around the time I was getting my Ph.D., some of my fellow students who had specialized in studies of the family talked of setting themselves up in business as marriage counselors. Surely the market was there. Although I had never had a course in The Family, I too thought from time to time about setting up a "practice." In one of my favorite fantasies about professional practice, I imagined a white clapboard house fronted by a very thick and very green lawn enclosed by a white picket fence. On a post near the gate would be a discreet shingle with my name and degree neatly lettered, and then one word: "Justifications."

I would be a specialist in ideological work. Surely the markets were there: people who wanted to do something difficult to reconcile with their principles; people involved in disputes with others and who needed reasons and arguments to promote a point of view; people who were slow in debate, and thought only too late about what they should have said to their antagonists. Ideology as an ideology-neutral skill: the paradox was attractive to someone with an ear for irony. However outrageous, there was surely precedent. Establishments had their propagandists and mouthpieces. Princes had their Machiavellis; in the seventeenth and eighteenth centuries, English governments had used writers and scientists as official wordsmiths. Poets used to sell love-lyrics to aristocrats for the latters' use in wooing, and they kept files of flattering dedications (with only the name of the dedicatee left blank) in hopes of winning further patronage. Presidents retain speechwriters to convey sincerity, and celebrities retain press agents to tell the world that they are "very private persons." Corporations have their public relations departments and their advertising agencies. Why not have the same services for ordinary individuals in affluent industrial societies whose cultural pluralisms made traditional legitimacies increasingly problematic and hence increasingly up for grabs?[1]

My fantasy was frivolous, and I never did hang out that shingle. But my interest in the relevance of ideology to individuals and groups pursuing aims through human interaction in specific circumstances never waned. The attempt to legitimate action and the "structures" that recurrent actions produce and reproduce seemed to me a universal feature of human behavior, occurring at all "levels" of social life, from the most abstract and formal levels of foreign policy and international relations to the most specific and intimate levels of interpersonal relations. It also seemed clear enough that structures varied from place to place and changed over time. Beliefs about propriety and legitimacy also changed, and these changes revealed that the relationships between structures and beliefs were not inadvertent, although exactly what they were was often not entirely clear.[2]

The sociology of knowledge, that subfield of sociology that took these relationships as its objects of study, typically focused its attention on comprehensive systems of ideas in their relationships to whole social systems, thus doing what I call a *macro*sociology of knowledge.[3] In this book, the analysis of relationships between some of the beliefs of communards and the social structures in which they live has constituted in my

1. Of course, there are such services available: psychotherapies perform such services to some extent, so do lawyers. "How-to" popular books do it also.

2. Robert Merton pointed this out many years ago in his discussion of a paradigm for the sociology of knowledge. In many studies it was not clear whether the asserted relations were causal, functional, involving "elective affinities," or some other connection. See R. K. Merton, "The Sociology of Knowledge," in *Social Theory and Social Structure* (Glencoe: The Free Press, 1957).

3. Virtually all of the major figures in the history of sociology of knowledge (Marx, Scheler, Durkheim, Sorokin, Lukács, etc.) were analysts of macrostructures. Mannheim occasionally dealt with smaller (but not much smaller) units, like "generations."

mind a *micro*sociology of knowledge because the magnitudes of the ideas and the social structures I have considered are smaller than those ordinarily considered by sociologists of knowledge. The beliefs treated here are relatively specific *norms* rather than entire moral philosophies, and the structures are rural communal "families," rather than nations, classes, or major institutional complexes.

"CYNICISM" AND THE SOCIOLOGY OF KNOWLEDGE

Regardless of the magnitudes of the variables, however, there are common problems that arise as a consequence of doing sociology of knowledge that researchers too seldom confront directly, particularly when strongly felt ideas are at stake. One of the most interesting of these problems is the tendency of the sociology of knowledge to impugn, weaken, or undermine ideas when analysis of them reveals their self- and group-serving functions.

The problem is posed clearly by the empirical analysis undertaken in this book. If the idea of urban apocalypse serves the interests of survival-equipped communards, is that sufficient reason for casting a cold and skeptical eye on it? If the idea of equal rights for children serves the purposes of those adults who initially had neither the time nor the inclination to be middle-class parents, is that sufficient reason for being cynical about their motives? If the affirmation of "authenticity" in interpersonal relationships serves the interests of people so situated that their dense interactional textures make them ill-able to afford emotional disguises, isn't that reason to regard "openness 'n honesty" as simply another self-serving element of ideology (like belief in cultural pluralism by ethnic minorities or in low taxes by the wealthy)? Or on the other hand, when groups are caught in contradictions between the ideas they profess to believe and their day-to-day behavior, is their hurried ideological repair work best understood in an ironic, contemptuous, and cynical manner?

My answer to these questions is no, at least insofar as the communards at The Ranch dealt with them. But the answers provided by the major tradition of the sociology of knowledge would seem to be a resounding YES—in part because one of the major motives informing the sociology of knowledge as an intellectual enterprise has been the desire to "unmask" or "demystify" ideas by revealing the "real" interests or functions they serve. The "unmasking" theme has probably been as prominent in the analysis of "small" ideas as it has been in the macrosociology of knowledge, and it did not begin with the analysis of the small ideas of communards.

It was Raymond Aron who first planted in me the seed-idea of the microsociology of knowledge with two offhand remarks he makes in *The Opium of the Intellectuals*.[4] In that book, he suggests that the practice of surgery is not conducive to an elevated view of the human spirit ("M*A*S*H" has taught us something about that). Elsewhere in the same book, Aron implies that the best way to dampen the ardor of a political revolutionary is to give him (or her) a research project—preferably on revolutionary movements. In formal terms I take these two throw-away remarks to imply hypotheses in the microsociology of knowledge. First, on surgery: the routine practice of poking around in the internal organs of human beings is likely to increase the surgeon's reserve toward noble invocations of the power of the human spirit (although it may increase his respect for organic functions as well). Second, on revolutionaries: the rigors (and delights) of research itself are likely so to absorb the attention and energy of revolutionary researchers that they may lose sight of the forest of revolution as they wander into the trees of research design and method and sources and data (irrespective of the possibly dampening effects of substantive historical knowledge of past revolutionary movements).

Now, there is a sour and "conservative" quality to such typically "French" insights, a tradition going back to La Rochefoucauld and Montaigne.[5] Such insights take a skeptical or diffident or "aristocratic" stance toward the claimed au-

---

4. Raymond Aron, *The Opium of the Intellectuals* (New York: Norton 1962).

5. The insight is not much weakened by one's ability to cite Marxist-Leninist-Maoist scholars whose commitment to revolution has not been dampened by their research, or by one's ability to cite surgeons who develop respect for "the will to live" as a causal variable.

tonomy of utopian or other ambitiously elevated ideas. The insights imply a touch of disdain, a posture of reserve, especially toward passionately espoused ideas, setting them in *contexts* (surgery in hospitals; research in academic institutes) that suggest the susceptibility of the ideas to modifications by those contexts. The posture says, in effect, hang cool in the face of Abstract Moral Conviction; meet it not with hostile counterargument or passion-in-kind, but with Olympian tolerance and a decent respect for practical reason. Praise the Lord, of course, but pass the ammunition; acknowledge the dignity of the "will to live," but don't forget the penicillin; struggle toward revolution against capitalist exploitation, but in the meantime apply for a Guggenheim, put your kids in private schools, lock your door at night, stay out of rough neighborhoods, and keep that cottage at the beach to recoup your energies for the struggle ahead.

Insights like Aron's also point, usually in a sardonic mood, toward either (1) the self- and group-serving character of moral ideas: (a) the revolutionary researcher may discover— and sincerely defend—the importance or indispensibility of research to the revolution; (b) the professionally cool surgeon may discover his reserves of moral outrage when a devout Christian Scientist (committed to the therapeutic power of prayer) refuses to give parental permission to perform an emergency appendectomy on his child; or (2) the discrepancies or contradictions between expressed moral postures or convictions and the behaviors of everyday life: (a) the heart surgeon may speak to the news media with the ritual modesty of a Healer, while stealing hearts from his medical competitor in the interests of scientific priority; (b) the radical researcher may continue to preach revolution while living the cautious and circumspect life of a middle-class scholar.

Such insights, by stressing the absence of disinterestedness (the self-serving character of moral ideas) or the duplicity of moral statement (when contrasted with the behavior of those who utter it), are likely to weaken belief in moral ideals, therefore weaken commitment, and therefore obstruct the progress or slow the momentum of attempts to sustain and promote these ideas through time. In this sense, then, such insights have a sour and cynical quality.

I am not concerned here with the validity of these insights. Regardless of their empirical validity, however, they (and the implicit hypotheses they contain) do have the merit of asserting a relationship between socially structured daily practice (surgery and/or research) and the ideas brought to these practices and eventually carried away from them. They are therefore one model of what I mean by the microsociology of knowledge: they connect small ideas to small social structures, and they provide a model for the interpretation of that connection: circumstances shape conviction.[6]

This model is a little troubling in part precisely because of its sour and conservative bent, which suggests that ideals are frail but circumstances powerful, human profession weak but circumstances decisive for ideological posture. Nevertheless, I think that this model is sufficiently accurate to merit respect. Moreover, it has the charms of irony working for it, and I try never to underestimate the power of intellectual seductiveness—the model and the seductiveness that Eric Hoffer (a practitioner of the French insight) exhibits when, for example, he says that if the Jews had called Jesus "Rabbi," there might have been no Christianity, and if the Roman Church had made Luther a bishop, there might have been no reformation.[7] Will you "buy" that idea? Well, in the marketplace for cynicism it's an attractive and saleable idea, but can you afford the price?

Although there's a lot to be said for the Aron-Hoffer perspective, it seems expensive to me, not only because it seems to lead to a sour and constricted view of human possibility and to esthetic commitments that rely for pleasure on

---

6. Of course, consequences shape conviction too. Joseph Conrad used the following as an epigraph for Lord Jim: "It is certain that my conviction increases the moment another soul will believe it." These days we call that "reinforcement." Whatever we call it, I think it is important to understand that in the dialectic of ideology and material forces, the *empirical* question of which is dominant is likely to depend on the *phase of the interaction* extant at the time and place with which particular studies are concerned. Clifford Geertz's work is especially good at pinpointing this. See his The Interpretation of Cultures (New York: Basic Books, 1973).

7. Eric Hoffer, The True Believer (New York: Harper, 1951).

ironic skepticism or the confirmation of disillusion. It also fails to illumine the occasional tendency of people to act upon their avowals of passionate commitment in ways that seem directly detrimental to their practical interests or circumstantial convenience. Such instances are intellectually troublesome because we are weak in theories designed to account for them. Marxists use a notion of false consciousness, an idea with more knots in it than a Boy Scout training manual. "Idealists," phenomenologists, and utopians, committed to a theory of intrinsic motivation to explain the "constructed" character of cultural reality, frequently neglect the systematic impact of *given* or inherited cultural circumstances or social conditions on the structure-*creating* activities that claim their attention. That leaves us with notions of visionaries, saints, martyrs, heroes, and the obsessively dedicated, whose inner commitment to ideals is sustained in the face of high practical costs to themselves, which commitment must surely be an embarrassment to those who see sanctions where others see norms, or to those who see rewards and interests lurking behind every moral claim. Even so equable an experimental psychologist as B.F. Skinner shows rare irritation and impatience with those so devoted to illusions like "freedom" or "human dignity" (whose pursuit increases human suffering) that correlations between behavior and positive/negative reinforcements (which, according to Skinner, aim at net reductions in the amount of human suffering) are less than perfect.[8]

The sour perspective is not only theoretically troublesome for what it fails to explain; it also implicitly raises the difficult question whether cynicism is the only appropriate response to an observed self-serving relationship between moral ideas and the circumstances of the persons or groups who espouse them. On what grounds are moral claims weakened or regarded skeptically when it can be shown that they are self-serving for those who affirm them? Should we, for example, be skeptical about the value of a civil liberty like "free speech"

8. See B. F. Skinner, *Beyond Freedom and Dignity* (New York: Alfred A. Knopf, 1971).

because the celebration of it far more clearly and directly serves the interests of professional intellectuals (the people who espouse it most forcefully and who need it in their day-to-day work) than the interests of the politically dumb or apathetic who, indifferent to expressing themselves on public affairs, can get along OK without it? Should discrepancies between preachment and practice be regarded with a knowing cynicism as evidence of the duplicity or "phoniness" of preachers, for example when a police officer, sworn to enforce the laws against gambling, ignores the ladies playing bingo in the church basement to raise money for a worthy cause? Or should his selective inattention be regarded as a reasonable accommodation to conflicting claims and circumstances that he does not entirely control?

I am presuming here that most readers would not be disposed to discipline the police officer for dereliction of duty nor cast a cold eye on free speech simply because it plainly serves the interests of those who most energetically espouse it. But that readers would probably not be so disposed might well give them pause to reconsider the grounds of what I take to be a "normal" tendency to be cynical about apparent duplicity in others and suspicious of the rhetoric and content of ideas that turn out to be self-serving. I raise these questions about the moral and theoretical grounding of the relationship between ideas and interests not to provide *ad hoc* answers to these specific questions (they are answered *ad hoc* every day by every group and every person who must cope with that relationship), but to attempt to develop a perspective that may illuminate the general discussion of the questions.

INTELLECTUALS: "FALSE CONSCIOUSNESS" AND THE SOCIOLOGY OF KNOWLEDGE

In the United States, the discipline called the "sociology of knowledge" is practiced mostly as a subfield of sociology whose subject matter is primarily those groups and institutions prominently characterized by a high degree of intellectual creativity. Sociologists of knowledge usually wind up studying science and scientists, art and artists, theories and theorists, ideas and ideologists. But in the Marxist tradition, the sociology of knowledge is less a substantive subfield of specialization than a distinctive perspective that is, in principle, applicable to all subfields of specialization because all arenas of social life are characterized by a set of constitutive ideas (which define their preoccupations) and by groups of people struggling to realize those ideas under conditions not entirely of their choosing.

As a perspective, the sociology of knowledge implicit in the examples from Aron and Hoffer, and in the tradition that comes down through the Marx and Engels of *The German Ideology* and the Mannheim of *Ideology and Utopia,* is less than satisfactory because its tendency is to explain *away* ideas and beliefs by attempting to specify the social conditions (usually class) that generate them and the interests (usually—though not always—class interests) they serve—which may be why Mannheim (naively, as it turned out) had to conceive of intellectuals (whom he credited with potentially undistorted vision) as a "free floating" stratum without class interests.

Some would say that the tendency of this tradition is "reductionistic."[9] I say "explain *away*" to minimize reification (although some reification is inevitable in any effort at abstract thought) by emphasizing that it is *people* who "have" ideas (although I have in this book attempted to make the nature of their "possession" problematic) and that the analysis of ideas always affects the belief of people in them, and is usually *intended* to. Despite its talk about dialectics, and despite recent concern by Neo-Marxists with the "reproduction of culture," the major tradition of the sociology of knowledge treats ideas (considered as cultural phenomena) as dependent variables (after Marx's dictum about the relation of existence and consciousness) and the political and economic circumstances in which they are borne and espoused as independent vari-

---

9. "Reductionism": a term usually employed pejoratively to indicate unsuccessful or illegitimate attempts to "reduce" a complex set of phenomena to a few simple conditions or causes. Freud attempted to understand culture by reducing it to a sublimated expression of repressed erotic gratification. Durkheim fought attempts to reduce "social facts" to psychological elements. Successful reductionism is sometimes called "science."

ables.[10] To explain *away* a cultural phenomenon is to take an idea that its believers believe is true or beautiful or good, that they *experience* as "real" or as fundamental or as autonomously "their own" (a property of their own being), and reveal its felt reality or autonomy as induced or manipulated, as epiphenomenal, as an "expression" of something more fundamental—in short, as dependent upon the circumstances in which the groups or individuals who "carry" the ideas (we are, let us not forget, "carriers" of culture in much the same sense that some people are "carriers" of disease) are more or less *caught;* "caught" in part because these circumstances are given at the beginning point of any analysis.

10. The very language of "dependent" and "independent" variables, like the language of "infrastructure" and "superstructure," imprisons one in a vocabulary that is misleading, one from which theorists have struggled to extricate themselves. A little late, Engels tried to explicate the "Marxist" view of the dialectical relation between material and ideal factors. Weber tried not only to emphasize the influence of ideas (e.g., "the protestant ethic") on economic development, but also to emphasize the use of economic clout to defend the autonomy of the values defining "status honor." Peter Berger has perhaps been clearest in his simultaneous emphasis on the society-in-man (subjective, ideal) and man-in-society (objective, material) perspectives (see chaps. 2 and 3 of *The Social Construction of Reality*). Durkheim, it seems clear, understood all this by his twin injunctions to "consider social facts as things" and to regard the *conscience collective* as a simultaneous representation of the interiority and exteriority of culture. Contemporary Marxists have come late to this convergence. If Marx wanted to stand Hegel on his head, Louis Althusser (without crediting Durkheim) seems to be trying to stand Durkheim on his head by interpreting the *conscience collective* not as a fundamentally "religious" phenomenon, but as the evidence of the ways in which capitalist institutions reproduce the culture of capitalism by their control over the repressive apparatuses of the state *and* the ideological apparatuses of the "private" sector. Althusser is quite aware that the equivalent hegemonic functions he assigns to the repressive apparatuses of the state and to the "ideological" apparatuses of nonstate institutions wipe out the distinction between the "public" and the "private." Indeed, he asserts that maintaining that distinction is one of the conditions of bourgeois domination. But maintaining it also wipes out the distinction between force and consent, something he apparently chooses not to see. See Louis Althusser, *Lenin and Philosophy* (New York: Monthly Review Press, 1972).

If the hegemonic functions of ideology were as unambiguous as Althusser suggests, there would be little way (except by vulgar imputation) of account-

Now, explaining away ideas is generally not an onerous task for intellectuals, so long as they don't *like* the ideas they're explaining away, can impute them to fools or knaves or victims, and identify the ideas as illusions, deceptions, distortions, or lies. Conservatives like Aron and Hoffer tend to focus their sociology of knowledge on ideas of the Left; Marxists focus theirs on bourgeois ideology. The role of Enlightener is an almost unimpeachably noble one,[11] and intellectuals who think of themselves as enlighteners are likely to be *eager* to explain away false or misleading or exploitive or deceptive or otherwise illegitimate ideas because "accounting for" them by reference to the circumstances in which they are espoused (e.g., by reducing them to interests or, say, to psychopathology) *discredits* them. By such demystification, that is, by revealing the "real" interests or functions that ideas serve, intellectuals apparently weaken (and usually *aim* to weaken) the convictions of those who adhere to these ideas, and they strengthen the antipathy of those who oppose them.

One of the major aims, then, of intellectuals as enlighteners is to forewarn the naive or the intellectually unwary about the

---

ing for the primarily ideological differences that have fragmented the socialist movement from the very beginning. My own view is that Althusser is not sufficiently *materialist*, in the sense that his emphasis on the *relations* of production (i.e., an *abstraction*) distracts attention from the *materials* (i.e., the *objects*) of production, which are essential features of the *conditions* of production whose consequences are seldom fully foreseeable. The introduction of attractive and inexpensive printed cotton into England from India not only had important consequences for the British textile industry; it also affected the class and status system by making *fashion* an important variable in economic production, by making *taste* available to the lower classes, and by promoting an (eventually unsuccessful) attempt to establish sumptuary laws designed to maintain class distinctions in permissible modes of dress. In this case, apparently, the availability of printed calicoes (and the consequences of their public approval) was sufficient to overcome the ideological attempts to limit their distribution. See Chandra Mukerji, *Graven Images* (forthcoming).

11. "Almost" unimpeachably because there are probably still some traditionalists for whom the application of reason to social affairs is *in itself* a threat to tradition. Alvin Gouldner points out (1976) that "conservatives," to the extent that they *use* rational discourse in the defense of tradition, are not traditionalists.

dangers of "false consciousness," which here means too much attention to the reified words and images and principles in ideas themselves, and too little reflexive attention to their sources and to the relevance of their consequences to the interests of their purveyors. When a beautiful young woman with a wonderful smile promises her TV viewers that love and marriage will come to those who overcome their foul breath by using her toothpaste, amateur microsociologists of knowledge in the viewing audience will respond skeptically with a "she's only saying that because . . ." the toothpaste company (or advertising agency or somebody) is paying her to say it. The credibility of the message is discounted or impugned by the circumstances of its delivery.[12]

Advertising, however, is only a vulgar case (and a specially bizarre—because so transparent—case) of self-congratulatory messages offered in a spirit of apparently utter obliviousness to the differences between the claims or overtones of The Word (or the suggestions and associations of The Image) and the interests they serve. The eagerness of intellectuals to use the sociology of knowledge to debunk claims and expose or "unmask" ideas by impugning their sources and consequences, however, is in general limited to ideas they dislike. Ideas they regard favorably are likely to be spared analysis from the perspective of the sociology of knowledge because analysis that questions the sources and premises of ideas risks discrediting or impugning them.[13]

12. In this case, the credibility is diminished despite the fact that *accounting for* a claim or some other idea does not necessarily prove it false or misleading. An *ad hominem* accounting does not logically dispose of an argument, but it usually in fact weakens the credibility of the arguer, which, perhaps, is an accounting for the widespread use of *ad hominem* discourse. Murray Davis suggests the use of the term *ad socium* to cover the practice of impugning ideas by imputing them to despised *groups* (rather than persons). On advertising and ideology see Stuart Ewen, *Captains of Consciousness* (New York: McGraw-Hill, 1976).

13. Except, perhaps, for Stalinist commitment to "correct" ideas. Is it possible that the persistence of Stalinism is rooted in the orthodox Marxist conception of ideas as epiphenomenal? as meaningful *only* to the extent that they promote or obstruct revolutionary interests? If that be the case, understanding it would not impugn pro-revolutionary ideas. It would, however, impugn all other ideas and provide the political grounds for suppressing them.

Most sociologists of knowledge probably do respect the ideas that serve the interests of the groups with whom they identify their own interests. Marxists, for example, usually respect the ideas that serve the revolutionary interests of the working class (as distinguished from the ideas that the working class, at least in the U.S., actually believe they believe). Similarly, liberals and conservatives will espouse and defend ideas that serve the interests of their respective constituencies. But few, if any, of them routinely apply the reflexive method and spirit of the sociology of knowledge to their *own* ideas—perhaps precisely because this tradition of analyzing only disliked ideas has created an ethos of contempt for ideas that may be so understood.[14]

There is a specific kind of false consciousness operating here. The perceived risk of weakening the appeal of ideas one likes by applying the sociology of knowledge to them leads to its selective application to disliked ideas. Mannheim, of course, tried to correct this tendency by universalizing its application to all ideas. But in doing so he got caught in the analysis of his own ideas, producing an epistemological relativism that weakened the grounds of his own credibility—thus confirming, in a sense, the reluctance of sociologists to be analytically reflexive about ideas with which they identified themselves.[15]

False consciousness in this context, then, is the result of an inability or a reluctance or a failure to risk the credibility of one's own beliefs (or those one has sympathy for) by passing them through the fire of sociological analysis, which constitutes a critique of their contextual sources and consequences. False consciousness is present in ideological discourse when discussants are so wrapped up in the rhetoric or symbolic content of their ideas that they overlook the fact that those ideas are grounded in the aims or premises of the community

14. This book is, in part, an attempt to overcome that limitation since I am using the sociology of knowledge to understand some ideas for which I have considerable sympathy.

15. Karl Mannheim, *Ideology and Utopia* (New York: Harcourt, Brace, 1936).

that validates them;[16] or when they ignore or are selectively inattentive to the consequences these ideas help to bring on.[17]

A rare and striking example of this false consciousness is contained in *The Bridge Over the River Kwai*: the "heroic" British officer in the Japanese prisoner-of-war camp is so obsessed with the importance of maintaining the morale and discipline of his captured troops that he fails to see that in putting them to work building a railroad bridge for the Japanese he is contributing to the enemy's war effort by doing the best job that British engineering skills can accomplish. The *ideas* of morale and discipline, *in themselves*, took precedence over the national purposes and the military functions they were intended to serve. Morale and discipline became "reified" ideas (in Mannheim's terms, "functionally rational" but not "substantively rational" ideas) whose changed meaning under prisoner-of-war conditions eluded the British officer until the very end, when the war and the killing suddenly intrude on his work to remind him of what he has done.

IDEOLOGICAL WORK AND FALSE CONSCIOUSNESS

But false consciousness is seldom so clearcut in complex societies because one of the things that groups are ideologically at odds with each other about is precisely the question of the extent to which their beliefs are reified as "theory" or "moral principles" rather than grounded in social contexts and in the "praxis" of pursuing interests. A great deal of ideological discourse is concerned with the question of false

16. Thomas Kuhn (1962) set off an epistemological debate that has still not ended by arguing that even the paradigms that govern the routine day-to-day work of scientists are rooted in and sustained by the norms of scientific communities.

17. An extreme case: in a recently published autobiographical fragment, the late poet W. H. Auden confesses himself to be a man so committed to the *Word* that a piece of literary pornography could produce greater sexual excitement in him than any human being could. But he was surely reflexive enough about it to cast doubt on whether it constitutes "false" consciousness. "Sick?" Perhaps. Deluded? Certainly not. W. H. Auden, "The Early Years," *The New York Times Book Review*, January 29, 1978, p. 3.

consciousness; that is, whether the beliefs of groups or individuals are "appropriate" or "inappropriate" ("correct" or "incorrect") to their interests, or whether "the unity of theory and practice" is broken by contradictions between what believers profess and what they do and the consequences of what they do—contradictions between words and deeds and outcomes.[18]

It may, for example, seem absurdly contradictory to those who are sensitive to the relationship between ideas and circumstance for a prince of the Roman Church, in splendid robes, to promise his ragged parishioners that the wretched will inherit the earth, or for a Republican Party leader to affirm the work ethic from a golf cart in Palm Springs, or for a liberal proponent of busing-to-achieve-integration to put his children in private schools, or for radicals who claim the right of political dissent to attempt to prevent "racists" or "fascists" from being heard on a university platform.[19] But attempts to resolve these "contradictions" can be (and have been) made not only by an appeal to reified principles selectively inattentive to the circumstances that seem to impugn them, but by grounding those attempts in practical interests which appeal to contextual meanings in order to synthesize the "scandal" of contradiction, and hence neutralize imputation of false consciousness.

Thus the cardinal may do his ideological work by arguing that the splendor of the robes is not his but reflects the glory of the Church, which belongs to its ragged believers and which protects their interests by caring for their eternal souls.

18. Gouldner (1976) points out that it is only since the beginning of the age of ideology (i.e., when political discourse is grounded in rational argument rather than revelation or tradition) that discrepancies between theory and practice constitute a vulnerability that may be attacked by one's political opponents.

19. Indeed, it is not only intellectuals who are fond of pointing out the self-serving character of beliefs or the glaring discrepancies between professed belief and apparent circumstances. It is the very stuff of political debate for people with one set of interests to be selectively sensitive to such vulnerabilities in the claims of those with opposed interests. Intellectuals may do so more abstractly and systematically but not necessarily more incisively than those in the thick of political combat.

The Republican Party leader may argue that the golf cart in Palm Springs is a just reward for a life devoted to the work ethic and an emulatory ideal that serves as an incentive sustaining the pursuit of self-interest through work. The liberal integrationist (back-to-the-wall) may defend removing his children from the public school system by arguing that, although he endorses integration, he doesn't feel that he should exploit his own children to bring it about. And Herbert Marcuse, as is well known, has defended the heckling and shouting down of Right-wing speakers on the grounds that the principle of free speech, while generally valuable for its tolerance of dissent, is, under late capitalist conditions, "repressive" of radical and revolutionary ideas, in part because Establishment and Right-wing views have greater access to media and other public platforms than have Left-wing views.[20]

In concrete cases, then, ideological work enables those engaged in intellectual combat to attempt to persuade their critics and their own constituencies (more or less plausibly in different cases) that apparent discrepancies between preaching and practice are in fact illusory and can be successfully resolved. However clearly "false consciousness" may be abstractly defined, it is usually a *contested* matter in the concrete case.

Ideological controversy arises not only from debates over the consistency of theory and practice regarding "agreed-upon" interests like equal opportunity or free speech. It also arises from disagreements about what those interests themselves are.[21] False consciousness, for example, has been imputed to "Tory workers," anti-feminist women, and black "Uncle Toms" by more militant workers, women, and blacks

20. See Herbert Marcuse, "Repressive Tolerance," in *A Critique of Pure Tolerance*, by Barrington Moore, Jr., Robert Paul Wolff, and Herbert Marcuse (Boston: Beacon Press, 1965). Marcuse claims in effect a sort of "affirmative action" for radical ideas because the principle of free speech, like the principle of equality of opportunity, has not succeeded in serving the interests of minorities by actually bringing about equal representation.

21. For a wonderful essay on the history of the idea of "interests," see Albert Hirschman, *The Passions and the Interests* (Princeton: Princeton University Press, 1977).

who see the interests of their respective groups quite differently. Franklin D. Roosevelt (and some of his patrician allies)
was similarly seen by some of his wealthy Republican
enemies as a "traitor to his class" (upper) because of his New
Deal policies. But such people do not supinely accept being
characterized as afflicted with false consciousness or as having sold out the interests of their people. And ideological
work in defense of their conception of their interests has appealed not only to reified principles ("President of *all* the
people," "Biology is destiny," etc.), but also has in fact asserted the contextual appropriateness of their ideas to the
interests of workers, women, blacks, and capitalists. Arguments are made, for example, that FDR's policies "saved"
capitalism at a time when public dissatisfaction with its performance was at an all-time high in the U.S. and hence provided a sympathetic ear to socialist ideas; the moderating role
unsympathetically characterized as "Uncle Tom" is said to
have mediated the delicate relations between segregated
black and white worlds at a time when a race war might have
meant genocide for blacks; conservative women's organiza-
tions assert that they are defending the dignity and interests
of women to the extent that the fate of women is still tied to
housewifely roles, and they attack those feminists who, in
derogating housework ("Fuck Housework!") derogate one of
the major sources of self-respect for many women; and Tory
workers, particularly if they are comparatively well paid, may
argue that they have vested interests in a *status quo*, even if
they are exploited by it. Indeed, it can be argued that all oppressed groups, short of those in desperate straits, have interests in a *status quo* since whatever small gratifications they can
wreak from an oppressive social order are likely to depend on
the stability of that order.[22] Again, these examples show that,

22. With a premise like this, the question is not why so *few* oppressed
groups in the U.S. are revolutionary but why so *many* are. On the other
hand, Erving Goffman, in *Relations in Public* (New York: Basic Books, 1972),
describes the President of Columbia University looking over his trashed office after the 1968 troubles and wondering sadly how people could do such a
thing. For Goffman, the more important question was how come they do it
so infrequently.

however clearly interests or false consciousness are defined in theory, they are still likely to be contested with ideological work in the specific case.

INTERESTS, LEGITIMACY, AND THE SELF-SERVING CHARACTER OF IDEAS

But perhaps the *most* important point that the examples clarify is that the revelation that ideas serve interests does not *always* impugn or undermine ideas. Unlike Immanuel Kant, who left to us the principle that self-serving ideas and actions cannot be "moral" (a principle that, as we shall see, suggests a "protestant" ethic), I want to suggest that *whether* the self-serving character of ideas impugns them is a variable that depends primarily on the level of consensus regarding the *legitimacy* of the interests involved, and the *reflexive candor* with which the relation of ideas to interests is made plain.

Legitimacy itself is a variable that, at any historical moment, ranges from very high consensus to no consensus at all. Claims by the aged on fixed incomes that they deserve special tax benefits are not impugned because the claim is self-serving for the aged, and many routine moral-political claims are of this sort. Their self-serving character does not impugn them because consensus on their legitimacy is high, and their self-serving character is not disguised. On the other hand, few Americans would probably agree with Marcuse that radical ideas deserve affirmative action. Reflexive candor is relevant to the legitimation of interests and circumstances because candid expression of the relationship of ideas to interests denies to sociologists of knowledge (and other critics) the opportunity to "unmask" or "demystify" that relationship. Indeed, it was partly the "unmasking" spirit, by now traditional in the sociology of knowledge, that made abstract ideas and elevated principles seem unsavory when it could be pointed out that they served *hidden* interests. But Mannheim's impulse was correct: the "unmasking" spirit is itself incomplete if it does not, regardless of the risks, apply its reflexive method to itself. If it does not, unmaskers are themselves vulnerable to the suspicion that they are pursuing hidden (and therefore illegitimate) interests.

There are a number of complex ironies working here. For one thing, the tendency of sociologists of knowledge to restrict their analyses to ideas they dislike confines the sociology of knowledge within its role as an ideological weapon and leaves its reflexive analytic power unused. Reflexively unsentient, sociologists of knowledge abandon the ideas they like or respect to the prospect of being impugned by enemy-unmaskers who will use the sociology of knowledge as a weapon against them. In chapter 2 of *The Dialectic of Ideology and Technology,* Gouldner points out that Marxists are reluctant to be reflexive about their own ideas because reflexivity seems to promote neutrality or detachment, rather than ideological struggle. But this apparent prospect seems to rest on the presumption that candid recognition of the self- and group-serving character of ideas impugns them and only *therefore* weakens the will to struggle in behalf of them. Yet I have tried to make clear that not all ideas are impugned when their self-serving character is made plain. Ideas are impugned when they *deceptively* claim or imply that they are *other* than self-serving (and must therefore be "unmasked" by their opponents), and when the level of consensus is high, that the interests the ideas serve are illegitimate or unjust.

This failure to distinguish clearly between the self-serving character of ideas and the legitimacy (or illegitimacy) of the interests they serve obscures the grounds on which ideas are impugned and has the ironic consequence of discouraging sociologists of knowledge from being reflexively analytic about their own ideas—hence making those ideas vulnerable to "unmasking" by others who dislike them, on what I take to be a *mistaken* assumption that the revelation of their self-serving character is sufficient to impugn them.

But the apparent persuasiveness of this mistaken assumption reveals a second powerful irony, because lurking behind this "unmasking" impulse, usually unrecognized, is that Kantian sort of "protestant ethic": the ascetic notion that the harder it is to sustain one's moral beliefs, the more profound becomes one's moral achievement—as if in order to be warranted a moral claim had to be founded on the suffering or inconvenience it caused the claimant. Bernard Shaw put it well: "The English think they are being moral when they are only being uncomfortable." Shaw may have been too hard on "the English," but the hair shirt is sociologically ironic because in regarding ideas as epiphenomenal or as instrumental to material interests, sociologists of knowledge (of *all* people) might be expected to *respect* ideas that enable people to get on with their lives more successfully, rather than, like Kant, to regard these ideas as mere or otherwise unworthy *because* they are self-serving. What, after all (asks the historical relativist), are moral ideas *for?* To suffer in the name of? Or are they tools and instruments, *culture*—like shovels, rakes, and chain saws—to help people get through their days, and in helping them through, providing some pride, even ennoblement, for having got through safely (and, indeed, some comfort and succour for injuries and defeats in the process)?

That a sort of protestant ethic lurks triumphant here is indicated by the fact that, when the self- and group-serving functions of apparently elevated moral ideas are pointed out, the pointing is likely to be done cynically, in a spirit of "laying bare" the truths behind the masks, as if the revelation of their functionality somehow dishonored them. Do the well-placed believe in equality of opportunity? How convenient for those who already have a competitive advantage! Do the disadvantaged believe in affirmative action? in the dignity of subcultures? How convenient for them! Do professional intellectuals regard the First Amendment as the cornerstone of our democracy? Well, of course, they have interests in free speech and social criticism that most ordinary citizens seldom have public occasion to use. Do university professors in the humanities believe that a liberal education enriches the human spirit? No doubt many do. But wait—in an era of tightened budgets, if too many potential students agree with these professors, work loads may be increased, speed-ups may occur; and there's an idea now gaining currency among educators (and other taxpayers) that a "liberal education" may be a waste of time for many young people ("overeducated" and "underemployed"), that there are other, alternative, and more efficient ways of becoming qualified to lead a productive and satisfying life. There is always ideological work to do.

"*. . . as if* the revelation of their functionality somehow dishonored them." But these examples reveal that it is not the functionality of the ideas (for the groups or individuals who espouse them) that dishonors them (if, indeed, they are dishonored), but the *judgments* made about their legitimacy or illegitimacy *vis-à-vis* larger constituencies. Readers already familiar with the kind of reasoning that cross-tabulates two variables will have observed a four-fold table in the making here. The variables are (1) whether the ideas to be analyzed are or are not materially self-serving for their espousers, and (2) whether the interests the ideas serve are judged to be legitimate or illegitimate by a high consensus of larger constituencies. Cross-tabulating these two variables generates the following four categories or cells representing varieties of judgment:[23]

1. Ideas that serve the interests of the groups that espouse them *and* whose interests are judged as legitimate. In such circumstances ideological claims are likely to be regarded as "reasonable," "appropriate," or "correct"—like the claim

23. Many writers on ideology and the sociology of knowledge discuss the problem posed by the fact that there is no standard usage of the term "ideology." Anthony Giddens, for example, distinguishes between those who oppose ideological claims to the claims of science or truth and those who see the *general* interests expressed by ideology as different from the (merely) sectional interests expressed in the pejorative use of "ideology." See Anthony Giddens, *Central Problems in Social Theory* (London: Macmillan and Co., 1979). Geertz, on the other hand, distinguishes between the analysis of ideology as an expression of interests and ideology as an expression of strain in the society. See Clifford Geertz, "Ideology as a Cultural System," in *The Interpretation of Cultures* (New York: Basic Books, 1973). I do not delude myself that, by proclaiming my own usage and arguing for its clarity and utility, consensus on usage will thereby be achieved. I use the term as Gouldner does (and to some extent Habermas) to refer to modes of discourse that require "rational" grounding and to argument requiring logic and evidence—as distinguished from argument based on revelation or authority or tradition. I intend this to blur the science/ideology distinction, though not to wipe it out: science is a particularly persuasive mode of ideological discourse. With respect to Geertz's distinction, I am attempting to understand ideology both as an expression of interests *and* as a response to strains generated by groups seeking aims under conditions they do not entirely control.

that the aged deserve special tax benefits or that physicians and other professionals should have the autonomy to determine standards of professional competence.

2. Ideas that serve the interests of the groups that espouse them *but* whose interests are judged as illegitimate (because they are disguised or because they threaten more general interests or for other reasons). In such circumstances ideological claims are likely to be regarded as greedy, deceptive, seductive, or manipulative. These are the ideas that are apparently successfully impugned when their self-serving character is pointed out. Sometimes such ideas will be pejoratively characterized as "ideology," or *merely* self-serving. Marxists will place "bourgeois ideology" in this category; and when affirmative action claims are characterized as "reverse racism," they are implicitly being placed in this category. Advertising claims that go right to the edge of lying belong here too.

3. Ideas that do *not* serve the interests of the groups that espouse them but the interests they *do* serve are judged to be legitimate. In such circumstances ideological claims are likely to be regarded as noble, saintly, heroic, or altruistic because they involve sacrifice or martyrdom for those who espouse them (although, of course, the conferred nobility may compensate for the sacrifice). This is a relatively rare category (since self-serving ideas are likely to be regarded as "normal"); it conceivably includes cases of transcendent "religious" or "spiritual" dedication, like the Dutch who hid fugitive Jews during the second World War or the Abolitionists who ran the stations on the Underground Railroad, or Soviet dissidents condemned to the Gulag, or Japanese Kamikaze pilots.

4. Finally, ideas that neither serve the interests of the groups that espouse them *nor* any other interests that are judged to be legitimate. In such circumstances ideological claims are likely to be regarded as foolish, irrational, far-out, visionary, obsessive, or insane. Perhaps even rarer than Category 3, this one is likely to be a "pathological" category

that might include schizophrenic and other seriously "disturbed" people (and their followers), weird cults, victims who blame themselves, or other self-haters bent on suicidal paths for no discernible legitimate reason.

Now, I know that there are several problems in the utilization of these categories.[24] Since each cell requires an interpretive judgment to fill it with real cases, there may be little consensus on which ideas belong under what headings. Critics of medical care may challenge the legitimacy of the claim by physicians to autonomy in determining standards of professional competence, preferring to place such a claim in Category 2 as "ideology." Some will want to judge the noble and the saintly (in Category 3) as foolish (thus placing them in Category 4); others will want to call the foolish or the insane "martyrs." All that is in the nature of ideological disputation. But I am less interested in placing ideas (and their espousers) in their proper categories (thus reifying them) than in making plain the insight that it is not the self-serving character of an idea that impugns it, but a judgment that it is illegitimate.

MEANWHILE, BACK AT THE RANCH . . .

That clear insight has important consequences for understanding the ways in which ideas and the material circumstances in which interests become manifest do or do not accommodate to the pressures exercised by each on the other. Based upon their mistaken fear that the self-serving character of an idea impugns it and therefore weakens the will to struggle in its behalf, the failure of sociologists of knowledge to turn their analytic tools to the analysis of ideas they favor has obscured our understanding of the ways in which beliefs and the circumstances of everyday life interact in a never-ending process (indeed, a "dialectical" process), in which interests emerge and recede, become more or less salient and pressing, and in which struggles over the legitimacy of those interests

24. Compare this four-fold table with the diagrams in Giddens's *Central Problems in Social Theory*, pp. 190–91.

need the reflexive analytic attention that the sociology of knowledge at its best can offer.

If the ruling ideas of an age are the ideas of the ruling class, then the "radical" or "alternative" ideas might be expected to come from revolutionary or otherwise dissatisfied groups and classes. On the whole they do, but like any other human group that lives with ideas, they must continually adapt their convictions to their circumstances (and vice versa) in the realistic pursuit of their interests, which are not always clear. Convictions, we have learned, are "relative"; circumstances condition their meaning, changed circumstances may create pressures to change them, and this process can be painful because what people "believe" tends to become a property of their *being*. Such identification with one's own beliefs creates risks to the identity in being reflexive about their sources and consequences.[25]

Despite these risks, and although analysis of the relationships between the ideas of communards and their social circumstances makes these relationships appear to some extent as structurally fixed, they have of course undergone changes as communards have struggled with their beliefs, their interests, and their everyday lives. As I have shown, some of their beliefs have been modified. They do ideological work on the concept of "brotherhood"—redefining it to suit the exigencies of circumstance. Ideological work gets done on ideas about technology to bring them into line with the communards' interests in "survival." They do ideological work on the meaning of "welfare" to reconcile it with conditions that threaten their self-sufficiency. Circumstances that require the

25. The sense of property in ideas tends to be characteristic of intellectuals, which makes them behave not unlike other owners when the value of their property is threatened—by competition, expropriation, absorption, reflexivity, or by changed circumstances. Such behavior may be especially frequent among those intellectuals who either have relatively little in material interests to modify their "purity" or intransigence about ideas (e.g., students or young, dissident intellectuals), or those intellectuals who are so heavily "invested" in their ideas (for example, intellectual leaders of social movements or "schools of thought") that circumstantial pressures to modify them may involve heavy "losses."

formal education of The Ranch's children have obviously placed some pressures on the belief in minimum formal socialization. Similarly, when a commune's ideological commitment to "consensual decision making" (i.e., effective veto power by small minorities) leads to political paralysis (i.e., no decisions, drift) or a tendency toward authoritarianism (usurpation of power by *ad hoc* leaders on specific issues), a "reversion" toward majority rule or parliamentary procedure may occur. Or a solution may be found in another direction by invoking "encounter" or other critical and self-critical techniques (i.e., more ideological work) to overcome the resistance of minorities and induce assent. In either case, appropriate ideological justifications are not difficult to imagine.

Although these instances illustrate some of the ways in which communards yield some ideological ground to the pressures of social structure and other circumstances (while yet attempting to maintain some consistency in what they believe they believe), it is at the same time clear that the communards at The Ranch are not always eager to accommodate their beliefs to contextual pressure. They have yielded neither their belief in free sexual choice nor their belief in sexual nonpossessiveness to the unavoidable tensions that accompany them. They have achieved a marked alteration in "normal" age-grading by "living up to" their belief in extending a wide range of freedoms and normally "adult" privileges to their children in spite of the risks to their legitimacy doing so entails. They have maintained their unalienated, pastoral style of familism (and their poverty) in spite of the opportunities for commercial exploitation that their land offers.

In these instances, they have not yielded to the pressures of circumstance; rather than "accommodate," they opt to "struggle against circumstances" (against the threats to the group represented by sexual freedom and jealousy; against potential criticism of their child-rearing and the threat this represents; against pressures to increase their wealth by sacrificing ecological or other "principles") to maintain what they believe they believe. Both processes, the day-to-day accommodations and struggles, require *ad hoc* judgments (and the ideological work to render them persuasive) made at the level of "everyday life," judgments that attempt to reconcile, in ways that can command legitimacy, the sometimes conflicting claims of ideology and practical convenience, while doing minimum damage to either their beliefs or their interests.

In either case, self-serving processes are at work. Where remedial ideological work has been done modifying some of their beliefs (brotherhood, technology, welfare, decision making, sex and drugs for children), it has been done to enable them to pursue their interests more effectively under threatening circumstances without unambiguously "selling out" their beliefs. Even where they have been able to maintain their convictions largely intact by a successful struggle against threatening circumstances (sexual freedom, the decline of age-grading, "out-front" intimacy, unalienated work), that success has been made possible by their control over *other* circumstances (ownership of the land, insulation from interference by social caretakers, the education of their children in their own school, the density of interaction) that help support the viability of their ideals and render the threatening circumstances relatively tolerable.

In the past (and in some of my work) I myself adopted a skeptical and sometimes cynical attitude toward ideas whose self- and group-serving functions I could see through, as if ideas owed a personal obligation to me to be heroic and transcendent of circumstance. And their general failure to fulfill that obligation (administered, as they were, by imperfect persons under less than ideal conditions) evoked my most severe negative sanction: scorn. But then I began to understand, partly through this commune research, that my own cynical attitude was itself an expression of a severe, ascetic, and inevitably disappointing ethic: the Judeo-Christian hair shirt. The test of your beliefs was whether you suffered for them; if you felt guilty, grim, or tight, you must be doing something right—like D.H. Lawrence's hero in the novel *Kangaroo*, who wandered the world looking for things not to give in to. That view sees virtue as resistance to temptation (in this case resistance to the practical comfort or gratification self-serving

ideas can provide), instead of (its original sense) as *competence*
or excellence at accommodating ideals to circumstances.[26]

This does not, of course, mean either that I like ideas because they are self-serving or that I like them when I regard
the interests they serve as legitimate. It would take an Orwel-
lian 1984 to create such nicely integrated psyches. Like anyone else, I have been trained to respond favorably to heroic
sentiments, and when Dylan Thomas urges me not to go
gentle into that good night but to "Rage, rage against the
dying of the light," I am moved both because of and in spite
of the intransigence of the feeling. And I would resist the
cautionary warning that rage may be counterproductive. But I
also respect ideas when, rather than reifying them, the
people who are committed to day-to-day living with them
(under circumstances not entirely of their choosing) are ready
to do both the remedial ideological work to keep the ideas
vital and the organizational work to keep the interests viable.[27] That, I think, is why I like The Ranch as much as I do.

But I think too that the reason it was so difficult for me to
understand why I was so happy to be among its inhabitants is
to some extent a result of my sociological perspective on
ideas. Like the law, which is said not to "respect" persons, a
relativist sociology of ideas should have some difficulty respecting beliefs. For out of the almost limitless number of
ideas that people somewhere sometime have believed are
self-evidently true, beautiful, good, reasonable, or useful,
surely it must seem astonishing (and to some extent arbitrary)
that any given group or individuals should have hit upon the
specific set of convictions they happen to have.

Perhaps there is "no way out" of this relativism. But I have
found that the *logical* dilemma of relativism is *merely* theoreti-

---

26. Among the several meanings of "virtue" listed in *Webster's Collegiate
Dictionary* (2nd Ed., 1949) is this arresting one: ". . . an excellence of any
kind; as, to make a *virtue* of necessity" (emphasis in original).

27. Sometimes this is not possible. Groups and individuals may paint
themselves into ideological corners from which the only escape is martyrdom
or "selling out." Societies erect monuments to heroes and heroines of culture
who "died for what they believed," but they shake their heads in bewilder-
ment at the events in Guyana.

cal; it has not prevented me (nor does it prevent others) from making the practical judgments of good-better-best and bad-worse-worst that people need to sustain their sense of order and meaning while getting through their days. I have been helped through these decisions by a reflexive practice, by alternations of resolution and irony; by the businesslike resolve made diffident by an ironic appreciation of its arbitrary sources and sometimes incalculable consequences, and by the languor of reflexive irony stiffened by the world's demand that resolve be rooted in an appeal to criteria (arbitrary or not) that an ultimately political constituency will validate.

I like most of The Ranch's convictions. But because I am a sociologist, my own conviction is that I don't *understand* any of these convictions unless I can find their relevance to the circumstances (historical and contemporary) in which they are espoused and to the material interests of the social groups that carry them through time and preside over such lives and careers as ideas may be said to have. It is in this spirit that I have tried to understand the sources of some of the ideas of communards and the relationship of these ideas to the daily lives communards face, and to see in this ethnography larger lessons for the study of ideological work.

7

REPRODUCTION AND CHANGE
IN CULTURE
AND SENSIBILITY

The argument of the book is about completed. The meaning of moral ideas resides in the contexts through which groups give them life and carry them through time. Genuine convictions are usually self-congratulatory and generally serve group interests, and that this is so should not necessarily impugn those convictions. Where the relationship of ideology to the circumstances in which it must live is abrasive, remedial ideological work should be expected to prevent the abrasions from cutting to the bone.

Nevertheless, it should be plain that the integrative achievements of ideological work are not always successful, and even when successful they are seldom total. Vickie's uneradicated jealousy suggests the recalcitrance of sensibility to alteration by mere ideology; however apocalyptic the long run may be, the bills must still be paid this month, and the temptation to exploit commercially the timber resources at The Ranch will not go away. Despite the successes of the counterculture (and I think they have been many, both fundamental and cosmetic), the "generation" that produced them has also inevitably *re*produced some of the culture and sensibility it ideologically disavowed, and this is a sort of definition both of a "failed" revolution and of the nature of social life.

THE RADICAL TRADITION

Nevertheless, much of the Monday-morning quarterbacking about the "failure of the sixties" misses an important point about revolution that Paul Goodman did not miss, even before the sixties got seriously underway: most revolutions (perhaps all of them) are lost or compromised when measured against the initial ideological visions that inspired them;[1] and this is as true of "microrevolutions" (in families, communes, and age, gender, or ethnic relationships) as it is of revolutions carried out at the level of the whole economy or polity. But short of a fascist counterrevolution (like Chile's in 1973), "failure" does not mean that important changes have not been accomplished, that "generational" mentalities have not been created whose residual influences may be permanent, that key groups of people are not left with altered sensibilities in altered circumstances, which may then permit new surges toward further democratic change when political and economic conditions are again ripe.[2]

But in saying this my aim is not to provide empty ideological comfort to survivors of the movement, nor to engage in optimistic platform rhetoric for the benefit of the still-faithful partisans ready and eager to promote that surge. The point is that the existence of continuous radical traditions (now ebbing, now flooding) makes it seem likely that each generation will continue to contain groups whose social placement renders the accessible tradition of radical ideas attractive, and that these ideas will be selectively invoked (and new ideas added) and applied to contemporary conditions.[3]

Many of the core beliefs generally associated with the counterculture constitute a peculiar mélange of old and odd traditions (pastoralism, anarchism, romantic bohemianism, apocalypse, Asian religion or mysticism, American Indian lore) synthesized in eclectic and syncretic ways with radical political and personal experiments in equality, sexuality, effusive "expressiveness," and other "liberations." Even the craziness and sly nihilism of the Yippies were continuous with a

1. Paul Goodman, *Growing Up Absurd* (New York: Random House, 1960).

2. American politics has long been characterized by Right-Left waxings and wanings. See Dennis Wrong, "The Rhythm of Democratic Politics," in *Skeptical Sociology* (New York: Columbia University Press, 1976).

3. See Karl Mannheim, "The Problem of Generations," in his *Essays on the Sociology of Knowledge* (New York: Oxford University Press, 1952), where he calls such groups "generation units."

Dadaism that predated the first World War. And some of their bizarre practices were continuous with those of the Parisian bohemians in the early nineteenth century that have been described by Cesar Grana.[4] Running a pig (from a New Mexico commune) for President in 1968 evokes Gerard de Nerval ostentatiously taking his pet lobster-on-a-leash for a walk through the Tuilleries, and Grana's description of Parisian garrets decorated like Tartar war camps evokes the tent-like, billowing madras decor of hippie apartments.

Moreover, adding to the complexity of these traditions is the fact that, despite their commitment to "alternative life styles," rural communards sometimes seem "conservative" or "traditional" in the sense that these terms are applied to rural or small-town folks who are skeptical of unfamiliar vibrations and wary of slick incursions of urban culture; like the isolated frontier families of our myths, they sometimes reveal a distrust of strangers and a craggy severity of mien.

But the very fact that the rural communes of the counterculture carry this complex mix of traditions, synthesized in fresh ways, suggests that there may be relatively permanent groups or strata to keep these traditions alive and carry them down the generations with movements (now a trickle, now a torrent) of dissent, defiance, rebellion, withdrawal. It is the continuity of these traditions that suggests to me that we have here neither a simple anachronism in late twentieth-century American communards attempting to live like nineteenth-century pioneers (although, of course, not *just* like them) nor a mere sideshow in the drama of social and technological change. But even as a sideshow, it is one that keeps affecting what goes on in the main tent. There are, after all, those tears in the tent fabric, those chinks in the cultural facade: the sexual revolution (including feminism), more racial equality, the diffusion of sacred attitudes toward the land and the fragility of its ecology, the decriminalization of marihuana, the spread of yogic disciplines, massage and encounter as weekend recreation at your local community center, to say nothing of blue jeans as high fashion and the strong hippie impacts on pop music and the graphic arts.

4. Cesar Grana, *Modernity and its Discontents* (New York: Harper and Row, 1967).

I have no wish either to catalogue the accomplishments to which the counterculture has contributed nor to exaggerate their importance. Some may well be merely cosmetic, and some are easily interpretable as evidence of the genius of American institutions for absorbing dissent and co-opting innovation in ways that provide new commercial opportunities for some (entrepreneurs in ecology, entertainment, religion, health, pop psychology, and other forms of private "fulfillment") without affecting the fundamental distribution of wealth and political power. But I think too that the hypersensitivity of the Left to the ease with which "life style" changes can be co-opted may have desensitized the Left to the potentially Schumpeterian ironies and dialectics in the achievements of the counterculture. Joseph Schumpeter saw the freedom fought for and institutionalized by capitalist entrepreneurs as having unintentionally created a stratum of discontented intellectuals who would "nibble away" at the foundations of capitalism.[5] The luxury of late capitalism has also created a stratum that believes in its right not merely to success but to psychological "fulfillment," and if success does not indirectly bring fulfillment in its wake, it will be sought directly. What this means is that states of consciousness (e.g., "fulfillment") are rendered problematic, and hence manipulable. If you feel unhappy or unattractive or empty or anomic or unfulfilled, or trapped by lost opportunities and wracked by nameless longing, and you can't make a revolution, there are some things you can do: talk it out, find a group, take a pill, get a guru, turn your head around. Never mind the co-optation, the charlatanism, the "privatization," the narcissism, the pathetic "me's" struggling to be heard; the point is that one of the basic achievements of the "generation" may be a mind-set *aware* of the *induced* character of its own dissatisfied consciousness and hence ready to reject those inductions for more promising ones deliberately chosen. For if the hostility of conservative, liberal, *and* radical, cultural establishments is any measure of a perceived threat, then surely "narcissistic" self-absorption with how one's consciousness got that way can't be all bad.

5. Joseph Schumpeter, *Capitalism, Socialism, and Democracy* (New York: Harper and Bros., 1942).

Whenever I hear the "generation" that came to maturity in the early 1950s described as "the silent generation," I am always a little surprised, because it wasn't silent for me. The radical and/or "bohemian" groups I lived and moved with around New York and Berkeley didn't make any big headlines or the network news, but most of us were quite aware that we belonged to a deviant tradition (more accurately, several traditions of deviance or dissent) that went back a long time. Moreover, that most of us were students and young enough not to have accumulated heavy responsibilities to, or interests in, the established order made most of us relatively safe from the constraints of McCarthyism, which "silenced" so many others who were more vulnerable to its sanctions. As I remember the 1950s, most of us did and said what we damn pleased, in part because we could afford to.

Now, I don't know why I (unlike, say, my own brother) began moving with or identifying myself with these groups. Nor do I know why some people became hippie communards when others whose social backgrounds and psychological make-up seemed very similar did not. Nor do I know why some hippies become communards while others do not, or why some stay communards while others do not; just as I don't know why Baudelaire or Rimbaud were the crazies they were, or why Count Henri de Saint-Simon or Auguste Comte ("fathers" of sociology, indeed) were the different kinds of crazies they were.

It does seem, however, that such people somehow get free from the threats and promises, the rewards and punishments that an established order uses to keep its members from misbehaving; somehow, they are induced to resist reproducing the dominant culture. Perhaps, like Bobby McGee, they've got nothing left to lose; perhaps they hear the rhythms of that proverbial different drummer coming through the spheres clearly enough to prevent them from even imagining the possibility of a misstep in their march. Perhaps their deviant traditions can provide enough subcultural reinforcement to neutralize sanctions from the dominant culture. Perhaps, as in Joseph Schumpeter's dialectical (but non-Marxist) analysis of capitalism, unique historical junctures present unanticipated opportunities for radical actions but tie the hands of authorities attempting to restrain or repress them, which process, in turn, weakens that authority further; or some magical combination of these and still other conditions in just the right weighted mix.

Although I don't know why such people opt for deviant traditions, I suspect it begins early, when one hears teachers and/or parents say of certain children: he's (she's) a dreamer, that one; head's always in a book; rather look at pictures of far-away places than play with the other kids. This one's "sensitive," that one's "gifted"; this one's "difficult," that one's "different," the other would rather be off in fantasyland than remembering that Helena is the capital of Montana or that the chief export of Chile is, or was (as I was taught), potash. I've always been tempted to think of such people as "oriented to culture," as distinguished from attentive to practical circumstances and contexts; as preoccupied with *relatively remote* symbolic levels of experience, rather than with getting a Gold Star or a Smiling Face from the teacher, or with otherwise getting along favorably in their day-to-day relations with peers and powers that be.

I do not delude myself that these happy (or unhappy) few constitute an eventual elite of sensibility (after Stendhal's image of his readers), or an Elect of lumpenproletarian Saints (after the Sartrean image of Jean Genet). But I do think it useful to indicate that in each generation there seem to be larger or smaller groups of people who are more interested in, or oriented to, the *abstractions* of cultural traditions (dominant or deviant) than in the practical realities or concrete social relations that dominate the now of everyday life.[6]

---

6. I say "more" interested to indicate that I do not believe that preoccupation with "culture" or symbols occurs in a manner utterly insulated from practical economic or political circumstances and constraints, or that preoccupation with practical matters can proceed without the invocation of culture or ideas—as Daniel Bell implies by radically separating what he calls the cultural "realm" from the polity and economy (see *The Cultural Contradictions of Capitalism*, New York: Basic Books, 1976). Artists, ideologues, and visionaries must cope with the mundane political and economic realities of their milieux, just as engineers, businessmen, and dentists depend on occupational cultures and professional styles to proceed through their mundane routines.

What eventually becomes of these interests and orientations depends upon a variety of circumstances I can't specify, but which at given points in time involve the social placement of the group and the access that placement provides to a body of *available ideological tradition* that can be put to work in that context in behalf of the realization and legitimation of its symbolic visions. I deem this discussion relevant here because, at the height of their powers between 1967 and 1971, communes attracted large numbers of these symbol-preoccupied people from both major divisions of "the movement": the counterculture, whose "hippies" were more interested in cultural revolution and personal liberation than in capturing political power; and the New Left, whose members were more interested in political and economic transformation, which they saw as requisites without which cultural changes and deviant life styles would either be repressed or co-opted.

POLITICAL AND CULTURAL RADICALISM

There is, nevertheless, an inherently uneasy relationship between political and cultural radicalism. There is a book that remains to be written tracing the history of the relationships among and the traffic between political and cultural radicals. At some points in history they seem to have been able to make common cause for a while. At other points they bitterly diverge. Sometimes those who begin as cultural radicals drift by the logic of their lives into revolutionary political commitments; at other times those who begin as political radicals lose their commitments to revolutionary action and devote their energies to personal liberation, cultivate odd private gardens, or innovate in one or another cultural sphere— all the while adjusting and accommodating their convictions to the contemporary conditions they must face (as this book and this very paragraph will be said by some to be doing).

The mutual disdain of the hippies and the New Left after their paths began to diverge was paralleled more than 150 years earlier by the mutual disdain between the cultural radicals of bohemian Paris and the St. Simonians, whose revolutionary ambitions were broader and more politically programmatic.[7] Their "need" for each other is hinted at by Herbert Marcuse's argument that unless revolutions are carried out simultaneously at both the political level and the more intimate levels of personal "life style," they are likely to fail or to boomerang or to be co-opted since the hippies may be crushed at any moment by the power of the state (or absorbed by its institutions), and the Left has a tendency to turn puritanical, ruthless, or authoritarian if political power is transferred without corresponding cultural changes and personal "liberations."[8]

The marriage of the politically and culturally radical impulses is difficult to sustain for many reasons, which ordinary democratic politicians, faced with gathering majority coalitions, know a lot about. But one important reason unique to radical movements is that each has a tendency toward typical excesses, which go in different directions. The politically radical excess is represented by terrorism, which is "excessive" not because I think so but because (short of overt civil war) it usually goes beyond what even a radical political constituency is willing to support.[9] The culturally revolutionary excess is represented by anarchic and anomic craziness, which trails off into a variety of forms of *ressentiment*, freakiness, personal derangement, hospitalizable insanity, and suicide, all of which alienate parts of *its* potential constituency.

7. A similar phenomenon may be seen in the relationships of Greenwich Village "bohemians" and the International Workers of the World (IWW) just before World War I. See the account by Robert Humphrey in *Children of Fantasy* (New York: John Wiley, 1978).

8. Herbert Marcuse, *Counterrevolution and Revolt* (Boston: Beacon Press, 1972). There is a sense in which the New Left and the counterculture *competed* for the allegiance of youth. In my view the New Left suffered its sharp decline in the early 1970s not primarily (as some have argued) because of economic recession and the end of the Viet Nam War, but because it gradually became clear that "alternative life styles" were going to be tolerated (perhaps even co-opted) by Establishments but that political revolutionaries were going to be harassed or worse.

9. There is also the tendency to exaggerate the size of the constituency because of the geographically concentrated character of radical actions—the "today Berkeley, tomorrow Dubuque" phenomenon.

But each of these excesses is also founded on an important partial truth, which is a source of such strength as they have. The terrorist excess seems to be founded on the insight that ruling classes will not generally relinquish their power and privilege peacefully, and that urban industrial democracies are particularly vulnerable to commercial or industrial sabotage and other guerilla activities that attempt to bring business as usual to a halt, to polarize the political center, produce a political and economic crisis, and hence generate the possibility of civil war. But for political radicals to become professional revolutionaries or active terrorists, radical changes may be required in their sensibility and in the "humane values" that may have led some of them to a radical vision to begin with.

The culturally revolutionary excess is founded on the insight that a revolution is not completed by the capture of economic institutions and political power; a revolution is not radically complete until it goes to the root—until, that is, profound changes are wrought in tacit cognitive, moral, and esthetic premises or categories, in the largely taken-for-granted folkways they generate, and in the modalities of feeling they induce, which, willy-nilly, can trap political radicals (regardless of their *political* success) into "reproducing" the dominant culture.[10] Like the insights of political radicalism, which produce their own distinctive "excesses," cultural radicalism too may require "outrageous" violations of extant canons of "decency" or "common sense" (notice how the quotation marks help undermine the taken-for-granted character of these concepts and hence make them more vulnerable to challenge) as cultural radicals become reflexively aware of how deeply socialized some of these conceptions are, how effectively they may obstruct personal liberation, and how difficult they are to overcome.

10. On the reproduction of culture, see Pierre Bordieu and Jean-Claude Passeron, *Reproduction in Education, Society and Culture* (Beverly Hills, Calif.: Sage Publications, 1977), particularly for its discussion of the ways in which French higher education reproduces elitism regardless of the efforts of Marxists to radicalize it. See also Alain Touraine, *The Self-Production of Society* (Chicago: University of Chicago Press, 1977).

Given these difficulties of avoiding the inadvertent reproduction of culture, some cultural radicals have seen their true task as "mind-blowing": the transformation of bad taste into good, vice into virtue, ungainliness into grace, in ways that may drive them to the very edge of (and over) the abyss of derangement. Indeed, one of the features of a culturally radical perspective over the past decade has been to challenge as culturally oppressive the very criteria that define insanity.

MIND-BLOWING: THE DESOCIALIZATION OF SENSIBILITY

Both political and cultural radicalism, then, contain dialectically related insights and excesses that can lead to outrageous violations of sensibility.[11] The ubiquity of the term "mind-blowing" in the vocabulary of the counterculture catches some of the importance its adherents attach to achieving changes in consciousness and sensibility. First used primarily to refer to powerful drug experiences that radically altered cognition, perception, and feeling, the term was gradually broadened in common usage to include a variety of experiences that shook up one's ordinary psychology and that, in "blowing one's mind," exposed some layers and corners of consciousness rarely otherwise seen, and revealed some of the tacit assumptions on which one's ordinary organization of understanding was based.[12]

Mind-blowing is, in a sense, the desocialization of sensibility, and the apparent frequency with which it could be ac-

11. The outraged public response to "The Armory Show," the first major exhibition of post-impressionist painting in the U.S., reveals some of the potentially hostile consequences of violating esthetic sensibility. See Humphrey's discussion in *Children of Fantasy*.

12. While this was going on in the popular culture, it was also going on at more elevated levels in the universities—where Kuhn's work in the history and sociology of science undermined the certainties of "normal science" by revealing that they were sustained by the (largely unstated) norms of scientific communities—and where "cognitive" psychology, sociology, and anthropology "blew minds" by revealing some of the unsuspected ways in which language and meta-culture affect ordinary consciousness.

complished in some parts of the counterculture (group sex, comfortable nudity among strangers, the devaluation of privacy, religious rebirths) was itself mind-blowing, for we have been taught that socialization is powerful indeed, and the depths to which it reaches may be inaccessible to deliberate attempts to alter it. We know, for example, that people socialized to dietary laws may experience real nausea at the prospect of eating forbidden foods, that women and men socialized to traditional sexual morality may experience real impotence or frigidity with sexually forbidden others, and that attempts to deal with such problems may take years of psychiatry and still not be successfully solved. Is it surprising, then, to find communards blithely going about "turning their heads around" by violating deeply socialized rules about child-rearing and age-grading and coupling and sexual possessiveness, and preparing for apocalypse by elevating bare survival into a major moral triumph at a time when it is no longer problematic for most Americans?

It is not so surprising if one remembers with what apparent impunity norms of sensibility and feeling have been violated in recent years and how quickly some of these modalities of consciousness may be resocialized. I can remember how shocked I was the first time I saw a visibly pregnant woman ignore the norm that "required" her to drape her bulging body in discreet "maternity clothes." It now seems unexceptionable to me, and I presume I am far from alone. Twenty-five years ago pop singers like Joe Cocker, Rod Stewart, or Patti Smith would not only have been regarded as not *good* singers, but as not singers at all (at least among white people); larynx surgery rather than concert tours and record contracts would have been recommended to them. In this short period the esthetics of the ear have been resocialized to hear the harsh and guttural sounds they emit as beautiful, at least for the millions who buy their records (although not for Herbert Marcuse and some other cultural radicals, whose tastes remain rooted in European *haute bourgeois* culture). When the use of "Ms." and other nonsexist language was introduced fewer than ten years ago, linguistic conservatives objected to the barbarity of the usage ("chairperson," "spokesperson," etc.), which they found offensive to the music and rhythm of the language. For many (although still far from all) the ear has been resocialized to "hear" such usage as normal. Despite recent legal reactions against "gay rights," public displays of homosexual affection are offensive to far fewer sensibilities (varying, of course, from place to place) than they were in the recent past.

All these events involve varying degrees and intensities of mind-blowing, and all of them utilize reservoirs of deliberate ideological work to accomplish their resocializations: the pregnant body is not shameful but beautiful; the harsh sounds and words of Rod Stewart offer antidotes of passion, urgency, and realism to the bland and soothing pieties of a Perry Como; language is culture, and the language of sexism confirms women in their subordinate status; and so on.

But mind-blowing takes more than consciousness raising or other forms of ideological work; if it didn't, discrepancies between beliefs and feelings would be less widespread than they seem to be, and the ideological disavowal of the honorableness of jealousy would be sufficient to exorcise suffering from it. In addition to ideological work, the desocialization of sensibility requires the presence of circumstances (either inadvertently extant or deliberately controlled) that induce or enforce ritual *enactments*, appropriately sanctioned or reinforced, which may then be productive of the feelings that feeling-rules (i.e., ideology) assert as proper or desirable and hence *re*productive of a culture, extant or incipient.

TEACHING, TRAINING, CIRCUMSTANCE, AND SENSIBILITY

The ways in which this process works are similar, regardless of whether examples are drawn from relatively intimate microinteraction or from macroinstitutional processes involving large numbers of people. At the microlevel they range from the relatively unmysterious ways in which Howard Becker describes novice marihuana users learning to identify drug highs and experience them as pleasurable[13] to the ways in which the position of the hands when a male takes the hand of his girl friend induces in the male feelings of dominance, protectiveness, and possessiveness that are lost when, as feminists are happy to show, the positions of the hands are reversed.[14]

Although these examples of the relationship between circumstance, enactment, and feeling involve relatively minute interactions, the forms in which they occur are similar in more abstractly and comprehensively structured *rites de passages*, in which initiations into desired new statuses may require "tests" of skill, endurance, knowledge, loyalty, or other values, which tests examine the readiness of candidates to cast off old sensibilities (as well as old behavior) for new ones. Novice nuns, for example, are not only taught to *behave* with humility but are also *trained* to *feel* humble by being required, when passing through a corridor, to walk with one shoulder brushing a wall rather than stride down the center of the passageway, although why this should induce feelings of humility (try it, you'll see that it does) may be mysteriously biosocial indeed.[15]

In established institutions that are part of a society's dominant culture, the reproduction as well as the transformation of sensibility is facilitated (although not always easily or successfully) by the relatively uncontested controls exercised by institutions over *teaching* (ideology or "indoctrination"), *training* (ritual enactment), and the circumstances in which both take place. It seems plain enough that societies and their major institutions (so long as they *are* societies and major institutions) are successful far more often than not at inducing their members not only to behave properly but also to *want* to behave properly and to feel virtuous or otherwise gratified for having done so. Religious institutions induce awe and reverence and piety in their communicants; nations induce pa-

---

13. Howard S. Becker, "Becoming a Marihuana User," in his *Outsiders* (New York: The Free Press, 1963).

14. Erving Goffman, *Relations in Public* (New York: Basic Books, 1971).

15. Katherine Hulme, *The Nun's Story* (Boston: Little, Brown, 1956).

triotism and pride in ethnicity; families induce feelings of warmth and intimacy and loyalty.

It is probably more difficult for major institutions deliberately to alter culture and sensibility than to reproduce them, but it is far more difficult still when such changes are attempted by politically or culturally radical groups that lack support from the general institutional culture and the power to command the requisite controls over teaching, training, and circumstance.

In orthodox Marxist theory, for example, overcoming "bourgeois mentality" requires revolutionary "praxis." Since existence determines consciousness, changes in consciousness require not only ideology but also radical ruptures in the routine *lived experiences* that shape consciousness: go south with the civil rights movement and experience the meaning of being treated as a nigger; participate in strikes, demonstrations, or civil disobedience and experience what it means to have the police withdraw the routine courtesies middle-class people expect from them; more, experience the terror of fleeing in panic before the billy stick of a cop in full riot gear with his blood up. Become a terrorist yourself; assassinate class enemies, bomb their establishments; burn your psychological bridges to the old sensibility so that you have vital interests in eradicating the old residues of restraint and guilt and shame, and in developing the kind of consciousness that enables you to feel that you have acted "correctly" and done right.

What political radicals try to accomplish (not always successfully or permanently) through institutional political praxis, cultural radicals try to accomplish by "inappropriate" behaviors that violate the more informal folkways or mores; such behavior aims to make problematic (hence weaken) the sometimes unexamined assumptions that help perpetuate cultural rules by *demonstrating* that they can be violated with some impunity: smoke marihuana publicly; come out of the closet; stop using underarm deodorant; flaunt your overweightness; don't shave (don't shave your legs); have an open affair with someone thirty years older (or younger) than you; wear a flag; ceremonialize the public destruction of your television set; buy no Christmas presents; ask what the Super

Bowl is; take the door off the bathroom; watch your spouse have sexual intercourse with someone else; organize your own Woodstock; have a "conversion experience."

But like terrorism, mind-blowing can be counterproductive. The internalizing of shame, guilt, or disgust may be deeper than one thought, and the resources for overcoming them may not be present. Although norms may be weak, sanctions can still be strong; and fear of sanctions or the anticipation of anomie and moral chaos can be compelling. You may be shunned if you consistently flaunt your overweightness or smell sweaty; you can lose your job if you come out of the closet; being chased by a cop or a racist mob can scare the hell out of you and discourage your participation in further demonstrations.

Although social scientists know a good bit about socialization (the ways in which appropriate behavior is learned), internalization (the process by which culture is transmitted to cognition, perception, and emotion) is still largely a black box about which cognitive and experimental approaches in social psychology have taught us a little, but it is also a process about which there seems to be considerable ambivalence about knowing more. The prospect of knowing how to induce given states of consciousness evokes the bugaboo of "brainwashing," taps fears of psychological "manipulation," and threatens belief (illusion or not) in the moral autonomy of individual consciousness. China's "Great Cultural Revolution" tapped such fears in the West (to say nothing of what the Red Guards did to its unwilling victims in China), and such fears have been overt in the hostile reception by many to behavior modification programs, the Skinnerian psychology of "reinforcement," and the sociological theory of sanctions on which such programs are based.[16]

At the same time it seems plain enough that these fears are rooted in a deeper fear: that it may indeed be possible to

16. See the review symposium on Skinner's *Beyond Freedom and Dignity*, in *Contemporary Sociology* (November 1972). See also John Finley Scott, *Internalization of Norms* (Englewood Cliffs, N.J.: Prentice-Hall, 1971), for an integration of Skinnerian psychology with a sociological theory of sanctions.

"manipulate" feeling deliberately; and that given a *desire* to alter one's own state of consciousness (and an inability to accomplish it autonomously or through "will power"), people may willingly (even eagerly) submit themselves to "behavior mod" programs to overcome, say, an addiction to excessive eating or to tobacco. Smoking and gluttony are surely bad habits, and the close study of their day-to-day reproduction can provide clues to their psychological organization and their cultural meanings, and therefore to the ways in which habit and desire may be altered. The legacy of *1984* is the apprehension that it may not be very far from public readiness to alter these bad habits to the readiness to alter vices like "bureaucratism," sexual inhibition, competitiveness, vanity, egoism, machismo, paternalism, and thoughtless spontaneity.

Although the evidence of how culture and sensibility are successfully reproduced provides clues to how they may be successfully altered, much of the success of institutions in relating teaching to training to circumstances in producing or reproducing appropriate consciousness or sensibility rests on the "natural" or taken-for-granted character of the association among ideology, enactment, setting, and experience. When these are understood as an "organic" unity, the experience of culture is not only mystified, but the mystery is also made to appear benign (as in many instances it is or may be). But when the curtain is drawn back and the Wizard of Oz is exposed at his control panel, manipulating atmosphere and frightening Dorothy and her none-too-brave companions half to death, not only is the Wizard revealed as a humbug, but Dorothy's innocent respect for mystery is betrayed, inadvertently liberating her rational anger and good sense. When, that is, the "organic" association of teaching, training, context, and consciousness is revealed as analytically separable (and therefore subject to deliberate, calculated intervention) an extra meta-variable is added to the mix.

In its objective dimension, Max Weber called this addend "the disenchantment of the world"; in its subjective dimension within individuals, we can think of it here as "reflexivity," or consciousness of induced consciousness, which complicates the relevance of teaching, training, and context to the internalization of culture.

REFLEXIVITY AND "LABELING" THEORY

Now, I have no wish to generalize the Oz phenomenon into a paranoid conspiracy theory. Fortunately or not, unanticipated consequences are ubiquitous, ironies are everywhere, know-how is imperfect, and most of us become exhausted before arriving at the heart of the mystery. But surely there are people out there very busily trying to get us to think and feel in one way or another. (I am trying to do it to you in this book, but I can't train you to hear my words as I hear them, and I don't control the circumstances in which you will read and respond to the words I write, although if I did, I would be sorely tempted to use those resources.) If knowledge is power and if power corrupts, most of us would likely already be puppets on some Big Wizard-Brother's string.[17] That may be one of the meanings of "ignorance is bliss." But for every blissful ignorance there is likely to be someone who thinks forewarned is forearmed. Clichés aside, conditioning is also ubiquitous, and reflexive awareness of that fact may constitute a weapon against it.[18] That possible resistance to conditioning may cast some light on why irony frequently seems to be the enemy of power—but not usually a very formidable enemy, because irony, apparently resistant to conditioning, probably functions more often than not to accommodate ironists to the conditioning they are in fact stuck with, rather than to alter conditions.

But reflexivity can also put one in a stronger position to choose the conditions that will condition one, which is what Skinner seems to mean by "freedom" and "dignity" and

17. There are, of course, those who think we already are, or are well on the way to becoming. See, for example, Herbert Marcuse, *One-Dimensional Man* (Boston: Beacon Press, 1964); see also Herbert Schiller, *The Mind Managers* (Boston: Beacon Press, 1973).

18. Skinner's sour attitudes toward "freedom" and "dignity" seem to rest on a popular conception of these values as referring to behavior that is, somehow, uncaused.

what Marxists used to mean by identifying freedom with the understanding of "necessity." Nevertheless, both recalcitrance to and choice of conditioning imply a decline of the belief in the *autonomy* of feeling,[19] and therefore an increased *interest* in the relations between conditioning and consciousness.

That interest, however, is politically *ambiguous* because it can just as easily promote "conservative" or "radical" consequences. Taught that helping a slave escape was a crime and a sin against God, Huckleberry Finn, upon reflection, decides that he will go to hell if necessary to help Nigger Jim escape. But Eliza Doolittle's transformation from Cockney flower girl into a "lady" is incomplete because Professor Higgins doesn't "treat her like a lady," thus leaving her in a kind of cultural limbo or anomie. Similarly, the efforts by communards to control their own contexts and training to make their teaching (ideology) more effective in radically blowing minds is balanced by the restorational efforts of other, perhaps formerly "alienated," people to turn their heads around by reintegrating themselves with powerful socializing institutions from which they may have become estranged—as in the reclamation through religious conversion of formerly burned-out or strung-out hippies, or in the practice of secularized and assimilated Jews rediscovering their ethnic and religious traditions, or in lapsed Catholics reembracing faith and ritual, or in formerly liberal or socialist critics of American capitalism rediscovering the value of corporate enterprise, inequality, and the traditional family.

One doesn't have to subscribe to "labeling theory"[20] to see labeling processes operating here. Huck Finn accepts being negatively labeled as a sinner and a candidate for hell; he has a freaky little subculture to support him. Eliza discovers that consciousness is historical: She may be a "lady" to many, but the security of that new identity depends on the way she is

---

19. That "choice" itself may, in some theoretical sense, be conditioned need not detain us here. I am interested here in a phenomenological account of reflexive responses to the awareness of conditioned consciousness.

20. On labeling theory, see Becker, *Outsiders*.

treated by others, and that treatment is uneven. She "is" not only what she eats (Professor Higgins's lady-training) but what she ate (Cockney), and her future is uncertain because it contains both her past and her present, and the past *in* the present. Similarly, reborn Jesus Freaks, neo-conservatives, Jews, and Catholics may be understood in part as reacting against attempts at negative labeling that characterize their pre-rebirth identities in such contemptuous terms as "freak," "ethnic disavower," "rootless nihilist," "ideologically bankrupt liberal," "relativist," and so on.[21]

I raise these issues here because I had to deal with strong labeling experiences during the commune research. In reflecting on my research experience at The Ranch and in attempting to sort out my relationship to the people there (and to others with whom I necessarily came into contact), I found that much of my own ambivalent or multivalent behavior while I was involved with the research was in part a response to my spasmodic awareness (now sharp, now dim) of the labeling influences that were operating on me. I mean not simply the specific pressures of getting the work done (inducing people to talk with me, coping with anti-research attitudes, etc.), but also my awareness of how the very processes of sustaining my research association with the counterculture evoked labeling actions (both positive and negative) from others who attempted to tell me "who" I was and how I should feel. Let me provide some sharp examples of the process:

1. *The Grocery Store Incident.* One day in the middle of the research at The Ranch, I drove into town with Maxwell, Abe, a few of the children, and a load of dirty laundry. On the way back from the launderette, we stopped in the village at the

21. Of course, the reaction against negative labeling attempts may be not only to disavow them, but, like Huck Finn, to affirm them. It always seemed to me, for example, that the work of liberal sociologists like S.M. Lipset, Nathan Glazer, and Daniel Bell was *addressed* primarily to the Left, but that their rejection by the "new" Left and their stigmatization as enemies of the Left *confirmed* them gradually in their new identities as "conservatives." Like Huck Finn, who proudly affirmed his labeled identity as "sinner," they affirmed theirs as "neo-conservatives."

grocery store owned by the National Rifle Association member. His eleven- or twelve-year-old daughter was at the cash register behind the counter at the front of the store. While Max and Abe went to gather up a few items, I asked the girl for a package of True cigarettes. She looked behind her at the cigarette-display rack but couldn't find any Trues. Then my eye lighted on a boxful of packages of candy cigarettes lying on the counter. Pointing to the candy (and thinking of the children waiting in the car), I said, "well, if you don't have any True cigarettes, give me a pack of False cigarettes." The joke fell flat; it apparently frightened her, and she ran to the back of the store to get her father, who came forward with an angry stride and ordered us filthy hippies out of his store.

2. *The Car-Rental Incident.* One of my commune visits was to an extremely isolated group that lived in an old abandoned mining camp in the wilds of the Trinity Alps in the extreme north of California, about forty miles from the nearest paved road. I made this journey in a rented car. The last several miles of the harrowing trip to this commune entailed a series of hairpin turns up a mountain on a "road" that was hardly more than a rocky path full of patches of melting snow, with yawning precipices on the down side. After finally reaching the commune, I discovered an oil leak under the car, and further investigation revealed a punctured oil pan. One of the local communards helped repair it by cutting a wedge out of a block of wood, widening the puncture somewhat, and jamming the wedge into the crack. If I were careful, he said, the pan would hold enough oil to get me back to the rental agency without damaging the engine. The wedge held, the oil pressure remained normal, but when I returned the car to the rental agency and reported the cracked oil pan, the rental agent became angry and abusive, insisting that an accident report be filled out. His abusiveness may have been partly a result of the fact that I looked rather scruffy after a few days in the wilderness: dusty, unshaven, unclean, unslept. In filling out the accident report, he asked for my employer's name. When I answered "the University of California," a contemptuous smirk spread across his face, as if the nature of my

employment explained what he took to be my irresponsibility in damaging the car. "What department, *philosophy?*" he asked, with dripping sarcasm. "No," I said. "Political *science?*" he inquired further, still dripping. "No, sociology," I said. "It figures!" he said triumphantly. As he got more abusive I decided to drop my composure, and told him that I was sorry about the car but I was in no mood to take any shit from him. When I rented the car I had told the agent about the unpaved roads I expected to travel, and I had bought the maximum insurance anticipating the possibility of something like this happening. We were both angry by then, and we might have come to blows had not the local cop on the beat walked in out of the rain to have a cup of coffee.

3. *The Mexican Border Incident.* I took a short respite from the field research in the spring of 1971 to become Visiting Professor at the University of California in San Diego. One warm, windy Saturday late in the spring, a young woman friend and I decided to drive to Tijuana, spend the afternoon shopping, and have dinner. As we approached the border gate in my white convertible with its top down, I noticed that a Mexican border guard was searching the trunk of the car immediately in front of mine. The search reminded me that I had recently read that Mexico had tightened its border inspections because of drug trafficking. When the search was done and the car was waved on, I pulled forward and was halted by the guard. I was wearing shorts and sandals and a light jacket with its hood up over my head and tied with a drawstring against the wind. The guard came over, stood beside the car, and very deliberately said "Lemme see your hair." Instantly, I realized that he would think that the hood was over my head to hide my long hair. I was right. When he saw my hair, he smiled thinly and, making circular gestures with his arm, told me that I would have to turn around and go back. This is ridiculous, I thought; "there must be some mistake," I harrumphed. I was no hippie drug smuggler going to a rendezvous with his source of supply. I was a middle-aged professor going to lay a few innocent tourist dollars on the Mexican economy. I asked the guard if I could speak to someone in authority. He rested his hands lightly on

his gunbelt and said just a little ominously that *he* was the authority, and repeated with finality that I would have to turn around and go back. I did. I stopped at a San Diego police office at the border, told a sergeant what had happened, and asked if the matter could be straightened out. I got a lecture instead. The sergeant informed me that the Mexican border guards were under direct orders from what he called "El Presidente" to stop any suspicious-looking characters. The guard's authority was final, he told me. Then he said "that's the way it is in a revolutionary government [apparently referring to the Mexican revolution and the name of Mexico's dominant political party]; there's no appeal. And as bad as Mexico is, Russia's worse." Pausing then, he added "and Czechoslovakia is even worse than Russia." And if I were a professor, he advised me, I ought to tell my students about such matters. And that if I didn't want to be mistaken for an undesirable character (he said, looking me up and down), I ought not to look like one.

4. *The Escape from the FBI.* Manfred was the first communard from The Ranch I ever met. A muscular man, then in his late twenties, he was one of the communards working on The Ranch's access road when I first visited with the Medical Clinic team in 1970. One Saturday in Berkeley, I ran into Manfred and three friends of his with whom I was unacquainted and I invited the group to have a drink with me at my house. While we were there talking, one of Manfred's friends telephoned his own apartment in Berkeley and was told by his roommate that a telephone message had been left there for Manfred by one of the communards from The Ranch informing him that The Ranch had been visited by agents from the FBI looking for Manfred, and that unless he was ready to be picked up, it seemed wise for him not to return to The Ranch. A Viet Nam veteran, Manfred had been arrested for possession of narcotics (a couple of years previously at Logan Airport in Boston) on his return from the war. He had jumped bail in Massachusetts and headed for California, where he had lived peacefully for some time at The Ranch. The discussion, following the news that he had been traced, considered several plans for his escape. The four of them de-

cided that Manfred's best course was to be driven into the
Sierra, where he, an experienced woodsman and backpacker,
could pick up the John Muir Trail and walk to refuge in
Canada. There were at least a couple of important decisions
for me to make. First, I was faced with deciding whether I
would assent to providing aid and shelter to a fugitive. The
prospect made me uneasy, but it seemed hardly conceivable
for me to refuse. Manfred had been kind and helpful to me in
the initial period of the research, and I was fond of him. He
had been foolish to jump bail on what could have turned out
to be a minor charge, but it seemed equally foolish to advise
him to turn himself back in to the legal machinery. He was an
outlaw in any case, far better suited to surviving in the primitive reaches of the counterculture than to defending himself
in court. His plan was to become a fisherman on the northern
coast of British Columbia—something, it seemed to me, better than the paltry legal help toward which I might have di-
rected him, and far better than a stretch in prison at public
expense. But the plans were not simple to arrange. There was
the matter of finding a car and a driver, of checking the routes
and the probable weather, and of gathering the necessary
equipment. The time it took for these problems to emerge and
the time it was apparently going to take to solve them presented me with my second decision. I had appointments that
were going to keep me busy that evening and most of the
following day, and I suddenly found myself apprehensive
about leaving these people (three of whom I didn't know at
all, and one not really very well) and whomever else they
might round up, headquartered in my small cottage to plan
the great escape. As I reflected upon it, the apprehension
seemed increasingly mean, given the emergency and given
their apparent assumption that I was one of *them*, a friend
who could be trusted. There wasn't much in my house worth
worrying about being ripped-off, and I had no reason to believe that this was a realistic prospect. Strangers-in-
inadvertent-possession-of-my-castle: *that* was the issue; turf,
mine. I told them to feel free to use the house, where things
were that they might need, said I'd be back as soon as I could,
wished them good luck, and left. I returned the next evening

and they were still there, although just getting ready to leave, the arrangements having been set. I gave Manfred an old Marine Corps tank jacket of mine, a twenty dollar bill, and a vigorous embrace, and sent him on his way. A few months later I received in the mail an audiotape cassette from a little town on the British Columbia coast, containing a long oral "letter" from Manfred, recounting his adventures, describing the fishing boat he worked on, and his accumulating savings toward the purchase of his own boat. Manfred returned to the locale of The Ranch (although not to the commune) about three-and-a-half years later, his legal difficulties settled, and went to work as equipment manager for a local rock band (and bouncer at their concerts). When I saw him last, early in 1976, he was sitting in a cafe in town with three handsome women doting on his charm. I remember it clearly, because the story does not have a happy ending. Later that year, Manfred died of gunshot wounds inflicted by a local notable in a fight over money allegedly owed.

The first three incidents exemplify labeling processes that surely *could* have confirmed me in my identity and consciousness as a "hippie." I was not only negatively stereotyped and ritually degraded, but these actions were undertaken by persons whom I was ideologically prepared to counterstereotype, and for which counterlabeling I could count on subcultural support. It was easy enough to write off the grocery-store owner as a Neanderthal (and his unaccountably frightened daughter as a victim of his brutality), and we did exactly that and had a good rueful laugh about the incident with the other communards at The Ranch when we returned. It was easy enough for me to neutralize the contempt of the car-rental agent by counterlabeling him as a frustrated college graduate in a low-paying, dead-end job, acting out his resentments against the University of California (much in the headlines in those days)—especially in contrast to the sensible, practical problem solving by the auto mechanic at the remote commune. It was easy enough to see the absurdity of the bumbling, quasi-military mentality of the Mexican border guard and the San Diego police sergeant, whose stupid intransigence could confirm "our" superior moral status and rationality against "their" dumb rigidities.

The fourth story is a sort of reversal of this labeling process. In this case, I was also labeled, but the labeling was flattering rather than degrading; it was assumed that I was one of them and that I would do what I could to help. Indeed I did do what I could, but like the second and third incidents, in which I used such respectable middle-class resources as I could command to resist the negative labeling, I did not entirely identify myself with the four near-strangers planning the great escape in my house. In fact, although I was not aware of it then, I sometimes wonder: did I help Manfred escape from the FBI to strengthen my then-fragile credentials with The Ranch? I may never know the answer to that question, but it is a real question because it is certain that the communards at The Ranch trusted me more after the escape than they did before.

Such processes of labeling and counterlabeling are "normal" in human interaction, and persons normally respond to them with gestures that avow or disavow the label. Ambivalent or contradictory responses (such as I now and then affected) are also not uncommon toward efforts at labeling; but a *reflexive* response goes beyond these by attempting to make the labeling process itself problematic, and hence to evade the reification of identity.

If reification is labeling writ large and abstract, labeling at the level of concrete human interaction is the attempt to fix an identity (and its appropriately positive or negative feelings) on persons who, having biographies as well as present roles in situations that have histories as well as (more or less temporary) extant "structures," are always more complex than any identity or label can allow. People, of course, may use their accumulated biographical resources and their knowledge of history to disavow or otherwise resist the simplified labels that we all attempt to impose on others to reify meaning and thus sustain our fragile sense of social order. But the resources to bring this off successfully are stratified, like other cultural resources; and reflexive consciousness of the ways in which the labeling process induces feeling can render the feeling itself problematic, therefore increasing somewhat our resources for sustaining the sense of our own complexity by transforming sensibility into *induced* sensibility, that is, from subject into object, or resource into topic.

This is not an *argument* for introspection; I want to *demonstrate* something. If it seems excessively abstract, I can make it concrete by describing what I did to cope with influences that I was *aware* were bearing upon me. After one or another particularly illuminating research experience at The Ranch, for example, I often had the impulse to flee the scene to plusher or more familiar surroundings (and sometimes did—to the town library or a good local restaurant), not merely to make field notes before the observations and experience faded from memory, but also to consider their meaning *in a context relatively insulated from the influence of the commune itself.* I needed that insulation to counteract forces that were having a strong impact on my feelings, feelings I had no wish to deny but only to control and understand. (I liked these people, disliked those; felt warm and comfortable with this experience, but isolated and threatened by that one. *Why* did I?)

Sometimes, after a period of research in the field, I would drive back to the city and instead of going home to my empty house, I would go directly to the then-new Hyatt Regency Hotel in San Francisco. While the feel and smell of the commune were still fresh in my senses, I would stand in the Hyatt Regency's seventeen-story lobby, drink at one of its chic bars, and think about which of these two evocative symbols of culture represented the future: the commune, with its kerosene lamps, its outhouse, its organic gardens, its odors of perspiration, greasy jeans, and fresh bread, its canning, cheese making, apple picking, egg gathering, goat milking, and its solemn familism; or the Hyatt, with its soaring, stunning lobby, its ivy-hung balconies, its indoor trees and fountains, its gallery-like lounges, its fashionable promenaders, and its silent and ornate glass elevators, like imperial dumbwaiters, lifting and lowering their cargoes of tourists from the delights of the lobby floor to the delights of its revolving top-floor lounge.[22]

22. See the evocative analysis of the Hyatt-Regency by Todd Gitlin, "Domesticating Nature," in *Theory and Society* (September 1979).

In retrospect, I think my doing that was a way of symboliz-
ing in extreme terms two of the worlds I was living in: hippie
communes and the upper-middle-class cosmopolitan world
of a senior professor at the University of California. But more
than that, it was a way of attempting to balance or neutralize
the powerful effects of the commune on my consciousness, *as
if I dimly understood that I needed mixed and contradictory conditions of reinforcement to retain a hold on my impulse to protect the
full biographical complexity of my own sensibility* (for analytic
purposes?—that would be nice ideological work), against
the labeling forces attempting to circumscribe it within a simplified role.

There are some who may argue that my resistance (by attempting to render the labeling process itself reflexively problematic) to identifying myself fully with the labels that were
thrust upon me virtually guaranteed my inability to achieve a
full phenomenological understanding of the experience of
those with respect to whom I was reluctant to identify myself
fully. There may be some truth in that; it may be that that kind
of understanding requires the "surrender" of one's precious
ego to the demands of a group that offers or imposes "membership." But I do not think it is the whole truth. "Surrender"
is a momentary act whose consequences are incalculable, and
an act of "surrender" does not wipe out biography or history.
"Phenomenological" understanding always occurs from the
point of view of a surrenderer conditioned by his or her own
past. Besides, phenomenological understanding was never
one of my major aims; those aims were more modest: an
ethnography of ideas and a sociology of them.

Others may argue that this preoccupation with myself
exemplifies one form of contemporary narcissism, one of the
more unfortunate residues of the failures of "the sixties."[23]
There is no doubt some truth in that too, but again I do not
think it is the whole truth. Becoming aware of the historically
and circumstantially induced character of one's own sensibil-

23. For recent criticisms of contemporary narcissism, see Richard Sennett,
The Fall of Public Man (New York: Vintage Books, 1975); and Christopher
Lasch, *The Culture of Narcissism* (New York: W. W. Norton, 1978).

ity requires some reflexivity about that fact, not simply for individuals to maintain a practical sense of their own abstract "freedom," but for ethnographers to maintain a practical sense that the inferences and interpretations they make from their research were not predictable from the start (given an unreflexive sensibility) and therefore banal. Reflexivity requires an "I," and no apologies for the first person are needed, unless the reflexivity turns up nothing fresh—in which instance the pejorative "narcissistic" is surely deserved.

Nearly thirty years ago David Riesman introduced the idea of "other-direction" to refer to a then-emerging "character structure" driven not by a firm sense of moral rectitude internalized early in childhood, but by a heightened sensitivity to the expectations of others, which could not be taken for granted.[24] Riesman seemed less than sanguine about other-direction at the time (surely it was not his favorite character structure) because he associated it with a kind of cynical relativism, with a desire for "conformity," with a nihilistic readiness to manipulate the ambiguities of situations to one's own advantage—and with a loss of that firmness of moral character that he identified with the "inner-direction" of an earlier era.

Because of his genuine concern for moral priorities (which has characterized much of his work since *The Lonely Crowd*), Riesman may not have been entirely aware that his own conception of other-direction necessarily implied the diffusion of an increased capacity for what George H. Mead called "role taking," a projective or imaginative psychological device that, in Mead's theorizing, was an essential building block of minds, selves, and societies. Using one's psychological "antenna" (as Riesman called it) to intuit the expectations of others is a talent of imaginative *attention* whose growth and diffusion Riesman understood as an instance of psychological adaptation to an emerging social structure: urban heterogeneity brings persons into routine contact with groups whose folkways and mores are unfamiliar, and more people must

24. David Riesman *et al.*, *The Lonely Crowd* (New Haven: Yale University Press, 1951).

develop greater sensitivity to the expectations of more such others if gaucheries and serious unintended conflict are to be minimized in the conduct of cosmopolitan social life.

Despite the real dangers that Riesman saw in other-direction, it seems plain enough that the ubiquity of that phenomenon is a measure of the increase in what Mead saw as a distinctively human (and social) skill that, like any increase in human skill or power, is fraught with mixed moral potential. Surely it can (and did) create little Machiavellis on every street corner and in every office. But it also gave us the high ironies that have dominated modern art in the generation since Riesman wrote. I understand "reflexivity" as a psychological step or two beyond other-direction and role taking because its distinctive preoccupation is with making those processes problematic; it attempts to cope with one's own consciousness of the consequences of other-direction and role taking in oneself. If other-direction could produce a banal Machiavelliism, reflexivity has surely produced banal narcissism. But it can also produce (as oriental theology knew) an ego so bored with itself that it just might approach that dream-ideal of social science: the utterly detached observer.

In sociology, theoretical preoccupation with reflexivity has raised the ghost of infinite regress. Once one unlocks the Pandora's box of reflexivity, the demons of receding mirrors and infinite self-reflection jump out. But I think that, like "the relativist dilemma," "the problem of infinite regress" is *merely* theoretical. In fact, reflexive thinkers tend to become tired or exhausted by the regression of their own reflexivity. It loses interest to all but mystics and solipsists beyond two or three regressive steps, as it reaches the point of diminishing intellectual returns. Moreover, these dangers are reduced by the tendency of egos to become exhausted by their self-absorption, and this exhaustion can produce an almost ethereally detached researcher, one as ego free as it is possible for Western flesh to imagine.

Am I doing ideological work here? I surely am. Do these arguments seem self-serving for the kind of book I have written? They surely do. But one of those arguments is that the fact that this is the case should not necessarily impugn the case I have made.

APPENDIX: ETHNOGRAPHIC METHODS

It has taken me a long time to gain the perspective on beliefs and circumstances adopted in this book, and my failure to apprehend it earlier has functioned as a kind of bit in my mouth, preventing me from speaking clearly. I was simply reluctant to take what I had found in the communes and submit that data to the kind of "cynical" analysis suggested by the examples from Raymond Aron and Eric Hoffer in Chapter 6. In his enormously affecting play *Equus*, Peter Shaffer uses horses as a Christ symbol and the "sharp chains" in the horses' mouths as a metaphor for Christ's agonies. Much of the dramatic impact of the play is projected by Shaffer's psychiatrist-protagonist who is tormented by the feeling that, by relieving the equicidal obsession of his seriously disturbed adolescent patient, he is destroying the boy's deepest passions, his capacity "to worship," as the psychiatrist puts it. And in the concluding lines of the play, the psychiatrist expresses his own doubts about the wholesomeness of his successful treatment of the boy (thus extending the redemption metaphor) by saying that the sharp chain is now in his own mouth, "and it will not come out."

The idea is not new. It was given poignant and resonant expression earlier in the forceful writing of the British psychiatrist Ronald Laing: the idea that schizophrenia might well be a morally ennobled mode of being, and that normal rationality was a kind of spirit death, a reluctant accommodation to the unbearability of a truly imaginative religious consciousness. The idea is present in milder form in Ken Kesey's popular novel *One Flew Over the Cuckoo's Nest* and in the cult film

223

King of Hearts. It is surely a romantic idea, and I have no wish to romanticize insanity. Even Shaffer shows some ambivalence about the idea: an attempt is made to comfort Shaffer's psychiatrist by the woman who brought the tormented boy to the tormented doctor's attention. She reminds him of his great skill in relieving the suffering of others; she points out that it was the boy's very energy of worship that drove him at a gallop into the suffering from which he sought relief. The psychiatrist is not comforted; for him it is precisely an individual's unique suffering that confers authentic identity.

PSYCHIATRY AND ETHNOGRAPHY

Does it seem bizarre to cite *Equus* in an attempt to explicate what is, after all, a conventional problem in ethnography: developing a perspective on field research data? Unlike Shaffer's psychiatrist, I am not a redeemer (sociologists offer no relief), tormented or otherwise, and unlike Laing, I am not a moral advocate of either end of the passion-reason polarity. But I cite the case of psychiatry in general, and Shaffer's psychiatrist in particular, because of the interesting contrasts between psychiatry and interpretive ethnography, and because of their relevance to current thinking about the latter.

When a psychiatrist's understanding of a patient's problem is different from the patient's own understanding, the psychiatrist's mode is likely to be regarded by all parties to the therapy as fuller, deeper, or otherwise containing greater insight, particularly if it produces relief from symptoms (Shaffer's psychiatrist is interesting in part because of his own doubts about this). Indeed, whatever the psychological theory used by the therapist, all parties to the treatment tend to assume that the theory provides psychiatrists with a system of clinical interpretation enabling them to understand the meaning of symptoms and hence undertake a therapy to relieve them. The patient's very presence in therapy may be taken as evidence of the probable superiority of that system of interpretation to the patient's own.

Contrast this situation with that of an interpretive ethnographer. Ethnographers trained in sociology or anthropology bring to their research on human communities theories (functionalist, structuralist, cognitive, Marxist, interactionist, etc.) that both orient their observations and provide a guide to the interpretation of them. But when an ethnographer's understanding of an observed community is different from the understanding of members of that community themselves, there is likely to be far less consensus that the ethnographer's understanding is fuller, deeper, richer with insight, and so on—particularly if the community has an opportunity to debate or rebut the ethnographer's report (to say nothing of a replication by another researcher).

Whereas psychiatrists and their audiences are likely to assume that a psychiatrist's understanding is likely to be "better" than a patient's, it would seem the height of arrogance for an ethnographer to say of a human group: "I understand them better than they understand themselves." Part of this difference, of course, lies in the different situations of the psychiatrist and the ethnographer. Psychiatry is a healing practice; ethnography is not. Psychiatry is usually practiced at the invitation of patients (or their families), and even when it is not, the patient is often in some visible pain or other difficulty "requiring" treatment and cooperation. Ethnography is usually initiated by the ethnographer, sometimes aggressively, sometimes among communities not eager to cooperate, sometimes not even aware that they are being studied, and without the extension of even an implicit promise by the ethnographer that the ethnography will help them in any demonstrable way.

But this is not the whole difference, for Shaffer's psychiatrist seems to be in the grip of an incipient loss of faith in the *value* of the therapy he offers; the cure, he fears, may be worse than the disease. And once the *plausibility* (never mind the truth) of this insight is granted, the consensus that a psychiatric understanding is better than a patient's own begins to come apart.

Despite the fact that social science is not a healing practice, it has not been without a consensual justification, which once provided social scientists and the people they study with a common sense of the value of what they were doing. The justification goes something like this: scientific research produces knowledge; knowledge is in the public interest (it is surely better than ignorance); it is the obligation of publics to cooperate in the acquisition of knowledge (for example to provide basic demographic data to a census taker). Challenges to this consensus (for example, the arguments that the knowledge acquired by social scientists is distorted, biased, misleading, or otherwise flawed; that it does not serve the public interest but serves some groups more than others; and that it may actually do harm to the researched) have produced a crisis among social scientists about the value of their work comparable to the crisis of Shaffer's psychiatrist. Whereas he has grave doubts about whether he is actually healing, we have grave doubts about whether we know what we claim to know and about whether that claim does any good or any harm, and to whom in what quantities.

ETHNOGRAPHIC PROBLEMS AND
METHODOLOGICAL REMEDIES
AS IDEOLOGICAL WORK

This crisis of conscience has produced a variety of attempts at methodological remedy, some of which bear mentioning here. One school of thought, intent upon assuring maximum empirical accuracy of reported data, proposes greater rigor in field research, from more carefully and immediately recorded field notes, to the quantification of observations, to the documentation of even the minutiae of interaction, sometimes by the use of audio and videotape in the attempt to gather as comprehensive and accurate a recording of data as is humanly possible.[1]

Phenomenological viewpoints go further by emphasizing the *inevitably* distorted character of ethnographic reporting

---

1. No one, insofar as I know, recommends lack of rigor in field methods (although there are those who argue "anti-methods"). John Lofland has been particularly zealous in his efforts to make traditionally "soft" sociology "harder." See, for example his *Doing Social Life* (New York: Wiley-Interscience, 1976), and *Analyzing Social Settings* (Belmont, Calif.: Wadsworth Publishing Co., 1971). See also, John M. Johnson, *Doing Field Research* (New York: The Free Press, 1975).

that analytically imposes on communities the alien conceptual categories, theories, and epistemologies of researchers (which orient their observations, order their analyses, and ground their truth claims) without due respect to the communities' own conceptual understanding of the meaning of its social practices.[2] Corrective actions include varieties of *Verstehen* or participation that encourage the researcher vicariously or actually to absorb the point of view (or consciousness) of the subject, and techniques that place the instruments of research into the hands of subjects (for example, giving *them* the video cameras) so that what they consider relevant may be recorded and understood.

Another proposed way of avoiding the imposition of alien or premature ideas which distort is for the ethnographer to adopt a *tabula rasa* approach by attempting to suspend the application of *any* theoretical frame, at least until the data themselves begin to generate some ideas.[3]

Finally, Marxist or "radical" viewpoints emphasize the ways in which researched groups are exploited by sociologists and anthropologists who use them, without recompense, for their own interests (like personal profit from royalties on published books or academic salary increases) or for paying the piper who funds the research by providing perhaps damaging information about these groups to officials, governments, or other institutions that may not wish them well. Corrective action for some radicals involves the abandonment of "positivist" or functionalist pretenses of detachment, neutrality, or objectivity (with built-in "elitist" or

2. For phenomenological approaches, see the essays collected in George Psathas, ed., *Phenomenological Sociology* (New York: Wiley, 1973). See also Alfred Schutz, *The Phenomenology of the Social World* (Evanston, Ill.: Northwestern University Press, 1967); and the collection of essays in memory of Schutz, *Phenomenology and Social Reality*, edited by Maurice Natanson (The Hague: Martinus Nijhoff, 1970). On the use of video in phenomenological research, see Bennetta Jules-Rosette and Beryl Bellman, *A Paradigm for Looking* (Norwood, N.J.: Ablex Publishing Corp., 1977).

3. Anselm Strauss and Barney Glaser, *The Discovery of Grounded Theory* (Chicago: Aldine Publishing Co., 1967).

administrative biases) in favor of roles as *advocates* for or
against the groups among whom they do research.[4]

In one or another way each of these departures is responding to the fact that the more traditional or "established"
modes of ethnography typical of the contexts in which researchers work have led them (like Shaffer's psychiatrist) in
directions that weakened their belief in the value of what they
were doing: to intellectual impasses, to cognitive problems
without apparent solution, to moral or political consequences
they were unwilling to accept. The desire for greater rigor in
ethnographic research responds to the *unreliable* status of
much ethnographic data (would another investigator report
the same finding?) in which the lines between ethnography
and investigative journalism are hard to draw.[5] And when
research that aspires to the status of "science" is described as
"journalistic," such description is a derogation that requires
ideological remedy. Doubts about the scientific propriety of
using theories developed in academic contexts to interpret
the life of a community that is being actively constructed or
"accomplished" every day in the behavior of its members is
responding to a variety of problems of *validity* in ethnographic
research. So too are doubts about the adequacy of survey
data and hurriedly taken notes in accurately rendering the
events they ostensibly describe. The search for greater validity involves attempts to make sure that reports accurately
record events that actually occurred, that events were not
"staged" for the benefit (deception) of the observer, that subtle linguistic codes and gestures are not misunderstood (and
the data they reveal lost between the gathering and the reporting); and it involves an effort to cite masses of data in

4. For a sampling of such views, see the collection of articles called *Radical
Sociology*, edited by J. David Colfax and Jack L. Roach (New York: Basic
Books, 1971). See also Steven Deutsch and John Howard, eds., *Where It's At*
(New York: Harper and Row, 1970).

5. See Jack D. Douglas, *Investigative Social Research* (Beverly Hills, Calif.:
Sage Publishers, 1976.) See also Herbert Gans, "The Participant-Observer as
a Human Being," in Howard Becker, Blanche Geer, David Riesman, and
Robert Weiss, eds., *Institutions and the Person* (Chicago: Aldine Publishing
Co., 1968).

support of every interpretation an investigator asserts. The search for greater validity sometimes also involves the adoption of unconventional epistemologies that assert that researchers do not understand a community until they understand how it understands itself. Extreme versions of this theme invoke an epistemological relativism[6] (which sees ways of knowing as generic to, and only sustained by, communities) and a radical subjectivism requiring a researcher to "become" a corner boy, a Middletowner, an alcoholic, a Jesus Freak, and so on to render their lives in an epistemologically valid way.[7]

Getting "all the way into" the lives of the group one studies may, of course, increase the likelihood of researchers being "captured" by them, particularly if researchers are sympathetically predisposed to begin with (Shaffer's psychiatrist may be a case of incipient conversion) or if they are in the grip of doubts about the value of their own previously routine research perspectives. "The conversion of a scholar to the values and beliefs of the people studied," says anthropologist Daniel Crowley, "is a commonplace of field research." Such conversion occurs not only among anthropologists in extreme circumstances *vis-à-vis* exotic people; there is a long literary tradition stretching from Herman Melville's "Benito Cereno" to Conrad's "Heart of Darkness" to George P. Elliott's "Among the Dangs" to Castaneda's work (properly regarded as imaginative literature rather than anthropology) to the counterculture's *value* of having one's "mind blown" by extremely unusual experiences. Conversion occurs in more mundane ways too when, for example, among domestic sociologists researchers are "radicalized" into adopting positions of advocacy (for the poor or the black or the aged or

6. The wave of epistemological relativism seems to have been enhanced by the influence of Thomas Kuhn's work as well as the influence of phenomenology. For an interesting treatment of this matter see Bennetta Jules-Rosette, "The Veil of Objectivity," *American Anthropologist* (November 1978).

7. On "becoming the phenomenon" see Hugh Mehan and Houston Wood, *The Reality of Ethnomethodology* (New York: Wiley, 1975); and Bennetta Jules-Rosette, *African Apostles* (Ithaca: Cornell University Press, 1975).

children or the otherwise oppressed) as research demonstrates to the investigator's satisfaction that the ritual neutrality of established social science actually militates against the interests of these groups with which investigators may have come to identify themselves. (It may occur on the other side of the political spectrum too when, for example, the ardor of Aron's revolutionary scholar is cooled by socialization into a conservative academic community.)

Conversion, radical subjectivism, advocacy, phenomenologically based methodological revisionisms all occur and develop strength, it seems to me, under conditions where "established" modes of research are not serving researchers comfortably or well because they lead to cognitive, affective, or political consequences researchers are reluctant to accept. The growth of alternative approaches in sociology—existential, phenomenological, ethnomethodological, Marxist (each to some extent generational, since they resonate the student experience of the 1960s by younger sociologists)—provide some intellectual ground for breaking away from established field methods that were theoretically fragile enough to begin with but not easily broken or cast off until recently because intellectual constituencies were insufficiently developed to affirm and reinforce these newer approaches.

UNSOLVED PROBLEMS

By now, however, there is a substantial tradition in sociological field work of steeping oneself in the lives one studies, of attempting to get "all the way into" their experience (and all the way out of the assumptions undergirding one's own) in ways that enable the researcher to feel more *engagé* and closer to the cutting edge of perhaps startling theoretical insights about the fragility of social order and meaning. Much of this research is informed (if not actually "motivated") by an apparent desire to break through existing conventions of "established" ethnography: to see the world it studies from an "other" perspective; to celebrate and affirm that perspective or to debunk or otherwise expose its claims; to render the alien familiar through participation in its mysteries, or to render the routine strange by suspending the "normal" assumptions that give it "obvious" meaning; to adopt perspectives that make prostitutes, homosexuals, ethnics, children, or other outsiders and exotics more respectable and sympathetic, and teachers, physicians, and other fortunates less so.

Despite some impressive accomplishments by these newer ethnographic approaches, doubts remain whether they speak directly and forthrightly to the problems that generated them. Even greater rigor is not exempt. Greater rigor and accuracy in the reporting of ethnographic research are, of course, always desirable, and it is an absurd and thankless task to argue against them. But like everything else, rigor has a price, and in the marketplace of research the point is always not to pay too much for it. One pays too much for it when one's emphasis on rigor in field methods leads to a neglect of the substantive payoffs (new understanding, fresh insight) for such rigor. The danger here is that the rules of rigorous ethnographic practice can degenerate into still one more set of barren methodological strictures dutifully and mechanically invoked as a rationale by those who may have little to offer in substantive fresh insight or new understanding of the groups to whom the rules have been applied.

The most important thrusts toward rigor in field work have come from ethnomethodology and cognitive sociology. Both are informed by their sensitivity to Alfred Schutz's emphasis on taken-for-granted assumptions in practical reasoning that underlie the sense of the "common" in "common sense." Suspend these taken-for-granted assumptions, and one's sense of the orderliness of the world evaporates; the "common expectations" inherent in most conceptions of status and role (which are built up into conceptions of social structure) similarly dissolve. Harold Garfinkel has been especially good at revealing the disorienting consequences for one's sense of the coherence of life by inducing people to behave *as if* these expectations did not exist. Aaron Cicourel has gone further by emphasizing how, analogous to the "deep structures" of grammar, there must be universal cognitive rules ("interpretive procedures"), a set of meta-norms that enable people mutually to recognize the relevance of surface rules to specfic situations, thereby generating "meaning" and a sense of social structure.[8]

Attempts at empirically discovering how these processes develop and how their results are accomplished involve enormously detailed work, sometimes requiring the use of audio and videotape to reconstruct the subtle linguistic and other communicative interaction through which meaning and a sense of social structure are generated. Such work can either be very profound or very trivial. Since its aim is to render explicit "what everybody knows" or "what everybody does" (and *how* they know it and do it with varying degrees of competence) in revealing themselves as more or less adequate cultural performers, its *substantive* value as illumination depends on the extent to which what *was* implicit was so *deeply* implicit, so unconsciously taken for granted (i.e., its sources *forgotten* or never known) that its revelation comes as a startling, liberating insight.[9] But when the enormously detailed *method* reveals only "what everybody knows," and what they *know* they know, and *that* they know how they know it, the work falls under the heading of what unfriendly critics of sociology used to call "the documentation of the obvious," which may have its methodological virtues but which turns out to be banal or boring to those whose interests are substantive rather than methodological.

In the latter instance we have a qualitative equivalent to what C. Wright Mills in the 1950s called "abstracted empiricism," referring implicitly to the survey work of Paul Lazarsfeld and his disciples at Columbia University's Bureau of Applied Social Research. Lazarsfeld could codify his methods of survey design and analysis and pass those down, but he could not pass down his inventiveness and originality of mind. Mills' criticism of "abstracted empiricism" was a criticism of those sociologists whose chief competence was technical and who hence chose research problems to demonstrate the utility of their techniques, instead of selecting

8. Aaron Cicourel, *Cognitive Sociology* (New York: The Free Press, 1974).
9. Some of the studies in Harold Garfinkel, *Studies in Ethnomethodology* (Englewood Cliffs, N.J.: Prentice-Hall, 1967), do this particularly well.

methods appropriate to problems chosen for their perennial theoretical or substantive importance. Whereas the availability of statistical techniques and computers (to process the data generated by them) promoted big-budget, large-sample surveys, the availability of film, audiotape and videotape enables the most subtle forms of microinteraction to lie before us preserved as data. The substantive importance of what they reveal, however, still rests with the originality and insight of researchers rather than with the accuracy of the codes or the machines.

Advocacy, which takes a quite different tack in ethnographic research, seems benign enough, so long as it's not disguised and so long as it can be shown that a research posture of neutrality invites inferences that researchers do not want their audiences to make, and that, if made, may harm the researched group or community. But a deliberate posture of advocacy is also likely to promote selectivity and systematic bias in the perception and use of data; and regardless of whether this is done deliberately, it is likely to invite counteradvocacy that invokes evidence and argument neglected by the advocate. Selectivity and bias also occur, of course, in approaches that claim detachment or neutrality, but the claim itself constrains discussants to behave as if they had a common interest in arriving at the truth, instead of going for each other's jugular. Situations of advocacy, however, necessarily involve winners and losers, and if the advocate loses to the counteradvocate, harm rather than benefit will have been done to the group for whom the advocate speaks—although it's not likely to do the advocate much harm.[10] Under these conditions doubts may be raised whether the advocate's advocacy is group serving (for the client group) or simply self-serving.

Postures of advocacy have gained strength partly as an effort to avoid harming the groups that provide data to a social

10. Sacco and Vanzetti's advocates survived their martyred flesh. Radical groups have from time to time used the trials of "political" criminals as occasions to promote a political cause, with sometimes beneficial but sometimes harmful consequences to their clients.

scientist. There is much agitated talk in research proposals these days about "protection of human subjects," but the discussions have barely scratched the surface of the subtle moral problems that lie hidden underneath. It is very difficult to do extended field research without developing sympathies for or antipathies to the subjects/objects of one's study. Living for extended periods among "others," particularly under relatively insulated conditions, generates strong pressures to become one of them (the "my people" thing among anthropologists), and the loyalties so engendered can motivate strong desires to speak in their behalf, to defend them against detractors, to maximize their strengths and minimize their vulnerabilities—to become their catcher in the rye.

The opposite of advocacy occurs too, although probably less often and for an obvious reason: if you don't like the people you're studying, that fact will be hard to hide, particularly if you're with them for a substantial period of time. But if the research is to continue, you'd better learn to hide it well because groups that are busy sustaining their own lives don't have much reason for tolerating enemies (*manqué* or not) living among them. Probably the most familiar way of hiding it is the scientific posture. Objectivity, neutrality, detachment, and the assertion of *theoretical* interests (as distinguished from practical problem-solving ones) effectively *distance* researchers from their subjects and hence function not only to disguise negative valence but to protect researchers from being experientially affected in ways they'd prefer not to be. That, of course, is not *all* the scientific posture does, but it does suggest the hypothesis that ethnographers who use the traditional scientific posture are less likely to be (or become) *fond* of their subjects than ethnographers who use the newer approaches.

Nevertheless, the moral problems of "protecting human subjects" are not nearly solved by being "for" them rather than against them and surely not by a ritual show of neutrality. You may be "for" them in interpretive ways that they reject (so that with friends like you they need no enemies— which I sometimes fear may be my own status *vis-à-vis* communards); and you may be "against" them (say, for insufficiently living up to their professed aims) in ways that motivate them to try harder, for which they may be grateful (although not likely). In either case, whether you are protecting or harming human subjects is a subtle, elusive, perhaps imponderable question to which serious practical answers are not available.

Like advocacy, the phenomenological injunction to understand how a group understands itself also seems benign enough, given its rootedness in sociology's traditional preoccupation with "meaning." George Mead saw the social aspects of the self rooted in the projective-imaginative capacities of human beings to "take the role of the other," and Max Weber's very definition of *social* action emphasized the extent to which action "takes account of" the meaning assigned by others to situations. The sociological stricture to see from the point of view of the "other" is a pervasive feature of interactional sociology's traditional concern with meaning. But these strictures describe the *beginning* of sociological analysis rather than its conclusion, and contemporary phenomenology says little, insofar as I know, to help us through a situation in which there are discrepancies between an ethnographer's understanding of his or her observations in a community and the community's own understanding— except a general bias in favor of the "reality" of the meaning ascribed by the community.

Some help may be offered by the insight that a community's self-understanding, like an individual's, is likely to be self-serving, and ethnographers' sensitivity to that probability can direct their attention to the ways in which specific circumstances condition those understandings. The *use* of such seeing, however, requires *alternation* by ethnographers between the point of view of the community and the point of view they bring to its study, and reflexive awareness by ethnographers of the interaction between the two. The tension, of course, can be exhausting, and it is probably easier to adopt either a scientistic stance or to "surrender" one's ethnographer's status to a kind of quasi-membership in the community.

Finally, however commonplace or rare conversion is among ethnographers, it is always fascinating and sometimes awesome, especially when a rational, sophisticated, scientifically trained Western sociologist or anthropologist is converted by an obscure or eccentric sect through dark and mysterious forces that may produce visions, trances, possessed states, rebirths, or other uncanny experiences whose impressive subjective "reality" cannot be ignored. But however impressive, conversion is not usually useful as interpretive ethnography because it is not often sufficiently reflexive or *self*-analytic. Social scientists know that extreme conditions may produce extreme and vivid experiences. Hunger, thirst, fear, pain, anxiety, depression, fatigue, drugs, isolation, sensory deprivation, and so on are all known to produce vivid sensations. Does it derogate the genuineness or "authenticity" of such experience (i.e., explain it away) to be aware of its circumstantial character? For many the answer seems to be yes. One of my vivid undergraduate memories is of a fellow student nearly suffering a nervous breakdown in a literary criticism course as the professor analyzed a Yeats poem line by line in an effort to show *how* the poet achieved the esthetic effects he did. The student shrieked out that the professor was destroying the beauty of the poem by picking it apart, a view that apparently rests on the Romantic assumption ("to dissect is to kill," said Wordsworth) that the *value* of an esthetic (or emotional) experience is in the mystery of its immediate impact, and that it therefore needs to be protected against analytic understanding.

This seems to be a rather widespread attitude toward esthetic and religious experience, but such experiences do not seem radically different from the strong emotions or other subjective states stirred, for example, in a patriot when the flag passes by in a Fourth of July parade, or different from any of the powerful feelings evoked by the circumstances of major ceremonial occasions like weddings, funerals, and other transition rituals. I can remember that during the televised funeral of John F. Kennedy I was so "genuinely" stirred by rage, grief, and despair that I quite lost control of my feelings. But I was comforted somewhat by my (reflexive) insight that circumstances were sufficient to "explain" my extreme response: virtually all of the major institutional symbols of Western culture were being simultaneously focused on the fragile emotional equipment of us viewers. Family, church, state, military, the heads of the world's great nations in solemn procession before us, commemorating and dignifying the loss. Even the economy came to a grinding halt; imagine, no commercials on TV!

Rather than "explain away" such powerful feelings, this kind of reflexive sociological analysis is a model of the Durkheimian insight about the simultaneous interiority and exteriority of culture *vis-à-vis* the individual person: cultural institutions "compel us and we love them; they constrain us and we find our welfare in our adherence to them and in that very constraint. . . . There is perhaps no collective behavior that does not exercise this double action upon us and is contradictory in appearance only." Marxists, of course, might disagree with Durkheim, seeing revolutionary struggle as the proper antidote to this kind of "tyranny" over the mind by the superstructures of capitalism. Nevertheless, conversion experiences, despite their profoundly "Durkheimian" character, frequently leave the converted in such a state of euphoria or anomie or intellectual paralysis that they will not or cannot be analytic about it, content instead to express their helplessness in "explaining" it, saying it cannot be understood but only undergone.[11]

REFLEXIVITY IN ETHNOGRAPHY

I don't know why an ethnographer would bother to do ethnography unless there were some reason to believe that a sociological theory could provide more valuable insight into the life of a community (or the perennial theoretical issues that the life of the community illustrates) than a system of self-reporting by members could or the celebrations by an advocate could or the intense reporting of a conversion experience could. Doing ethnography, especially in communities very different from the ones in which ethnographers normally reside, is a tension-ridden task. Powerful experiences

---

11. In *African Apostles*, Jules-Rosette confesses that her "conversion experience" was at root ineffable.

can be generated while doing the research, and the best ethnographies I know are maximally reflexive about those experiences: they use the experience of the ethnographer to generate further questions about what's going on. If I understand the reflexive principle properly, it should be applicable even to the extreme case of conversion, for it means nothing less than immediate (if sequential and alternating) detachment from one's ongoing experience to consider the fact of it: "Whaddya know, I just had a conversion experience; I wonder what that means? How did that happen?" Like an instant replay in a football game, the aim is to slow the machinery of interaction so that its constitutive processes may be understood.[12]

There is a sense in which what an interpretive and reflexive ethnographer does is analogous to what a literary critic or movie critic does, except that the "text" is observed behavior, utterance, and interaction, rather than words on a page or images on film privately prearranged for consumption in advance. In the nature of the case, critics are interpretive; but they are reflexive when they use their own response to text or image as more data for analysis of the experience of the artwork: I was particularly moved (or not) by this or that sequence in a book or film; why was I moved? How was it done to me? The answers to such questions require more than an analysis of text; they require an analysis of the modalities of feeling that are presumably common to authors and their readers (or film makers and their audiences), and that reflexive analysis requires that modalities of feeling be made problematic.

Pauline Kael, the film critic of *The New Yorker*, is a model of a reflexive critic, and reflexivity is an important component of what has been called "The New Journalism."[13] Such work is

12. *In Seeking Spiritual Meaning* (Beverly Hills, Calif.: Sage Publishers, 1977), Joseph Damrell attempts precisely the difficult task of slowing the machinery of interaction to describe his own visionary experience under the guidance of a Vedanta Swami.

13. See Tom Wolfe and E. W. Johnson, eds., *The New Journalism* (New York: Harper and Row, 1973). See also Wolfe's collections of essays, *The Kandy-Kolored Tangerine-Flake Streamline Baby* (New York: Farrar, Straus, and Giroux, 1965), and *The Pump House Gang* (New York: Farrar, Straus, and Giroux, 1968).

sometimes derogated by more traditional critics and journalists because of the prominent place occupied in it by the
first person singular. The prominence of the reportorial "I"
violates the creed of more orthodox journalists that they attend to the events rather than to the reporter's feelings about
them. Ethnographers are generally under a similar obligation,
and both are justified by a general appeal to "objectivity." Reflexivity, however, requires the presence of an "I," less as a
pretext for opinionatedness or bias or narcissism (though
surely these occur) than to deliberately evoke the *feel* of a set
of events as a problem for analysis.

Does a critic "know more" about a book (or a film) than the
author *(auteur)* does? Maybe; maybe not. Common sense says
no. But I remember an exchange years ago in the letters col-
umns of *Partisan Review* in which a novelist wrote complain-
ing of the review his book had received in an earlier issue of
the magazine. The novelist argued at some length that the
reviewer was utterly mistaken about a number of interpretive
comments he had made in his review. The reviewer replied
very briefly. "Sir," he addressed the novelist, "you do not
know what your book is about"—a comment that would
seem far less outrageous if it had been uttered by a psychiatrist telling a patient that he did not understand his own
symptoms.

Criticism is further comparable to interpretive ethnography
in the sense that, whatever the theoretical equipment brought
to the analysis of the subject, no single analysis is likely to
exhaust the meaning in that subject. Communities, like art-
works, may be more or less complex, capable of yielding a
variety of more or less plausible, more or less persuasive
"readings." But although one reading may be better than
another (for example, in explaining more of the evidence
more compellingly), any reading is inevitably less than complete. Moreover, like criticism, ethnographic case studies (including this one), however plausible and persuasive, do not
"prove" anything of a general substantive nature. Case
studies never do that and cannot do that, although their findings may weaken previously accepted generalizations and
shift the burden of proof. What they can do is provide as accurate a record as possible of a group's life (a sort of current

history), and rigorous field methods are valuable to this end. But they are theoretically interesting only when, out of the field observations come insights that transcend the time and place in which they occurred and that bear significantly on the stock of inherited thinking about the subject (or on the dominant theories in the discipline to which the ethnographer belongs). Findings may challenge the conventional wisdom about the specific group under study or the type of community it represents. Such findings may correct erroneous beliefs and contribute to a reorientation of public thinking. Findings may also suggest new concepts that link relationships in ways that were previously obscure or not clearly understood. They may therefore contribute to the formulation of new hypotheses to be tested by means other than ethnographic case studies and on populations radically different from those among whom the new concept was discovered.

Unlike criticism, however, reported ethnographies *interact* with the communities they describe and interpret in ways that may have direct impact on them and, perhaps, generate controversy and strife among their members. Even before the ethnography is publicly reported, the ethnographer interacts with the community in ways that may have the same consequences, and this fact brings us back to the crisis that promoted many of the newer ethnographic approaches. One aspect of this crisis is, as I have suggested, doubts about the wholesomeness of the entire research enterprise,[14] some of which are generated by the unanticipated consequences of the research: have I distorted the facts of their lives? Have I misinterpreted the meaning of the connections and the relations I observe or infer? Do I betray their confidence if the meanings I ascribe are different from their own? Do I injure them if the answers to these questions are yes?

Fears that the answers to these questions may be positive have prompted some of the attempts at solution I described

14. See John Seeley's comments on the wrenching consequences of the research that produced his remarkable book *Crestwood Heights* (New York: Basic Books, 1956) in his *The Americanization of the Unconscious* (New York: International Science Press, 1967).

above. Is this an *excessive* manifestation of conscience, a case of hearts too much predisposed to bleed? Why not adopt a posture of following the truth wherever it leads? "Follow the truth wherever it leads" is reminiscent of the theater's slogan "the show must go on." But if one raises the question "why must the show go on?" it may come out that the slogan, apparently expressing the troupe's sense of its professional obligation to audiences, is actually self-serving for the survival of the theater. Similarly, the scholar's injunction to follow the truth wherever it leads has been increasingly questioned as faith in the value of knowledge for its own sake has declined. In recent decades the questions of knowledge for what and knowledge for whom have been increasingly raised as the pursuit of knowledge led scholars along paths whose direction seemed obscure or ominous. Nuclear power, monitoring devices, databanks, behavior modification, relativism, the self-fulfilling character of political polling and media attention to events have all raised disturbing questions about the consequences of inquiry, which have constrained researchers to be increasingly reflexive about their own relationships to their work. I think that this is a wholesome development (despite the narcisstic risks) that promises added richness to ethnographic work.

BIBLIOGRAPHY

Abrams, Philip, and Andrew McCulloch. *Communes, Sociology, and Society.* London: Cambridge University Press, 1976.

Althusser, Louis. *Lenin and Philosophy.* New York: Monthly Review Press, 1972.

Aries, Philippe. *Centuries of Childhood.* New York: Vintage Books, 1962.

Aron, Raymond. *The Opium of the Intellectuals.* W.W. Norton and Co., 1962.

Auden, W.H. "The Early Years." *The New York Times Book Review,* January 29, 1978.

Becker, Howard. *German Youth: Bond or Free?* London: Kegan Paul, Trench, Trubner, 1946.

Becker, Howard S. *Outsiders.* New York: The Free Press, 1963.

———, and Blanche Geer, David Riesman, and Robert Weiss, editors. *Institutions and the Person.* Chicago: Aldine Publishing Co., 1968.

Bell, Clive. *Civilization.* London: Chatto and Windus, 1928.

Bell, Daniel. *The Cultural Contradictions of Capitalism.* New York: Basic Books, 1976.

Bendix, Reinhard. *Work and Authority in Industry.* New York: John Wiley and Sons, 1956.

Berger, Bennett M. *Working Class Suburb.* Berkeley: University of California Press, 1960.

———. *Looking for America.* Englewood Cliffs, N.J.: Prentice-Hall, 1971.

———, and Bruce Hackett. "The Decline of Age-Grading in Rural Hippie Communes," *The Journal of Social Issues* (Winter, 1974).

———, Bruce Hackett, and R. Mervyn Millar. "Child Rearing Practices of the Communal Family," in Hans Peter Dreitzel (ed.), *Family, Marriage, and the Struggle of the Sexes.* Recent Sociology, no. 4. New York: The Macmillan Co., 1972.

Berger, Peter. *Facing Up to Modernity.* New York: Basic Books, 1977.

———, and Thomas Luckmann. *The Social Construction of Reality.* New York: Doubleday and Co., 1966.

Bordieu, Pierre, and Jean Claude Passeron. *Reproduction: in Education, Society, and Culture.* Beverly Hills, Ca.: Sage Publishing Co., 1977.

Bottomore, Tom, and Patrick Goode, editors. *Austro-Marxism*. Oxford: The Clarendon Press, 1978.

Bridenbaugh, Carl. *Cities in Revolt*. New York: Alfred A. Knopf, 1955.

Cavan, Sherri. "Hippies of the Redwood Forest." Unpublished manuscript.

Cicourel, Aaron. *Cognitive Sociology*. New York: The Free Press, 1974.

Colfax, J. David, and Jack Roach, editors. *Radical Sociology*. New York: Basic Books, 1971.

Constantine, Larry and Joan. *Group Marriage*. New York: The Macmillan Co., 1973.

Cottle, Thomas. "Parent and Child," in David Gottlieb (ed.), *Children's Liberation*. Englewood Cliffs, N.J.: Prentice-Hall, 1973.

Damrell, Joseph. *Seeking Spiritual Meaning*. Beverly Hills, Ca.: Sage Publishing Co., 1977.

———. *Search for Identity*. Beverly Hills, Ca.: Sage Publishing Co., 1978.

Daner, Francine. *The American Children of Krsna*. New York: Holt, Rinehart, and Winston, 1974.

Davidson, Sara. "Open Land," *Harper's* (June, 1970).

———. *Loose Change*. New York: Doubleday and Co., 1977.

Davis, Fred. *On Youth Subcultures: The Hippie Variant*. New York: General Learning Press, 1971.

Deutsch, Steven, and John Howard, editors. *Where It's At*. New York: Harper and Row, 1970.

Diamond, Stephen. *What the Trees Said*. New York: Delacorte Press, 1972.

Douglas, Jack. *Investigative Social Research*. Beverly Hills, Ca.: Sage Publishing Co., 1976.

Eisenstadt, Shmuel. *From Generation to Generation: Age Groups and Social Structure*. Glencoe: The Free Press, 1955.

Ewen, Stuart. *Captains of Consciousness*. New York: McGraw-Hill, 1976.

Festinger, Leon. *A Theory of Cognitive Dissonance*. New York: Harper and Row, 1957.

Feuer, Lewis. *The Conflict of Generations*. New York: Basic Books, 1969.

Flacks, Richard. "The Liberated Generation," *The Journal of Social Issues* (July, 1967).

Foss, Daniel, and Ralph W. Larkin. "From 'The Gates of Eden' to 'The Day of the Locust,' " *Humboldt Journal of Social Relations* (Fall/Winter, 1975).

Friedenberg, Edgar. *The Vanishing Adolescent*. Boston: Beacon Press, 1959.

————. "Hot-Rods and Questionnaires," *Commentary* (November, 1961).

Gans, Herbert. *Popular Culture and High Culture.* New York: Basic Books, 1974.

Gardner, Hugh. *The Children of Prosperity.* New York: St. Martin's Press, 1978.

Garfinkel, Harold. *Studies in Ethnomethodology.* Englewood Cliffs, N.J.: Prentice-Hall, 1967.

Gaskin, Stephen ("Stephen and the Farm"). *Hey Beatnik!* Summertown, Tenn.: The Book Publishing Co., 1974.

Geertz, Clifford. *The Interpretation of Cultures.* New York: Basic Books, 1973.

Giddens, Anthony. *Central Problems in Social Theory.* London: Macmillan and Co., 1979.

Gitlin, Todd. "Domesticating Nature," *Theory and Society* (September, 1979).

Glock, Charles, and Robert Bellah, editors. *The New Religious Consciousness.* Berkeley: University of California Press, 1976.

Goffman, Erving. *Relations in Public.* New York: Basic Books, 1972.

Goodman, Paul. *Growing Up Absurd.* New York: Random House, 1960.

Gordon, Michael, editor. *The American Family in Social-Historical Perspective.* New York: St. Martin's Press, 1978.

Gottlieb, David, editor. *Children's Liberation.* Englewood Cliffs, N.J.: Prentice-Hall, 1973.

Gouldner, Alvin W. *The Dialectic of Ideology and Technology.* New York: The Seabury Press, 1976.

Gramsci, Antonio. *Selections from the Prison Notebooks.* Edited and translated by Quentin Hoare and Geoffrey Nowell Smith. New York: International Publishers, 1971.

Graña, Cesar. *Modernity and Its Discontents.* New York: Harper and Row, 1967.

Green, Arnold. "The Middle Class Male Child and Neurosis," *American Sociological Review,* 11 (1946).

Gross, Beatrice and Ronald, editors. *The Children's Rights Movement.* New York: Anchor Books, 1977.

Habermas, Jürgen. *Knowledge and Human Interests.* Boston: Beacon Press, 1971.

Hawkins, J. David. "The Dynamics of Conformity in Communal Groups of the Counter-Culture Movement." Unpublished manuscript, 1978.

Hedgepath, William, and Dennis Stock. *The Alternative.* New York: The Macmillan Co. 1970.

Hirschmann, Albert. *The Passions and the Interests*. Princeton, N.J.: Princeton University Press, 1977.

Hochschild, Arlie. "Emotion-Work, Feeling-Rules, and Social Structure," *American Journal of Sociology*, 85 (November, 1979).

Hoffer, Eric. *The True Believer*. New York: Harper and Row, 1951.

Hollenbach, Margaret. "Commune or Cult? The Family of Taos." Seattle: University of Washington, M.A. thesis, 1971.

Hulme, Katherine. *The Nun's Story*. Boston: Little, Brown, and Co., 1956.

Humphrey, Robert. *Children of Fantasy*. New York: John Wiley and Sons, 1978.

Jaffe, Dennis. "Couples in Communes." New Haven: Yale University, Ph.D. dissertation, 1975.

Jerome, Judson. *Families of Eden*. New York: The Seabury Press, 1974.

Johnson, John M. *Doing Field Research*. New York: The Free Press, 1975.

Judah, J. Stillson. *Hare Krishna and the Counterculture*. New York: John Wiley and Sons, 1974.

Jules-Rosette, Bennetta. *African Apostles*. Ithaca, N.Y.: Cornell University Press, 1975.

———. "The Veil of Objectivity," *American Anthropologist* (November, 1978).

———, and Beryl Bellman. *A Paradigm for Looking*. Norwood, N.J.: Ablex Publishing Co., 1977.

Kagan, Paul. *New World Utopias*. Baltimore: Penguin Books, 1975.

Kanter, Rosabeth. *Commitment and Community*. Cambridge: Harvard University Press, 1972.

———, editor. *Communes: Creating and Managing the Collective Life*. New York: Harper and Row, 1973.

Keniston, Kenneth. *Young Radicals*. New York: Harcourt, Brace, and World, 1968.

Kincade, Kathleen. *A Walden Two Experiment*. New York: William Morrow and Co., 1973.

Kramer, Jane. *The Last Cowboy*. New York: Harper and Row, 1977.

Kuhn, Thomas. *The Structure of Scientific Revolutions*. Chicago: University of Chicago Press, 1962.

Lasch, Christopher. *Haven in a Heartless World*. New York: Basic Books, 1977.

———. *The Culture of Narcissism*. New York: W.W. Norton and Co., 1978.

Lemert, Edwin. *Social Pathology*. New York: McGraw-Hill, 1951.

Lesy, Michael. *Wisconsin Death Trip*. New York: Pantheon Books, 1973.

Lofland, John. *Analyzing Social Settings*. Belmont, Ca.: Wadsworth Publishing Co., 1971.

———. *Doing Social Life*. New York: Wiley-Interscience, 1976.

MacRae, Donald. *Ideology and Society*. New York: The Free Press, 1961.

Mannheim, Karl. *Ideology and Utopia*. New York: Harcourt, Brace and Co., 1936.

———. *Essays on the Sociology of Knowledge*. New York: Oxford University Press, 1952.

Marcuse, Herbert. *One Dimensional Man*. Boston: Beacon Press, 1964.

———. "On Repressive Tolerance," in Barrington Moore, Jr., Robert Paul Wolff, and Herbert Marcuse (eds.), *A Critique of Pure Tolerance*. Boston: Beacon Press, 1965.

———. *Counterrevolution and Revolt*. Boston: Beacon Press, 1973.

Marris, Peter. *Loss and Change*. New York: Pantheon Books, 1974.

Marx, Karl, and Friedrich Engels. *The German Ideology*. New York: International Publishers, 1970.

Marx, Leo. *The Machine in the Garden*. New York: Oxford University Press, 1964.

Matza, David. "Subterranean Traditions of Youth," *The Annals of the American Academy of Political and Social Science* (November, 1961).

———. *Delinquency and Drift*. New York: John Wiley and Sons, 1964.

McPhee, John. *Coming into the Country*. New York: Farrar, Straus, and Giroux, 1977.

Mehan, Hugh, and Houston Wood. *The Reality of Ethnomethodology*. New York: John Wiley and Sons, 1975.

Merton, Robert. *Social Theory and Social Structure*. Glencoe: The Free Press, 1957.

———. *The Sociology of Science*. Chicago: University of Chicago Press, 1973.

Mukerji, Chandra, *Graven Images*. Forthcoming.

Muncy, Raymond Lee. *Sex and Marriage in Utopian Communities*. Bloomington: Indiana University Press, 1973.

Mungo, Raymond. *Famous Long Ago*. Boston: Beacon Press, 1970.

———. *Total Loss Farm*. New York: E.P. Dutton and Co., 1970.

Musgrove, Frank. *Youth and the Social Order*. Indianapolis: Indiana University Press, 1964.

Poggioli, Renato. *The Oaten Flute*. Cambridge: Harvard University Press, 1975.

Psathas, George, editor. *Phenomenological Sociology*. New York: John Wiley and Sons, 1973.

Ramey, James. *Intimate Friendships*. Englewood Cliffs, N.J.: Prentice-Hall, 1976.

Reich, Charles. *The Greening of America.* New York: Random House, 1970.

Reisman, David, et al. *The Lonely Crowd.* New Haven: Yale University Press, 1951.

———. "The Suburban Dislocation," *The Annals of the American Academy of Political and Social Science* (November, 1957).

Remmling, Gunter. *Toward the Sociology of Knowledge.* New York: Humanities Press, 1973.

Riley, M.W., M. Johnson, and A. Foner. *Aging and Society: A Sociology of Age Stratification.* Vol. 3. New York: Russell Sage Foundation, 1972.

Roszak, Theodore. *The Making of a Counterculture.* New York: Anchor Books, 1969.

Rothchild, John, and Susan Wolf. *The Children of the Counterculture.* New York: Doubleday and Co., 1975.

Rudikoff, Sonia. "O Pioneers!," *Commentary* (July, 1972).

Sahlins, Marshall. *Culture and Practical Reason.* Chicago: University of Chicago Press, 1976.

Schiller, Herbert. *The Mind Managers.* Boston: Beacon Press, 1973.

Schumpeter, Joseph. *Capitalism, Socialism, and Democracy.* New York: Harper and Bros, 1942.

Schutz, Alfred. *The Phenomenology of the Social World.* Evanston, Ill.: Northwestern University Press, 1967.

———. *Phenomenology and Social Reality.* Edited by Maurice Natanson. The Hague: Martinus Nijhoff, 1970.

Scott, John Finley. *Internalization of Norms.* Englewood Cliffs, N.J.: Prentice-Hall, 1971.

Seeley, John, et al. *Crestwood Heights.* New York: Basic Books, 1956.

———. *The Americanization of the Unconscious.* New York: International Sciences Press, 1967.

Seligson, Marcia. *Options.* Ashland, Md.: Lexington Books, 1978.

Sennett, Richard. *The Fall of Public Man.* New York: Alfred A. Knopf, 1976.

Shorter, Edward. *The Making of the Modern Family.* New York: Basic Books, 1975.

Simmel, Georg. *The Sociology of Georg Simmel.* Edited by Kurt Wolff. Glencoe: The Free Press, 1950.

Skinner, B.F. *Beyond Freedom and Dignity.* New York: Alfred A. Knopf, 1971.

Slater, Philip. *The Pursuit of Loneliness.* Boston: Beacon Press, 1970.

Smith, Henry Nash. *Virgin Land.* New York: Random House, 1950.

Strauss, Anselm, and Barney Glaser. *The Discovery of Grounded Theory.* Chicago: Aldine Publishing Co., 1967.

Thompson, Hunter. *Hell's Angels*. New York: Random House, 1967.

Touraine, Alain. *The Self-Production of Society*. Chicago: University of Chicago Press, 1977.

Veysey, Laurence. *The Communal Experience*. New York: Harper and Row, 1973.

Wallis, Roy. "Sex, Marriage, and the Children of God." Unpublished manuscript, 1977.

Warner, Sam Bass. *Streetcar Suburbs*. Cambridge: Harvard University Press, 1962.

Weber, Max. *The Protestant Ethic and the Spirit of Capitalism*. New York: Scribner's, 1930.

Whyte, William H. *The Organization Man*. New York: Doubleday and Co., 1956.

Wilkerson, Albert, editor. *The Rights of Children*. Philadelphia: Temple University Press, 1973.

Wilson, James Q. *Thinking About Crime*. New York: Basic Books, 1975.

Wolfe, Tom. *The Kandy Kolored Tangerine-Flake Streamline Baby*. New York: Farrar, Straus, and Giroux, 1965.

———. *The Pump House Gang*. New York: Farrar, Straus, and Giroux, 1968.

———, and E.W. Johnson, editors. *The New Journalism*. New York: Harper and Row, 1973.

Wolff, Kurt. *Trying Sociology*. New York: John Wiley and Sons, 1974.

Yablonsky, Lewis. *Synanon: The Tunnel Back*. Baltimore: Penguin Books, 1967.

———. *The Hippie Trip*. New York: Pegasus, 1968.

Zablocki, Benjamin. *The Joyful Community*. Baltimore: Penguin Books, 1971.

———. *Alienation and Charisma*. New York: The Free Press, 1980.

INDEX

Designer: Barbara Llewellyn
Compositor: Viking Typographers
Printer: Vail-Ballou Press
Binder: Vail-Ballou Press
Text: VIP Palatino
Display: Goudy Heavy Display (Spartan)